*f*P

MARIA A. RESSA

SEEDS OF TERROR

AN EYEWITNESS ACCOUNT OF AL-QAEDA'S NEWEST CENTER OF OPERATIONS IN SOUTHEAST ASIA

Free Press

NEW YORK   LONDON   TORONTO   SYDNEY

FREE PRESS
A Division of Simon & Schuster, Inc.
1230 Avenue of the Americas
New York, NY 10020

FREE PRESS and colophon are trademarks
of Simon & Schuster, Inc.

For information regarding special discounts for bulk purchases,
please contact Simon & Schuster Special Sales at 1-800-456-6798
or business@simonandschuster.com

Manufactured in the United States of America

10   9   8   7   6   5   4   3   2   1

Library of Congress Cataloging-in-Publication Data

Ressa, Maria.
    Seeds of terror : an eyewitness account of Al-Qaeda's newest
center of operations in Southeast Asia / Maria Ressa.
        p.   cm.
    Includes bibliographical references and index.
    1. Qaeda (Organization)   2. Terrorism—Asia, Southeastern.
    I. Title.

HV6433.A7852Q257 2003
303.6'25'0959—dc22   2003063140

ISBN 978-0-4516-3634-5

To the Heisenberg Uncertainty Principle

CONTENTS

CAST OF CHARACTERS

AL-QAEDA

OSAMA BIN LADEN: The emir and creator of al-Qaeda's global terror network.

DR. AYMAN AL-ZAWAHIRI: Al-Qaeda's second-in-command, who visited Southeast Asia in June 2000 with Mohammed Atef. He remains at large.

MOHAMMED ATEF (ABU HAFS): Al-Qaeda's military chief until his death during U.S. attacks in Afghanistan. He visited Southeast Asia in 2000 and green-lighted the Jemaah Islamiyah Singapore cell's truck-bombing plot against U.S. and Western embassies in Singapore.

KHALID SHAIKH MOHAMMED (KSM): Took over as al-Qaeda's military chief until his capture in March 2003. Considered to be the most significant arrest so far, KSM has been involved in nearly every major al-Qaeda attack since 1993. He has admitted to being the mastermind of the 9/11 attacks, a plot his cell hatched in the Philippines in 1994.

ABU ZUBAIDA: Al-Qaeda's operations chief until his capture in March 2002. He was in charge of logistics and support for al-Qaeda's associate groups in Southeast Asia. He sent operatives to help create and run training camps in the southern Philippines.

HAMBALI (NURJAMAN RIDUAN ISAMUDDIN): The only non-Arab sitting on al-Qaeda's leadership council at the time of his arrest in August 2003. An Indonesian cleric, he worked simultaneously for al-Qaeda and Jemaah Islamiyah (JI). As Jemaah Islamiyah's second-in-command and operations chief, Hambali was the primary recruiter for and planner of numerous terrorist operations throughout Southeast Asia, including the Christmas church bombings in 2000 and the Bali blasts in 2002. He began working with KSM in 1994, helping funnel money to the first al-Qaeda cell in the Philippines.

MOHAMMED JAMAL KHALIFA: Osama bin Laden's brother-in-law, he was sent to the Philippines in 1988 to create a financial network that would support operational cells activated in 1994. Much of that financial infrastructure still exists today.

RAMZI YOUSEF: The mastermind of the 1993 bombing of the World Trade Center, he fled to the Philippines and began training members of Abu Sayyaf, a group al-Qaeda helped create. Working with his uncle, KSM, Yousef set up the first al-Qaeda cell in Southeast Asia, which plotted to bomb eleven U.S. airliners. An accidental fire in their safe-house apartment foiled the plot and unearthed numerous other plans, including the blueprint for 9/11. Yousef was arrested in 1995 and is serving a life sentence in a U.S. prison.

WALI KHAN AMIN SHAH: An Afghan war veteran who fought with Osama bin Laden, he was sent to the Philippines in 1993 as an al-Qaeda sleeper agent, part of KSM and Yousef's cell. He was arrested in 1995 and convicted in a New York court but has yet to be sentenced.

ABDUL HAKIM MURAD: A high school classmate of Yousef, he was the first commercial pilot recruited by al-Qaeda for a suicide mission. Part of the Manila cell, he was arrested in 1995 and is now in a U.S. prison serving a life sentence.

SULAIMAN ABU GHAITH: An al-Qaeda spokesman who recruited and sent Mohammed Mansour Jabarah to Afghanistan.

MOHAMMED MANSOUR JABARAH: A nineteen-year-old Canadian-Kuwaiti sent by KSM one day before 9/11 to activate sleeper cells in Southeast Asia for al-Qaeda's second wave of attacks.

OMAR AL-FARUQ: An al-Qaeda sleeper agent sent in 1994 by Abu Zubaida to Southeast Asia. He was arrested by Indonesian authorities on June 5, 2002, and confessed to being "al-Qaeda's senior representative in Southeast Asia."

KHALID AL-MIDHAR AND NAWAF AL-HAZMI: September 11 hijackers who attended an al-Qaeda planning meeting organized by Hambali in Malaysia in 2000.

ZACARIAS MOUSSAOUI: On trial in the United States for September 11–related charges, yet very likely *not* the "twentieth hijacker," as he has been labeled in the press. He visited Malaysia twice in 2000 and had extensive contact with Jemaah Islamiyah's Singapore cell members.

JEMAAH ISLAMIYAH

ABU BAKAR BA'ASYIR: The emir and spiritual leader of Jemaah Islamiyah. Arrested in October 2000 and sentenced to four years in prison.

ABDULLAH SUNGKAR: Cofounder along with Ba'asyir, he met with Osama bin Laden and offered him the services of Jemaah Islamiyah. Died of natural causes in 1999.

FAIZ BIN ABU BAKAR BAFANA: A Hambali deputy, he brought a video-tape of a JI plot to Afghanistan for the approval of Mohammed Atef.

YAZID SUFAAT: Another Hambali deputy, whose apartment in Malaysia was used for an al-Qaeda planning meeting in 2000 and who hosted Zacarias Moussaoui. KSM claims that Sufaat, who has a bachelor's degree in biochemistry, worked on al-Qaeda's biological weapons program.

MOHAMMED IQBAL ABDUL RAHMAN (ABU JIBRIL): Another Hambali deputy, a fiery Muslim cleric who became Jemaah Islamiyah's primary recruiter for the jihad in Ambon.

FATHUR ROMAN AL-GHOZI: An Indonesian explosives expert who worked for Jemaah Islamiyah and al-Qaeda on a suicide-truck-bombing plot against U.S. and Western embassies in Singapore.

IBRAHIM MAIDIN: The leader of Jemaah Islamiyah's Singapore cell.

HASHIM BIN ABBAS: A Singaporean brother-in-law of Mukhlas (see below) who took part in the Christmas church bombings in Indonesia in 2000, and was part of the foiled plot to bomb the U.S. embassy and other Western interests in Singapore.

MUKHLAS: A key Hambali deputy, he is one of three people in Jemaah Islamiyah who worked directly with KSM (including Hambali). He ran a JI school in Malaysia and replaced Hambali as the head of Mantiqi 1, leading JI cells in Malaysia and Singapore.

IMAM SAMUDRA: The field commander of the Bali bombings, he lived for years next door to Ba'asyir, Hambali, and Abu Jibril in the neighborhood in Malaysia known as "Terror HQ."

ALI IMRON: The youngest brother of Mukhlas, he helped build the Bali bombs.

AMROZI: The middle brother of Mukhlas, he bought the explosives and the van for the Bali bombings. He was the first person arrested for the Bali bombings and was given the death sentence on August 7, 2003.

HASHIM SALAMAT: The founder and chairman of the largest Muslim separatist group in the Philippines, the MILF (Moro Islamic Liberation Front), which has set up training camps for al-Qaeda and Jemaah Islamiyah.

AGUS DWIKARNA: The head of Laskar Jundullah, a paramilitary group in Indonesia allegedly funded by al-Qaeda. He worked closely with Omar al-Faruq; the two acted as guides for al-Qaeda's senior leaders when they visited Indonesia in 2000. He was arrested in the Philippines in March 2002.

ABDURAJAK JANJALANI: The Filipino founder of the Abu Sayyaf, which he named after famed Afghan fighter Abdul Rasul Sayyaf. He was killed by government forces in 1998 and was replaced by his brother Khaddafy Janjalani.

NIK ADLI NIK AZIZ: An Afghan war veteran and son of an opposition Malaysian politician, he took over the leadership of the extremist group KMM (Kumpulan Mujahidin Malaysia) in 1999. KMM was co-opted by Hambali into the JI network.

NOTE: Jemaah Islamiyah's leaders created a clandestine umbrella organization known as Rabitatul Mujahidin, which includes all the armed Muslim groups in the region: the MILF, Abu Sayyaf, Laskar Jundullah, and several others. Although each of these groups has a separate leadership structure, for specific operations, they act essentially as part of the Jemaah Islamiyah and al-Qaeda terror network.

TIMELINE

1949

Darul Islam, an Islamic militia fighting for independence under Dutch rule in Indonesia, is formed. Much of this network would later evolve into Jemaah Islamiyah.

1965

After a series of massacres, a little-known general, Suharto, uses the military to suppress an alleged communist-led coup and deposes Indonesia's first president, Sukarno. Suharto stays in power for thirty-two years.

1971

Abu Bakar Ba'asyir, later dubbed the Asian Osama bin Laden, and his partner, Abdullah Sungkar, open the Pondok Ngruki Islamic boarding school in Solo, Indonesia, which later becomes Jemaah Islamiyah's first source of recruits. Although the clandestine organization didn't use the name Jemaah Islamiyah for more than a decade, at some point in the 1970s its leaders began creating their first network of cells and study groups.

1978

Hashim Salamat splits from the Philippine Moro National Liberation Front and forms a more Islamic-based separatist group, the Moro Islamic Liberation Front (MILF).

1980

Hashim Salamat begins sending Filipino Muslims to Pakistan and on to Afghanistan to join the first modern jihad—fighting the Soviets in Afghanistan.

1985

Abu Bakar Ba'asyir and Abdullah Sungkar flee Indonesia during a crackdown by Suharto, and settle in Malaysia, bringing the leadership of Jemaah Islamiyah with them. Sungkar begins sending Indonesian Muslims to fight the continuing war in Afghanistan, and he himself travels there to meet Osama bin Laden. Jemaah Islamiyah is co-opted by al-Qaeda, which begins training and funding Jemaah Islamiyah's key operatives.

1988

Osama bin Laden sends his brother-in-law Mohammed Jamal Khalifa to the Philippines to begin setting up a financial network in Southeast Asia that would support the terrorist operations cells he planned to create.

1991

Khalifa brings Filipino Abdurajak Janjalani to Osama bin Laden in Peshawar, Pakistan, where Janjalani is given support and operatives to create the Abu Sayyaf.

1993

The first group of Singaporeans, led by Ibrahim Maidin, goes to Afghanistan for training.

An al-Qaeda operative named Mukhlas establishes Jemaah Islamiyah's second school, the Lukmanul Hakim, in Malaysia. Many of the Bali bombers would later be connected to this school.

Wali Khan Amin Shah, who fought with Osama bin Laden in Afghanistan, is sent to the Philippines to create al-Qaeda's primary operational cell working with Khalid Shaikh Mohammed and Ramzi Yousef, fresh from having masterminded the bombing of the World Trade Center.

1994

Dozens of expert terrorists are sent to major cities of the Philippines to create al-Qaeda's operational cells. They include Mohammed Sadiq Odeh, who helped plan the 1998 East Africa bombings from the southern Philippines. The primary cell, led by Ramzi Yousef, is activated.

Al-Qaeda's operations chief, Abu Zubaida, sends Omar al-Faruq and other al-Qaeda operatives to the southern Philippines to help the MILF set up more training camps.

1995

A freak apartment fire alerts authorities to al-Qaeda's plans to assassinate the pope and bomb eleven U.S. airliners. The ensuing crackdown leads to the arrests of Abdul Hakim Murad, Wali Khan Amin Shah, and Ramzi Yousef. They are tried and convicted in a New York court.

1996–1998

More than one thousand Indonesians are trained at MILF camps in the Philippines.

1999

Osama bin Laden calls Hashim Salamat and asks him to open more training camps for al-Qaeda. Salamat agrees.

One year after riots and looting herald the end of Suharto's thirty-two-year rule in Indonesia, Abu Bakar Ba'asyir and Abdullah Sungkar move Jemaah Islamiyah's base of operations back to Pondok Ngruki, their school in Solo, Indonesia. Sungkar dies soon afterward.

Ba'asyir and al-Qaeda leader Hambali create Rabitatul Mujahidin, an umbrella organization that unites Jemaah Islamiyah with the MILF, Laskar Jundullah, KMM, and other Southeast Asian and South Asian groups.

Violence erupts in Indonesia: in Ambon, Poso, West Kalimantan, Aceh, and East Timor.

2000

Dr. Ayman al-Zawahiri, bin Laden's deputy, and Mohammed Atef, al-Qaeda's military chief, visit Indonesia to see if they can shift the base of al-Qaeda to Southeast Asia.

Jemaah Islamiyah carries out a series of bombings in Indonesia, which ends in the spectacular delivery of thirty-eight bombs to churches and priests across Indonesia on Christmas Eve. Six days later, the bombings are followed by five near-simultaneous explosions in the Philippines.

2001

A foiled robbery in Malaysia alerts authorities to the presence of terrorist cells. The crackdown in Malaysia begins in August.

One day before 9/11, Khalid Shaikh Mohammed dispatches Mohammed Mansour Jabarah to activate sleeper cells in Singapore for the "second wave."

Spain arrests the leader of its al-Qaeda cell and warns Indonesia of the presence of operatives and an al-Qaeda training camp within its borders.

Malaysia and Singapore issue warrants for the arrest of Abu Bakar Ba'asyir, but he continues living freely in Indonesia. Authorities in Jakarta repeatedly deny the presence of terrorists in their nation.

In December, Singapore foils a plot to truck-bomb the U.S. embassy and other Western interests in the city-state by arresting thirteen members of Jemaah Islamiyah.

2002

Fathur Roman al-Ghozi and Agus Dwikarna are arrested in the Philippines.

Omar al-Faruq is arrested in Indonesia and handed over to U.S. authorities. Information from him pushes the United States for the first time to raise its terror alert level to orange on the anniversary of the September 11 attacks.

On October 12, three bombs explode in Bali, Indonesia, killing more than two hundred people.

Within days, Indonesian authorities arrest Abu Bakar Ba'asyir. He would later be tried for treason but sentenced to only a four-year term in prison.

2003

By August, Indonesia arrests nearly ninety Jemaah Islamiyah members within its borders. More than two hundred are arrested in Southeast Asia.

On August 5, a suicide bomber sent by Jemaah Islamiyah attacks the J.W. Marriott Hotel in Jakarta's central business district, killing twelve people.

On August 11, Hambali is arrested in Thailand, but authorities across the region warn that Jemaah Islamiyah is plotting more attacks.

Indonesian intelligence officials say Jemaah Islamiyah may be getting ready to switch tactics: from bombings to assassinations.

The threat alert level has never been higher.

FACE TO FACE WITH OSAMA BIN LADEN

It is nearly two o'clock in the morning, and I am sitting in a cubicle on the sixth floor of the North Tower of CNN's headquarters in Atlanta, Georgia. Stacked around me are 251 videotapes from Osama bin Laden's personal collection. As I take another one from the pile, I can't help thinking, "When was the last time he touched this tape? What was he looking for?" Some sand spills out, part of the saga of this collection. Some savvy Afghans found them in one of the four houses allegedly owned by bin Laden in Kandahar.[1] Thinking they might be mistaken for al-Qaeda members if the tapes were found in their possession, the Afghans panicked and buried them after U.S. troops arrived. Later, through middlemen, they contacted CNN's Nic Robertson and Mark Phillips, who recovered the tapes and brought them to Atlanta less than a month ago.

It is now the end of September 2002, and the war on terror is in full swing. Nic had already aired a series of exclusive reports based on these "terror tapes," showing how al-Qaeda used videos to teach the basics of chemical weaponry, urban guerrilla warfare, assassinations, hostage taking, and other terrorist tactics. The tapes span nearly a decade and chronicle the interests and growth of al-Qaeda. All of them were recorded before the 9/11 attacks, except for one, a recording of news reports from different media organizations, including CNN, that show the disaster caused by simultaneous plane attacks and the collapse of the World Trade Center.

The tapes are graphic, at times horrifying and extremely alarming, always providing new insights into al-Qaeda's organizational structure, its strategies for training, its tactics and its recruitment methods. The fact that no intelligence agency around the world had seen these tapes, nor anticipated their contents and the extent and professionalism of the terrorists, showed how badly the West had underestimated al-Qaeda's fortitude, scope, and depth.

Because of the work I had done in tracking al-Qaeda's networks, CNN's investigative producer, Henry Schuster, asked me to come to Atlanta to look for any familiar faces—in my case, that meant any connections or links to al-Qaeda's network in Southeast Asia. Though the world's attention was focused on Afghanistan and Pakistan, I knew that the next major battleground would be to their south and east, in Indonesia, the Philippines, Malaysia, and other countries where al-Qaeda was busily setting up its training camps and financial networks and where it had already been active for years.

Some of the tapes are motivational propaganda, for the purpose of recruiting new mujahideen. One that I had already watched with our producers and Arabic translator, Hayat Mongodin, earlier that day, incites Muslims to join the jihad in Indonesia.

"This is what they're saying," Hayat told me as we saw pictures of horribly burned, often charred bodies. She translated, "Look at what your brothers are going through. Look at what you're closing your eyes to. They're burning mosques in order to put up synagogues and churches. This is a country of pride. Now it is a country of shame."[2]

The pictures dissolved into a map of Indonesia. She continued to translate: "Since the thirteenth century, Islam came to Indonesia spreading the word of Allah, replacing Hinduism. Now there are people working against you, behind your back, and they are killing your brothers. The government of Suharto [Indonesia's president until 1998] is treating the Muslims in such a harsh way, harsher than the colonizers." Then a more graphic image appeared—a man whose arm was being amputated as the camera panned to the tattered flesh on his back. "Look at this man," translated Hayat, "look at his back. You can't hide his torture. Even if your pens lie, his back won't lie. Be patient and strong in facing this."

The images were from the island of Sulawesi, where Muslims and Christians had been fighting, and the province of West Kalimantan, where brutal beheadings triggered by ethnic conflict between Dayaks (the old head-hunters of Borneo) and Madurese were portrayed as

Christians killing Muslims. Because the Dayaks were mostly Christian converts and the Madurese were Muslims, you could say the tape was technically correct—although religion wasn't the source of that conflict. This, I thought, was the key to al-Qaeda's success: in the anger it incites, its claims always lie on a foundation of unavenged truth.

At the time, the government of Indonesia was officially denying that al-Qaeda had come to the country, though some of its military investigators knew otherwise. Indonesia was fast becoming a stronghold. As the tape continued, the evidence leaped out: men training in a Kashmiri-style training camp, their faces covered with masks that had holes for their eyes and mouths. They were in the forests, running on a military-style obstacle course carrying homemade rifles. It was the first videotaped confirmation that Indonesia was becoming a key node in al-Qaeda's network. I was elated—and terrified.

By now, in the middle of the night, I am the only person on the entire floor. I am working through some of the other subjects in bin Laden's video library—tapes of news broadcasts that showed al-Qaeda's focus, including reports of Muslim conflicts in the Middle East, Chechnya, Kashmir, Bosnia, Indonesia, and the Philippines. Like he did with 9/11, bin Laden watched media coverage of the bombing of the USS *Cole* in 2000 and afterward even recorded news reports as the ship was moved from Yemen to the United States. It seemed that bin Laden monitored the news to see how al-Qaeda operatives and plots were doing and to get an idea of how much the authorities knew.

Finally, I reach the tape numbered 106 on the al-Qaeda registry. I press the PLAY button and watch news coverage of Pope John Paul II's 1995 visit to the Philippines. He had a record number of followers in what was then Asia's only Catholic nation; more than one million people came to see him at Luneta Park. Just weeks before he arrived, a freak chemical fire had led to the discovery of a plot to assassinate him by al-Qaeda operative Ramzi Yousef, the mastermind behind the first World Trade Center bombing.

The coverage that bin Laden or his associates had taped was CNN's. I was the correspondent on the story. I turn up the sound and hear my own voice, like listening to a ghost from the past. I try to picture bin Laden watching me. It is chilling. Did he laugh at my naiveté? Was he relieved at the simplistic picture my reports created? At the time, I had made the same mistake the CIA and FBI had about his terror plots in the Philippines, completely underestimating his organization's imagination and perseverance.

Even then, al-Qaeda members in the Philippines were planning what would become the 9/11 attacks, carried out because their discovery in 1995 had been ignored by authorities around the world. Now the Philippines, Indonesia, and neighboring countries had blossomed into one of al-Qaeda's most important centers.

What I didn't know was that in 1995 I had stumbled onto al-Qaeda's first-known cell in Southeast Asia. Although its plots would be foiled and most of its cell members arrested, al-Qaeda learned from its mistakes. Instead of sending Arabs to set up the next cells, al-Qaeda began to recruit from the regions it wanted to control. Over the years, al-Qaeda successfully infiltrated and co-opted homegrown Muslim movements around the world: in North America, Europe, the Middle East, Chechnya, Kashmir, Africa, and Southeast Asia. Groups from these regions have their own domestic agendas, but they are also pushing forward al-Qaeda's anti-Western goals. Through al-Qaeda, terrorist organizations around the world have exchanged tactics and information for more than a decade, fueling conflicts that, had they remained domestic issues contained within borders, may long ago have ended or been controlled. As I'll show in this book, this has been going on silently in Southeast Asia, slipping beneath the sensors of intelligence and law-enforcement agencies since 1988.

September 11 exposed something that had long been ignored— how al-Qaeda capitalized on the growth of radical Islam and anti-U.S. sentiment around the world. For me, it created a new framework for analyzing recent events. My discovery of al-Qaeda's network in Southeast Asia was like building links in a chain: each link led to the next, and forging the chain meant revisiting many of the stories I had reported on over the past fifteen years—particularly those that had struck me as instances of irrationality and senseless violence. For the first time, I began to understand *why* events had happened the way they did—mainly, what was behind the numerous, unexplained bombings and ethnic and religious riots I had reported on from the region. I began to realize much of the violence I had lived through had been fueled and exacerbated by al-Qaeda.

After 9/11, I looked up longtime contacts—investigators who had risen in the ranks in the Philippines, Indonesia, Singapore, and Malaysia. I realized they all were scampering to harness their resources and gather intelligence. My contacts were more than willing to share past intelligence reports. And for a short period of time, they desperately needed help. That was my window of opportunity. Often, because some nations lacked resources or the case officers didn't have time to go through unwieldy bureaucracies, investigators picked up the phone and called me—to find out whether a name was familiar or to brainstorm about the meaning of some new information.

Talking to investigators in different countries, often on deep background, I discovered what information they shared—or didn't share—with their neighbors. I was horrified at how crucial information would get lost when someone didn't see how it fit into the bigger picture. I saw firsthand how the United States underestimated the threat in the region.

The Philippines—because of the information it discovered in 1995—had much more information about al-Qaeda than its own intelligence or that of the United States realized. I began to collect intelligence documents. The joke in Manila now is that CNN's library is more extensive and better organized than the main Philippine intelligence database. Why? Because most Filipino case officers keep their own files and don't necessarily share them with others outside their units. There isn't a single, central data bank. The same situation exists in Indonesia and other countries in the region. This, on a simple scale, shows one of the main problems of this war on terror: the inability of law-enforcement officials and investigators on the ground to share their information with one another, let alone with other nations.

It didn't help that at the time al-Qaeda was gathering momentum, senior U.S. officials had little knowledge of the way things really worked in the region beyond the briefing papers they received in Washington. They had an inherent distrust of "third-world intelligence,"[3] and regional intelligence officers often told me they wished they had more information from the United States.[4] Intelligence agents are not only fighting to uncover information about terrorist networks, but after getting the information, they often have to fight, at great personal risk, to get their information passed up the chain of command, and struggle even harder to get the politicians to act on it.

Sometimes countries and institutions are so factionalized they can't even decide on a common agenda within their borders. In Indonesia, everything was in disarray. Imagine the office of the president—and the chief of intelligence—changing four times in four years. After the fall of Suharto, the most experienced information source, the military intelligence, had been discredited. The police, separated from the military in 1999 and now tasked with domestic intelligence-gathering, had no experience.

Ajaj Sahni, the head of the Institute for Conflict Management in New Delhi, summed up the intelligence dilemma for me: "Nation-states have still not gotten beyond the conventional position of interests of state. Each country thinks that it is, in some measure, on its own in this ball game. We talk about globalization, but I would like to emphasize that the only truly globalized enterprise today is terrorism."[5]

Much of what you will read in this book has never been published before. It is information I gathered from intelligence documents I collected over two years from Southeast Asia, the United States, Canada, and two European nations. I have used only information I have been able to cross-check with three different sources from at least two different countries.

I wrote this book because I was frustrated with the denial of public officials about the scope of the threat even as their countries' intelligence services gathered this information. This is the reality that lies beneath the surface. I've lived through many of the terrorists' attacks in the region. I've met victims and operatives. I've seen the violence the terrorists can unleash. And I believe the only way to stop the network from growing is to understand what they've accomplished, what they believe in, what they tell their new recruits, and, above all, to shift the paradigm of how we respond to this global threat.

CHAPTER 1

PICTURES DON'T LIE

An aide drew the curtains as the official took the CD out of his bag. The ground rules were clear: everything I would see or be told was for background purposes; I couldn't report this for CNN; I couldn't even tell anyone else this meeting took place. The date was December 12, 2002.

"This is highly classified, Maria," he said. "No copies exist outside of the military command." He pulled the CD out of its case, inserted it into the computer, and clicked the mouse. Seven files appeared on the computer screen. He clicked on one of the icons, and a black-and-white photograph appeared. Taken from 7,000 feet in the air, it showed the Philippines' southern island of Mindanao, huge tracts of forests making it extremely easy to see where the trees had been cleared and the land put to use.

"Let me explain," he said, pointing to a large, developed clearing with many structures. "This was the main Abubakar complex"—referring to Camp Abubakar, a sprawling complex and set of terrorist training camps that had been highly active for several years, despite one major government crackdown in 2000. The camps were run by the MILF, the Moro Islamic Liberation Front, for al-Qaeda and its associate groups. One of the camps, named Camp Palestine, was an exclusive Arab facility; another, named Camp Hodeibia, was for Jemaah Islamiyah, al-Qaeda's network in Southeast Asia.

"Camp Hodeibia was set up with al-Qaeda's help in 1994." He clicked on another icon. "When we looked through our files, we found this area had been photographed at the time. This is what it looked like. You can see here"—using the mouse to point to a long rectangular shape—"this long building is the barracks. Here, outside, you can see the clearing and something like an outdoor track which they set up. This must be their main area for training. Around the outskirts of the clearing, you can see a smaller series of structures, houses."

"Can we get closer?" I asked.

The official clicked on the mouse to zoom in closer. Now I could see the marks of the tracks and what seemed like fencing delineating the perimeter.

"Okay, that was in 1994," he said, closing the file. "Now look what happened in 2000."

In six years, the camp had grown significantly. Large swathes of trees had been uprooted to link the small original oblong area through a thick tunnel-like corridor to another large clearing farther south. It looked as if there was a T cut out of the forests, its base slightly enlarged and bulging. I used the mouse to zoom the picture in and saw that the running tracks had been moved from the original spot in 1994 to this bulge-like clearing to the south. At the base of the T was a small circular tract of land with several small structures and one rectangular building at its southernmost tip.

"See how they expanded?" he asked. Using the mouse, he traced the route. "Here, these trees were cleared to make room for this expansion. It's twelve by sixteen kilometers here. There are two bridges inside the camps. Here"—using the mouse to point to a small sticklike structure—"and here. And here's the football field. So we know as early as 1994, Hashim Salamat [the head of the MILF] had funding."

"But that's so early. Couldn't the Filipinos have set that up on their own?" I asked.

"No. No. Impossible. Hashim can't do it alone. That place is very inaccessible. Whoever made this had to have a lot of money and support. Look, it's in the northernmost, northeast portion of Abubakar."

In 2000, Philippine President Joseph Estrada had declared all-out war on the MILF and attacked the complex. But it had not been a successful war, and it was abandoned by his successor's regime.

"Are the al-Qaeda camps still operating?" I asked.

"I can't say they're al-Qaeda," the official replied coyly.

"But can I? Would I be accurate if I did?"

"We know there are foreigners there. A lot of Indonesians, Arabs, Middle Easterners," he replied. It was the intelligence I had been searching for. Despite the fact that the American war on terror was more than a year old, despite the Bali bombing, there were active al-Qaeda camps in the Philippines.

I took a deep breath. "Is the Philippines doing anything about it?"

"No. We're in peace talks now, right?" he answered, his voice heavy with irony. No Philippine government official wanted to say *al-Qaeda*. The evidence was filtering from its neighbors: more than a hundred al-Qaeda–linked terrorists had been arrested in Southeast Asia, and most of them confessed they had trained in camps in Afghanistan prior to the U.S. invasion, or in the Philippines.

"Ask your friend, Madam President," he added. When Gloria Macapagal-Arroyo took office on January 20, 2001, she pulled the military back and reversed the policy of her predecessor, saying she believed the way to lasting peace with the MILF was to negotiate.

"Look," he said, taking the mouse. "This"—holding it up—"is Abubakar. Then up here"—putting down a water bottle top—"is Hodeibia. Then there's a huge mountain, and you get to Bushra in Lanao del Sur."

In several intelligence documents, I had seen lists of foreigners training in three MILF camps, including Camp Bushra. One named fourteen men—from Indonesia, Egypt, Afghanistan, Pakistan, Kuwait, Saudi Arabia, and Qatar.[1] That report was dated August 24, 2001. Years before that and until today, thousands of Islamic militants, Filipinos and foreigners, have learned terrorist techniques in more than twenty-seven camps set up by the MILF in the southern Philippines. These training courses are not just patterned after the al-Qaeda camps in Afghanistan; they are run with al-Qaeda's support and leadership.

He clicked on the mouse again. "In Bushra, there are three camps, here—1, 2, 3. See them? One of them is Palestine, but we don't know which one. But here, this is target 1 . . ."

"When was this a target?" I asked.

"During the war."

"In 2000?"

"Yes," he said. "This is area 1"—using the mouse to encircle it—"this is area 2, and there's area 3. Area 3 is supposed to be the main camp, Bushra proper. You can see it's obliterated." All that remained was a clearing. No structures. "Area 2 is also obliterated." Then he clicked and enlarged area 3. "Now area 3—that still exists. There are structures still there, and the camp seems to be in relatively good condition, meaning someone is taking care of it."

"It's still being used?" I asked.

"Yes."

Incredible. One year earlier, I had wagered with several friends there would be an attack in Indonesia before the end of 2002 because government denial allowed the terrorists to work in peace. When the Bali bombings killed more than two hundred people on October 12, 2002, it was in spite of many signals that authorities had documented of a growing threat. Bali could have been prevented. The Indonesian police had had the names of every single one of the Bali plotters well in advance. But political gamesmanship—courting moderate Muslims by ignoring extremists—had prevented anyone from taking action.

Now I had the same churning feeling at the pit of my stomach. The lessons hadn't been learned. Indonesia may now be arresting terrorists, but the key American ally in the region, the Philippines, remained in denial about the existence of terrorist training camps. The terrorists still have a place to train and gather. If they can do that, another attack is certain.

Long before the United States was ever aware of it, Osama bin Laden had declared war on America in Southeast Asia, his first attempt to expand his influence. In 1988, he sent his brother-in-law Mohammed Jamal Khalifa to the Philippines to set up a financial infrastructure of charities and other organizations. Khalifa married a local woman and integrated into Filipino society, often asking politicians and Manila's elite to sit on the boards of his charities.[2] In fact, he had the help of the Saudi Arabian embassy to establish his first charity. That was phase one. A few years later, in 1994, when the financial support network was in place, bin Laden activated phase two by sending in several cells of expert terrorists. It is no coincidence that every single major al-Qaeda plot since 1993 has had some link to the Philippines: the attack on the World Trade Center in 1993; the 1995 Manila plot to bomb eleven U.S. airliners over Asia; the 1998 bombings of U.S. embassies in East Africa; the attack on the U.S. naval destroyer, the USS *Cole*, in 2000; the 9/11 attacks in 2001; the plot to truck-bomb U.S. embassies and Western interests in Southeast Asia in 2002; the Bali blasts later that year, and the J. W. Marriott Hotel attack in August 2003.

In 1994, one Filipino investigator picked up the underground movements and began to warn of an alarming trend he had discovered. Colonel Rodolfo "Boogie" Mendoza had combined hundreds of wiretaps and countless man-hours of surveillance into a 175-page report on the infiltration of local Muslim groups by international terrorists. It documented the dramatic 150 percent rise in terrorist acts from 1991 to 1994; the boom of madrassas, or Muslim religious schools (1,308 in number), and mosques (2,000); and a watch list of Arab nationals Mendoza believed were involved in spreading radical, jihadist ideas from the Middle East.

The statistics were alarming.[3] His watch list alone—those names he believed were connected to international terrorist groups—had more than 100 names on it.

The countries with the largest Muslim populations are in Asia: Indonesia, India, Pakistan, and Bangladesh. More than 230 million—nearly 25 percent—of the world's 1.2 billion Muslims live in Southeast Asia, influenced by its history, traditions, and cultures.

Locked between giants India and China, with 1 billion people each, Southeast Asia's 500 million people have often been ignored in recent history, but these chains of islands may hold the key to the future of Islam, and they certainly hold the key to the future of al-Qaeda. Unlike the Middle East or South Asia, Islam in Southeast Asia is moderate, malleable, and adaptable. Islam here is relatively new; it was brought in by traders in the thirteenth century rather than imposed by conquest, and Islam has merged freely with local cultures. Like most other religions in Southeast Asia, what lies underneath is still visible: at times, strains of animism and Buddhism peek through. Islam here has coexisted for centuries with other religions. In fact, Indonesia's 220 million Muslims are *abangans*—Muslims who fused Islam with Buddhism, Hinduism, and other beliefs like animism. Consequently, many hardliners in the Middle East patronizingly dismiss Islam in Southeast Asia as "not real" or "the fringes."

That is a mistake. Islam here is a work in progress, and as such has responded often successfully to the challenges of the modern world. The growth and appeal of radical Islam in the region is not only part of a global trend; it is also part of the march of progress. The war on terrorism here is a struggle for the soul of Islam.

Radical Islam's entry into the region coincided with a growing demand for democracy. Most nations in Southeast Asia have a colonial past: Indonesia was ruled for 350 years by the Dutch; the Philippines was ruled by Spain for 250 years; Singapore and Malaysia were ruled by the British. In the 1970s, these countries developed strongman leaders: Suharto, Marcos, Lee Kuan Yew, and Mahathir. By the late 1980s the cry was for democracy. Ironically, democracy—the nemesis of radical Islam—helped create the conditions under which the radical ideology could spread in Southeast Asia. It began with People Power in the Philippines in 1986. The ensuing chaos, reorganization of the political landscape, and shifts of power helped al-Qaeda infiltrate the MILF, the largest Muslim separatist group in the country, and the more extremist Abu Sayyaf. More than a decade later, the same thing happened in Indonesia, when massive, violent protests forced President Suharto to step down.

During times of sweeping change, people look for meaning, creating boom times for religion. Radical Islam in Southeast Asia was growing by leaps and bounds, spurred by the oil boom of the early 1970s. After the price of oil quadrupled, Saudi Arabia poured massive amounts of cash into Southeast Asia, building mosques and religious schools and spreading the austere version of Wahhabi Islam. That was followed by the overthrow of the Shah of Iran in 1979, a revolution that had a profound effect on Muslims' belief in Islam as a form of political power. Finally, there was jihad, the first modern holy war, in 1989.

The call to jihad against the Soviets in Afghanistan was highly appealing in Southeast Asia. In the Philippines alone, more than one thousand Muslims made the trip. They were joined by hundreds more from Indonesia, Malaysia, Thailand, and Singapore. When they returned home, they brought back the radical ideas—and terrorist techniques—they learned from the camps of Afghanistan.

The network al-Qaeda set up in Southeast Asia is not just its new center of training and operations; it is also a model for other regions, such as Chechnya and East Africa. Harnessing local groups, al-Qaeda has encouraged them to carve out autonomous Islamic areas that can be linked together worldwide. "He was able to tap different youths in different regions on different issues," Pakistan's former prime minister, Benazir Bhutto, told me, "by pegging it all as a war between Islam and the West, but in fact, he was damaging the regional conflicts for his own agenda, which was to topple important Muslim countries and seize power for himself."[4] Much like fascism and communism before, the goal is political power: using Islam as a tool for global domination. "Their goal is world dominion," says Philippine immigration commissioner Andrea Domingo, "and they are using religion as the battle cry."[5]

I sat down with Philippine president Gloria Macapagal-Arroyo in January 2003, less than a month after I saw the aerial photographs of the MILF training camps. About a year earlier, more than 600 U.S. special forces, part of 1,200 American troops, were sent to the Philippines, dubbed "the second front" after Afghanistan. Their focus was the extremist group the Abu Sayyaf, notorious for kidnappings and beheadings. I believed that American and Filipino troops were looking at the wrong people.

Based on hundreds of intelligence documents from more than half a dozen countries across the region, along with intelligence from at least three Western nations, including the United States, it was clear to me that the main al-Qaeda ally in the Philippines was the MILF, the largest Muslim separatist group in the country. Yet when the United States had tried to place it on the list of terrorist organizations, high-level American and Filipino sources told me that President Arroyo personally lobbied to keep it off. The MILF is interwoven into the social fabric of the south. It is strongly identified as a prime fighter for Muslims and enjoys popular support. President Arroyo's critics charged that she wanted to sign a peace agreement as a great vote getter for the 2004 elections, but a few days before my interview, Arroyo announced she would not be running for office in the 2004 elections.

Never having been elected president herself, Arroyo's reign was highly political, wracked by infighting and intense lobbying. She came to power in January 2001 on the wave of protests that threatened to derail her country's fragile democracy. It was a bastardized version of the mighty 1986 People Power revolt, which captured the world's imagination and peacefully ousted then-President Ferdinand Marcos, who had been in power for twenty-one years. Those heady protests brought democracy to this country, but in the decade that followed, the political infighting, rampant corruption, and a sluggish, barely moving economy all took their toll on its once idealistic people.

The Philippines practiced one-man, one-vote democracy. A high illiteracy rate ensured election campaigns would cater to the lowest common denominator, turning campaigns into rock-and-roll parties with politicians banking on name recognition rather than issues and platforms. By the 1998 presidential elections, Joseph Estrada—an aging movie star known for playing underdog roles—won the polls. Under him corruption became so flagrant, his society rebelled. He became the first Philippine president to be impeached for corruption, and the trial—held by the senate—was so flawed that, during the televised proceedings, when a decision was made not to accept key evidence against the president, some senators walked out and the people took to the streets.

The protests, dubbed People Power 2, lasted around the clock for nearly a week. It was history strangely revisited: The middle class and elite flocked to the streets against Estrada while his poorer supporters held their own demonstrations in another part of the city. The military was the deciding vote, planting the seeds for its further forays into politics. Less than a week into the civil disorder, the military abandoned Mr. Estrada and threw its lot behind his vice president, Gloria Macapagal-Arroyo. A little less than two years into his six-year term, Mr. Estrada was deposed.

On January 20, 2001, in the middle of a massive crowd of people on the main highway, EDSA (Epifanio de los Santos Avenue), where People Power had succeeded in 1986, Gloria Macapagal-Arroyo took the oath of office as her nation's fourteenth president. But the power of the people was tainted by a key difference between 1986 and 2001: The protests that brought Arroyo to power deposed a duly elected president, not a dictator. That would haunt the first few months of her presidency as Estrada's supporters attempted to launch a third People Power revolt against her on May 1, 2001. For a while, Filipino society split on economic lines: Mr. Estrada's supporters came from the bottom rung, while Mrs. Arroyo was backed by the middle and elite classes. She survived the split, attempting to unite her fractured people, but the damage had been done. Through the beginning of her term, Mrs. Arroyo was constantly forced to compromise her vision in order to maintain the unwieldy coalition that brought her to power. By announcing she would not run for office in 2004, she defanged the political lobbyists and empowered her administration by effectively declaring her political debts paid.

I had done many one-on-one interviews with her for more than a decade—first when she was a trade undersecretary, then a three-term senator, a cabinet member, the vice president—including the day after she took office as her nation's leader. At 4 feet, 9 inches, this petite, energetic woman was fun to interview. She was lively, honest, at times impatient, but always willing to engage in a debate.

So now, in January 2003, my crew was set up, and I was going over my notes when her aides walked into the room at Malacañang Palace. Our interview was in her study: a two-camera shoot, which meant there were at least fifteen other people listening to our conversation. We stood up. The door opened, and she walked in—wearing a suit that was the same color as mine. Wearing nearly identical red, we looked at each other. My cameraman, Andrew Clark, was horrified. She laughed and ducked back out. "Let me change!" she said.

When she returned, she sat down, and we began by discussing her decision and some general topics of the day. Her main goals now, she said, were political and economic reforms, setting the stage for the 2004 elections and setting the policies to win the war on terror.

"We have the terrorist threats, and that's the biggest security concern." She outlined a comprehensive strategy. "We have to tackle it in several ways: a military solution, a political solution, cultural solution, economic solution: they are all important. The military solution is to make sure we win the victories. The political solution is to continue to talk peace with those who are willing to try peace—to give peace a chance. The cultural solution is that there is that threat to make the terrorist war a religious war. Instead, we must make it an opportunity for religious understanding. And the economic solution, of course, is to remove the recruiting grounds for terrorism—which is not to be distracted from our fight against poverty."

In our last four interviews, I had grilled the president harshly about the MILF's links to al-Qaeda. Each time, Mrs. Arroyo had denied that they existed, characterizing the MILF as a domestic political issue. "After September 11, the MILF made it very clear that they are not linked to Osama bin Laden and al-Qaeda," she had told me earlier. "I think that their statement is a very big confidence-building step, and it makes our peace process even more successful."[6] Now that she was stepping down, I tried again. Her position had clearly changed.

"We are hoping that by dealing with the MILF both militarily and politically, that we can get them to understand that they must break all links—if any—with terrorist groups, and that there is life—there is more life for their people, who are of course, our people, if they go on the road of peace talks, laying down their arms and seeking to participate in development."[7]

It was something—hedged, perhaps, but far from a categorical denial of the evidence of the aerial photos. She continued, "I would not want to, I would not want to be detailed on intelligence reports, but what I can say is that our peace efforts are aimed at getting the MILF to recognize that peace is the better road for them than being linked up with terrorist groups."

The truth in the Philippines and Southeast Asia is something that anyone concerned about the future of terrorism needs to face. Few countries did it instantly, but the September 11 attacks were like a tidal wave, washing away the flimsy, outdated security and defense paradigms largely determined by the cold war. In effect, it was a pivotal moment that forced reexamination of recent history. Stripping away outdated notions revealed new, unfamiliar terrain that showed the extent and power of the infrastructure al-Qaeda had been building since 1988. In one Southeast Asian country after another, I witnessed a level of denial from political leaders who did not want to even admit there was a threat. There were several reasons: acknowledging the threat required taking action; sometimes, leaders were afraid of its impact on tourism; other times, officials had different priorities and terrorism didn't seem like an unmanageable problem.

These leaders' reactions were similar to the reactions triggered by Boogie Mendoza's pioneering report in the mid-90s. There was interest, but as long as there were no attacks, no one felt the need to take action. That only meant the terrorist cells could build their network in peace.

Mendoza's report was released on December 15, 1994, the same month Khalifa left the Philippines as Phase 2—the creation of terrorist cells—began. Intelligence sources say bin Laden himself had already made at least one trip to establish his network. A former CIA station chief in Manila placed bin Laden in the country in 1992. "Bin Laden presented himself as a wealthy Saudi who wanted to invest in Muslim areas and donate money to charity," the former CIA officer said. Then

President Fidel Ramos even allegedly authorized the use of a C-130 airplane to fly bin Laden from the capital, Manila, to Mindanao.[8] Others said bin Laden allegedly met with several government officials who helped him purchase property and set up bank accounts.[9]

Mendoza's report was largely forgotten, and Mendoza's career was even derailed by political opponents until the events of September 11 brought him back to the center of the action. Meanwhile, al-Qaeda had long since brought in its top guns—to Manila's red-light district.

CHAPTER 2

THE BASE

Outside the Manila Bay Club on Roxas Boulevard, car horns are blaring. Another Saturday night in the notorious red-light district of Malate. Boys selling cigarettes and mints stop by open car windows. If you lean your head out, you can feel the sea breeze. On one side of the road is the black ocean. On the other, bright neon lights and raucous music hit you as you approach. Taxis drop their passengers at the numerous clubs offering girls for sale. The drivers are really the guides: for the newbies, there's Firehouse, a little more laid back than some, girls dancing on a stage, wrapped suggestively around poles; for those wanting something more than suggestive, there's Manila Bay. When you walk in, the music is so loud it feels like the pounding of your heart. The promise of sex is palpable.

Girls come to you in different ways. You can sit at the bar, and inevitably someone will approach. She'll talk to you. You buy her a drink. If you're interested in conversation, you can stay there all night. Her job is to get you to buy her specially priced drinks. The tab may surprise you at the end of the night. If you ask her what she does, she may say she's a GRO—guest relations officer, a high-class euphemism for bar girl. Some encounters with GROs never go beyond conversation. But occasionally, if you get along well, she'll ask if you'd like her to go home with you. The limit is always up to you. That's really the thrill for most of the regulars. The power is always on your side. As long as you pay.

At Manila Bay, you can get special karaoke rooms. You and your friends can drink and sing, the girls helping you select your songs and sometimes singing for you—always ordering more drinks for everyone. Go a little farther to the back, and you may be invited into a special room. Here, everything is more blatant. Behind two-way mirrors, you can see girls in suggestive or sometimes lurid acts. In one corner, it's just a groups of girls sitting in bikinis with numbers, like beauty queens. All you have to do is point or give the number of a girl, and for a price, she's yours for the night. It's the ultimate buffet.

Although it looks gaudy and impersonal, the beauty of the red-light district in the Philippines is that it's neither. Few of the girls are hardened prostitutes. They're here because they left their families in the provinces and came to the capital looking for jobs, expecting to send money home. Some are hoping to find a foreigner husband—a Prince Charming to take them away from life in the Philippines. They're young. Still idealistic. Often gullible. The irony is that many of these girls are looking for romance. That, combined with the air of sex for sale, is what attracts the men.

Look at Carol Santiago. At twenty-eight years old, she's older than most of the other girls, but when the average height is 5 feet, 2 inches, at 5 feet, 6 inches she stands out. Slim at 105 pounds, long black hair, Carol is an Asian beauty.[1] She left her family in Davao City in Mindanao to look for a job in Manila. She didn't think it would be hard. After all, she's a college graduate with a degree in nutrition.

When Wali Khan Amin Shah and his friend Amein Mohammed walked in, Shah picked her out of the crowd. Carol sat and talked with the two Arabs. It wasn't out of the ordinary. Many Arabs come to the red-light district for a little R&R. The Arabs these Filipinas knew dropped the restrictions of the Muslim world. Although some came in flowing robes, most wore Western clothes, as Shah and his friend did.

That night in early 1993, Shah introduced himself to Carol as Osama Asmurai. Twenty-eight years old, with brown eyes, dark brown curly hair and a moustache, at 5 feet, 7 inches, Wali Khan weighed about 150 pounds. Compared to the other men who often came to Manila Bay, he was good looking. The three talked for a while that night, but it was difficult with the loud music. They spent much of the time drinking and watching the scene. Carol noticed there was something wrong with Shah's left hand: his ring and middle fingers were cut off. Later, he would tell her he was injured in an explosion while he was fighting in Afghanistan. When Shah asked if she was free for dinner the next night, Carol was thrilled.

She met him before coming to work in a restaurant nearby—across the street from the Army and Navy Club on Roxas Boulevard. In the open-air restaurant that served Filipino food, the two hit it off. By September 1993, Carol became the girlfriend of Wali Khan Amin Shah. She opened a bank account for him in her name, and she also registered a pager for him in Manila under her name. She told him her real name was Catherine Brioso, but that she didn't like using it at the club.[2] He told her he traveled under different names. She knew he had a passport from Afghanistan under the name Wali Khan Amin Shah. He also had a Norwegian passport in the name of Hashin Grabi.[3] She had a chance to see that for herself. In the two years or so they lived together, Shah traveled frequently, and he took her with him on some of those trips.[4] They went to beaches in the Philippines—Boracay and Cebu—but they also traveled together to Hong Kong, Bangkok, and Kuala Lumpur, where Shah attended to business. Until the day she was picked up by Philippine investigators, January 12, 1995, she said she had no idea her boyfriend was a terrorist.[5]

Carol had met Shah's other friends, and these are the names she gave to the police: Adam Ali, the alias of Ramzi Yousef, the mastermind of the 1993 bombing of the World Trade Center; Munir, whom police would later identify as Muneer Ibrahim, a rich Saudi Arabian businessman (and whom authorities still want to question); and Abu Omar, an alias for Ahmad al-Hamwi, from Turkey, tied closely to bin Laden's brother-in-law Khalifa. Al-Hamwi was the director of a nongovernmental organization Khalifa set up in the Philippines, the International Relations and Information Center, IRIC. Al-Hamwi is also married to the sister of Khalifa's Filipina wife.[6]

Later, with Carol's help, investigators would find out Wali Khan Amin Shah and Amein Mohammed were part of the financial network that funded what would be the first al-Qaeda cell in Manila. Lead investigator Boogie Mendoza would spend much time trying to track down Mohammed, a Yemeni member of the cell based in Malaysia's capital, Kuala Lumpur. Shah and Mohammed were both on the board of directors of a Malaysian trading company named Konsojaya, which channeled money from bin Laden to the Manila cell. It had incorporated in Kuala Lumpur on June 2, 1994. One other name stood out on the incorporation papers: Riduan bin Isamuddin, a Malay, born April 4, 1964. An Indonesian cleric who fled to Malaysia in the mid-1980s, Isamuddin would later take on the pseudonym Hambali. After 9/11, he would be one of only two non-Arabs to sit on al-Qaeda's leadership council.

Carol's first meeting with Wali Shah in 1993 is as good a date as any for the starting point of al-Qaeda's organized presence in Southeast Asia. There were plenty of local Muslim extremists, including some who had fought against the Soviet Union with bin Laden in Afghanistan in the 1980s, like Hambali, and others who studied with al-Qaeda leaders in Pakistan and returned to start local organizations, like Abdurajak Janjalani, the Filipino who set up the Abu Sayyaf. Some of those, investigators have concluded, were Middle Eastern sleeper agents embedded during that time, like Hadi Yousef Alghoul, would be imprisoned only after the September 11 attacks. He had lived in the Philippines since the early 1980s and was a cousin of Ramzi Yousef. Alghoul had married a Filipina and ran a women's clothing business. Yousef had another family member in Manila in the mid-1990s: his brother Adel Annon had literally set up shop in the Philippines, buying the Mindanao Meat Shop, a small store at the edge of the red-light district selling Arabic food and halal meat. According to intelligence sources, he was ready for his role in Yousef's "48 hours of terror," the planned attacks on eleven U.S. airliners. If these sources are correct, bin Laden and his network had plotted all this before 1994.

But not until the arrival in Manila of Wali Shah, Ramzi Yousef, and such other notorious leaders as Khalid Shaikh Mohammed (KSM) did al-Qaeda activate the cells and their plots. Using local women to solidify their new identities and establish them as members of the community is a strategy al-Qaeda operatives around the world use. Investigators have learned a good deal of information from the ex-girlfriends of terrorists. In all the time he was in the Philippines, KSM was known as Abdul Majid or Salim (Salem) Ali.[7] His English was fluent after attending two colleges in the United States. He was also fluent in Arabic, Persian, and his native Urdu. At times, he masqueraded as a wealthy Saudi sheikh. On other occasions he was a Qatari plywood exporter.

Yet surprisingly, in August 1994 in a seedy Quezon City bar, he introduced himself to the girls he met there as Shaikh Mohammed.[8] He was staying in a small, dingy motel in that suburb of Manila, about an hour away from the red-light district. It was the kind of place where the girls who are too old for Malate wind up. The bar at KSM's hotel, Sir Williams Karaoke, has since burned down, but back then it was on the second floor of the building. There, Rose Mosquera first saw Shaikh Mohammed with one of her friends, a girl named Precious who worked at the bar. The next night, she joined Precious and her friend at their table. He seemed pleasant enough. When he came back a third night, she asked him to sit with her at a table with her friends Helen and Jovy. He stayed with them for about an hour, shared jokes, and bought them all drinks. Before he left to go to his room upstairs, he asked her if she could come speak with him.

"I have a little problem," he said. "I need to open a bank account so I can send money I can use in Manila. As a foreigner, it's not so easy, and I wonder if you can help me with this?"

"What do you want me to do?" asked Rose.

"Just open a bank account in your name."

"Why would I do that?"

"Because I can help you with other things. I will take care of the account, and maybe you will let me help you with anything you want. Is there something I can do for you?"

"That's all I'd have to do for you? Open a bank account?"

"We can talk about this tomorrow. We can meet about one o'clock. Where can we have lunch?"

"We can meet at Wendy's down the street—at the corner of EDSA and Kamias. You know which one?"

"I can find it, and please everything must be kept secret—for my business, you understand?"

The next day, she met KSM at Wendy's. He was with two other Arab-looking foreigners. They had lunch, hamburgers and french fries. Conversation was natural. After eating, they rode a bus to go to Megamall, about a thirty-minute ride away, a sprawling shopping complex touted as the largest mall in Asia. They had her picture taken at the photo booth. Then they went to the bank in the complex. The three men helped her fill out the forms, and she opened an account in her name. When she was given the bankbook, she gave it to KSM and never saw it again. He and his friends also asked her if she could buy a cellular phone, and that's where they went next. They took the escalators to the third floor to look at phones. KSM found a nice model for which he paid 21,000 pesos, or about $800. By that time, it was 4:30 P.M., and she told her new friends she had to go to work. KSM gave her 500 pesos for taxi fare. She calculated the ride would cost about 100 pesos, so it was a nice gesture.

That night, KSM didn't show up at the bar. She had told him what she wanted in exchange for what she did for him, and she wondered whether he was now trying to get out of it. So she called his room.

"Hello, Mr. Shaikh?"

"Yes, hello, Rose."

"Mr. Shaikh, what about your promise to buy me a round-trip ticket to Davao?"

"Don't worry, Rose. I remember. Let's meet again tomorrow at Wendy's, and we'll take care of it then, okay?"

The next day when they met, KSM was alone. They had a pleasant lunch together and again took the bus to Megamall. They got off and crossed the four-lane highway in front of the complex. They basked in the mall's air-conditioning as they rode up the escalators to the fourth floor and entered the Williams Lines Booking Office. There, she told police, Shaikh paid 1,460 pesos for her ticket. After that, he took her shopping for a blouse and a skirt. Before she left him, he gave her 1,600 pesos for spending money on the trip and another 500 pesos for her taxi.

About a month later, she called the cell phone registered under her name. She was in Davao visiting her parents at that time, and she needed more money. KSM wired it to her. She last spoke with him in December 1994. She never heard from him again. Their transactions epitomized the world she lived in: money for favors.

KSM would meet other girls and actually get a girlfriend. That he did with his nephew, Ramzi Yousef. Using the names Adam Ali for Yousef and Salem Ali for KSM, the two men introduced themselves to Aminda Custodio and Jane Ramos in August 1994.[9] They were standing outside a busy intersection in the Espana neighborhood. The two girls had just come out of rehearsals for newer and better jobs: they were trying to go to Japan as "cultural dancers." In Japan, such Filipinas were known as Japayukis. Some of them could barely dance, but they could do the same thing GROs did back home: entertain men. Cultural dancers are sent by legitimate organizations allied with the Philippine Overseas Employment Association. They are paid in yen, and the money they send home makes them the new heroes of Manila's poorer neighborhoods.

Twenty-one year-old Aminda Custodio was a student in her second year at the National Teacher's College. She also worked at the Kentucky Fried Chicken near her house in Fairview in Quezon City and as a receptionist at a karaoke bar at the Manor Hotel. That was where she met Jane Ramos, who said she would introduce her to regular guests Yousef and KSM.

Yousef and KSM told the girls they were chemical engineers working for TIC Chemical Company based in Qatar. Aminda became Yousef's girlfriend, and KSM became Jane's boyfriend.[10] By that time, the two men were staying in a five-star hotel between Quezon City and the financial district, Makati. The Edsa Plaza Hotel was a symbol of status for the two young girls and their families, its expansive lobby and high prices beyond their reach. Aminda brought her twin sister and her mother to meet Yousef there. At one point, he visited their family home. Little is known about Jane Ramos, who would disappear soon after Yousef's terrorist cell was busted.

It is hard to know where the plots began and the good times ended. In early December 1994, KSM and Yousef rented a helicopter from the Airlink International Aviation School.[11] Yousef was considering several plots with attacks from the air, and they may have been on a test run. But KSM, who was piloting the chopper, flew over the Sheafa Dental Clinic on M. Adriatico Street near Malate. He pulled out his cellular phone and dialed the number of the dentist he was dating—or, in Philippine terms, "courting"—and told her to come outside and wave to him. It seemed that he wanted to impress her—or that was how Yousef told the story. A few weeks later, the two men went to a beach resort near Manila for scuba diving lessons.[12]

It seemed like fun and games, but KSM prepared years in advance and kept his cell tightly compartmentalized. Only his nephew, Yousef, knew his real name and the extent of his involvement. Yousef brought his high school classmate Abdul Hakim Murad, a commercial pilot, to KSM's Karachi apartment in July 1993, introducing KSM by the alias he would use in Manila: Abdul Majid. The three would meet two more times. Each time, the conversation would center on airplanes, "the mechanics of flying,"[13] and the potential ways to use planes for terror attacks.

Later that month, Yousef, Murad, and a third classmate used Murad's Karachi apartment for a terrorist plot to assassinate Benazir Bhutto, then the Pakistani prime minister. They planned to detonate a bomb near her home as she drove out. A police patrol stopped the men just in time. As Mrs. Bhutto explained: "The men said they had dropped their keys in the gutter and that they were looking for them. And at this stage, they were putting a bomb down there."[14] After the police left, Yousef apparently tried to pull the bomb out, and it accidentally detonated, sending shrapnel into his left eye and injuring his fingers. Murad brought him to the hospital and again met KSM, who came to visit.

In early August 1994, Yousef and Murad visited KSM's apartment again to meet Wali Khan Amin Shah, introduced to Murad by the pseudonym he used in Manila, Osama Asmurai.

Soon after, Yousef and Murad went to Lahore, Pakistan. There, Yousef spent eighteen days taking Murad through an extensive explosive-training workshop.[15] It was in a peasant village in Lahore; Yousef rented a warehouse. Parts of the building had no roof, but two rooms and the bathroom were enclosed. Murad stayed in the building throughout; Yousef went out once to buy food.

Yousef went over the strategies for getting through airport security with the right elements for making a bomb. He also went over the chemicals needed, meticulously showing Murad how high-density chemicals should be avoided because they can be detected by X-ray machines. He used his laptop computer to explain which chemicals should be mixed and in what proportions. Murad took notes on a spiral notebook.

Right after the training, Yousef left for the Philippines. Murad went on to Dubai, where he would get a call from Yousef in mid-December to come to the Philippines.

Yousef's return to the Philippines was through the back door—Basilan, the stronghold of the Abu Sayyaf.[16] Yousef's plan was to train members of the Abu Sayyaf in the use of explosives, but at some point, he became frustrated. According to a later interrogation report, "he saw the problem that the Abu Sayyaf Group's members only know about their 'assault rifles' and nothing more. He called them illiterates."[17] He

did not think the members of the Abu Sayyaf would be able to understand the complexity of his chemical mixtures. He would have to set
certain bombs himself.

Yousef had been training members of the Abu Sayyaf from the birth of
the group. In 1991, when Yousef came to Basilan with Abdurajak Janjalani to form the fledgling group, Janjalani spoke eloquently at the
mosques, enticing younger Filipinos to find Islam's true meaning. His
quiet demeanor won him converts, whom he asked to help him establish an Islamic state in Mindanao "where Muslims can follow Islam in
its purest and strictest form as the only path to Allah."[18]

   You could hear bin Laden's views powering his message. At one
point, Janjalani encouraged his men to kill their enemies, saying the
Koran supports this through the calling of jihad. He spoke about a
vision for an Islamic state patterned after the Caliphate of the Prophet
Mohammed, and condemned Muslim nations like Saudi Arabia,
Indonesia, and Libya for corrupting the true meaning of Islam.[19]

   Still, the Abu Sayyaf is also a product of its environment, and ideo-
logues like Janjalani are rare when the daily fight is to put food on the
table. The two provinces that are home to the Abu Sayyaf, Basilan and
Sulu, are predominantly Muslim and among the poorest in the nation.
They're known as "the Wild West of the Philippines": men with guns
rule the land, and the government and military are often ineffective,
unable to enforce the rule of law. Residents live in grinding poverty,
with no jobs, no justice, and little prospects for hope.

   This is not an ideal source for the sophisticated, educated terrorists
needed by al-Qaeda. In the words of Baser Hajan, who joined the Abu
Sayyaf when he was nineteen years old, "The rebels came to Lantawan
[in Basilan] and someone asked if I wanted to join them. I agreed. I was
fascinated with guns so I figured joining the Abu Sayyaf is the best
thing to do to realize my dream to own a gun."[20]

   It also got him a job and allowed him to travel—an unattainable
dream for many of the Filipinos who live in these areas. "We were given
food and clothes. Sometimes, I even went to Sandakan in Malaysia for a
weeklong vacation," he said. "We would go there by boat."[21]

   The line between criminal and ideologue is a hazy one for many
members of the Abu Sayyaf. Most of their members are poor and uned-

ucated with little religious training. Still, as promised, al-Qaeda supported the group with money and training.

On December 23, 1991, bin Laden's brother-in-law Mohammed
Jamal Khalifa met with members of Janjalani's personal staff at a
mosque in Basilan. He gave them 30,000 pesos, or about $1,000, to
bomb a church in Jolo.[22] Although they used only hand grenades, and
there were no fatalities, "it was the first terrorist operation" of the Abu
Sayyaf.[23]

About a month later, on January 29, 1992, Khalifa met with Janjalani at the Abu Sayyaf camp in Basilan. Wali Shah and Ramzi Yousef
came with him, and again money was delivered to the Abu Sayyaf.
This time, Khalifa gave 160,000 pesos, or $6,038, for two operations:
to assassinate an Italian missionary, Father Salvatorre Carzedda, and
to plant a bomb at the Basilan Public Market to disrupt elections in
the province. The fledgling group quickly accomplished both assignments.

The next month, on February 23, Khalifa met with Abu Sayyaf
leaders in General Santos City. He convinced them to create the Urban
Guerrilla Squad (UGS) to launch terrorist attacks in Zamboanga City:
to assassinate a radio announcer and to bomb Fort Pilar. On August 28,
a grenade thrown at Fort Pilar killed five people and wounded forty-
one others; the next month, on September 21, Greg Hapalla and two
others from radio station DXAS were killed. In April 1993, the Abu
Sayyaf clashed with troops in Tabuk, Isabela, in Basilan. Khalifa helped
the Abu Sayyaf with food, medicines, and ammunition.

Later, other al-Qaeda operatives would help in the training of the
Abu Sayyaf. In 1995, Islamic radicals from Kuwait, Qatar, Oman,
Bosnia, and Yemen would be among those who came to their jungle
camps to train the Abu Sayyaf members. One graduate said he met at
least nine "Arabs" whom he heard "talking on mobile phones and making overseas calls."[24]

Although it's never been acknowledged by the Philippine government, the Abu Sayyaf continued to work with al-Qaeda, even after
9/11.[25] In 1997, bin Laden funded the travel of three al-Qaeda members to Malaysia. They were met in Malaysia by Abu Sayyaf member
Ashraf Barreto Kunting, who acted as their intermediary and guide in
the southern Philippines. The three returned again sometime between
May and August 2001. In fact, based on the interrogation of three Abu

Sayyaf members, intelligence officials now know that two al-Qaeda members were inside the Abu Sayyaf base camp on Basilan Island one day after the September 11 attacks.

Yousef spent only a few weeks in Basilan in August and September 1994 before deciding to do his own bombing. He returned to Manila, established contacts with the members of the network in place, and began to fine-tune his bomb plans. Yousef was an expert and an innovator; the bomb he set off at the World Trade Center in 1993 had been used only once before in 73,000 explosions recorded by the FBI.[26] In Manila, he developed and tested what became known as his specialty (later taught throughout al-Qaeda camps).

Yousef learned to mix his own nitroglycerin from basic compounds he could easily buy on the market, especially the United States. His student Murad, who continued lessons in Manila, would later provide the formula to Filipino investigators, explaining that it produced nitroglycerin at such a low density that "even if you'll put it in the X-ray, you will never [detect it]."[27]

Still, nitroglycerin on its own is an extremely volatile mixture. Any slight movement can trigger an explosion. Yousef learned to stabilize it using cotton wool. This is how they could transport nitroglycerin: to the naked eye, it looks like cotton soaked in liquid. The cotton wool is extremely flammable and could trigger an explosion very easily. Yousef's genius came in the timer and detonator he developed. Using a Casio watch, he turned its alarm clock into the bomb's timer. At the set time, it would send an electronic impulse through electronic wires to the fuse—two 9-volt batteries—which sparked light-bulb filaments. A simple bulb filament, combined with a wristwatch and small batteries, was all that was needed to trigger the explosion.[28] Murad boasted, "Nobody in the world can make this timer except us."[29]

The batteries were the only metallic component of the bomb, and Yousef puzzled over how to get them through airport security and X-ray machines. Finally, he thought of hiding them in the hollowed-out heels of his shoes, which fall below the area the X-ray examines.[30] That same idea was used by Briton Richard Reid seven years later to try to blow up an American Airlines jet flying from Europe to the United States.

Before Murad arrived in Manila, Yousef tested his small nitroglycerin bombs at least four times, once with the help of his uncle, KSM. The first attempt was in November 1994, in Cebu City, a 45-minute plane ride from Manila. Yousef placed one of his bombs in the generator room of a shopping mall there. At the set time, the bomb exploded, causing minimal damage but proving that his device worked.[31]

The next test was on December 1, a Thursday night, a busy time in shopping malls in the Philippines because it heralded the beginning of the frantic Christmas season rush. I was at dinner with friends when I got a call from CNN that a bomb had exploded. I ran to the site, only a short distance away, at the Greenbelt Theater adjacent to a mall. By the time I got there, the police had already roped off the area. They had concluded that the bomb was under one of the seats. Still, the explosion wasn't large. It caused injuries, but no one was killed. I went back to dinner, and we never did find out the cause until two years later, during the New York trial of Ramzi Yousef's cell. The man who set the bomb under the seat was Wali Shah.[32]

Next, the plotters needed to know whether they could actually get the bomb elements through airport security. For this, Yousef had help. In what he admitted was his first operational role for al-Qaeda, KSM was responsible for casing airport security on a flight from Manila to Seoul, while Yousef took a flight from Hong Kong to Taipei.[33] KSM took concentrated nitromethane, an inexpensive liquid explosive readily available in the Philippines, and poured out the contents of fourteen contact lens solution bottles, taking care not to break the plastic security seals. He refilled the bottles with nitromethane and carried thirteen of the bottles in his bag while Yousef carried one.

To see if they could carry a detonator through the security checks, KSM took a metal bolt and taped it to the arch of his foot, following the model set out by Yousef. He then covered the bolt with a sock. Both men wore clothes with a lot of metal buttons and accessories to confuse the security scanner. Although they chose not to check in baggage, they carried bags in which they placed plenty of condoms to "support their cover story that their main purpose in traveling to the Philippines was to meet women." As expected, the metal detectors went off when KSM passed through it and he was asked to take off his shoes, but the police did not insist he take off his socks. When they proved they could get through airport security, they were ready for Yousef's next test.

On December 9, a day after Yousef signed a lease for an apartment at the Doña Josefa housing complex, he walked to the nearby Sheraton Century Park hotel in Harrison Plaza. At a travel agency there, he bought a one-way ticket for Cebu in the name of Armaldo Forlani, an Italian member of parliament. He got the name from the Atlas Almanac program in his laptop computer.[34]

Two days later, Yousef boarded Philippine Airlines flight 434 to Cebu, continuing on to Tokyo. He carried a computer bag that held the chemicals he needed for the bomb. Hidden in his shoes were the two 9-volt batteries. He sat near the back, in seat 35F. Soon after the flight took off, he asked if he could switch seats to be close to the front of the Boeing 747-200 aircraft.[35]

Halfway through the flight, Yousef went to the bathroom. It took him about two to three minutes to put the bomb together.[36] He returned to his seat and planted the device inside the life jacket under his seat. When the plane landed in Cebu, he disembarked. He had set the timer for 11:43 A.M.

The man who was in Yousef's seat when the plane left Cebu was a twenty-four-year-old Japanese engineer, Haruki Ikegami, who was heading home. Two hours into the flight, the stewardess noticed smoke rising from Ikegami's seat near the right side of the fuselage. A few moments later, the bomb exploded, nearly severing Ikegami's body into two and blowing a two-foot-square portion out of the fuselage. The explosion filled the cabin with smoke and caused a drop in pressure, which triggered the release of oxygen masks. Winds were howling through the cabin. People began to scream.

Behind Ikegami, Yukihiko Usui woke up when he heard the blast, his oxygen mask dangling in front of him. "I looked at the person in front of me," Usui said. He "was trying to ask for help."[37] Ikegami raised his index finger, then slumped backward into his seat. Authorities believe he lived another minute or so before he died. Usui tried to help but couldn't move. He felt intense pain: his legs were burned, and pieces of shrapnel from the blast had lodged in his skin. Four other Japanese passengers, a Korean man, and five others were injured by the blast.

Miraculously, the plane did not crash. The hole in the floor had severed the cables that controlled the plane's flaps, crippling the jet's steering, yet the pilot managed an emergency landing at Naha Airport in Okinawa about an hour later. For Yousef, it was a triumph. His bomb easily avoided airport security, and with just a little more tinkering, promised to cause an explosion large enough to destroy a commercial jet and kill all its passengers.

Soon after, Yousef summoned Abdul Hakim Murad from Dubai. Murad wasn't expecting that call and was reluctant to come to the Philippines. He had been trying to get his certification and get a job as a professional pilot, but Yousef convinced him. He landed in Manila on December 26, 1994, and checked in at the Las Palmas Hotel in Malate.[38] Yousef said he would pay for his plane fare but told him little else. He had many plans for him, but the first was a particular surprise.

Born on April 1, 1968, Murad, at nearly 5 feet, 9 inches, is a handsome man. From a relatively wealthy family in Kuwait, he has three sisters and four brothers scattered in three countries: Kuwait, the United Arab Emirates, and the United States.[39] Until he was captured, Murad lived a peripatetic life, moving easily among Kuwait, Dubai, Karachi, and cities in the West. He trained as a pilot in the Philippines, the UAE, Pakistan, and at four different flight schools in the United States.

The day after Murad arrived in Manila, Yousef picked him up and brought him to the apartment that would become their base. KSM had been staying there with him, but again, in a sign of how the cell was compartmentalized, he moved out before Murad moved in. KSM moved to another apartment on the other side of town, at the Tiffany Mansions in Greenhills, more than an hour away in Manila traffic.

The Doña Josefa Apartments in Malate are six floors high, in a white building with an open lobby and an airy feel. It's not luxurious. Certainly, KSM's new condominium was far more expensive. Close to the red-light district, the Doña Josefa Apartments are often used for short-term rentals by Middle Eastern tourists. For the terror cell's purposes, the location was perfect—a block away from the Papal Nunciature, the Manila home of the Vatican's ambassador to the Philippines, where Pope John Paul II was expected to stay during his upcoming visit.

Yousef told Murad they would try to assassinate the pope. Members of the Abu Sayyaf would help, he said, and they would claim credit for the group. In addition, there were several other attacks on the drawing board. By that time, Yousef had already discarded a plot to assassinate U.S. president Bill Clinton on his visit to the Philippines. Yet Yousef also talked of attacks on nuclear facilities in the United States[40] and attacks in France, Britain, and Sweden,[41] as well as at least three

plots using airplanes. The first was the most immediate: to use a crop-
duster plane to assassinate the pope. That was discarded once the police
announced there would be a no-fly zone in the capital during the
pope's visit. The second involved a light plane loaded with explosives,
which would be used to ram into the CIA headquarters in Langley, Virginia.[42] The third plot, which became the blueprint for 9/11, was to
"board any American commercial aircraft pretending to be an ordinary
passenger. Then . . . hijack said aircraft, control its cockpit and dive it at
the CIA Headquarters. There will be no bomb or any explosive . . . in
its execution."[43] Other target buildings in the United States included
the World Trade Center, the Pentagon, the Sears Building in Chicago,
and the TransAmerica Building in San Francisco.[44]

In the end, Yousef came back to his main plot: to plant the little
bombs he had perfected on eleven U.S. planes traveling from Asia and
set them to explode in midair. They would work on both that and the
pope's assassination simultaneously.[45]

When Murad entered apartment 603, there were already several
bottles of chemicals around the room. Earlier, Yousef and Shah had
established a shell company, the Bermuda Trading Company, as a cover
to purchase chemicals.[46] Yousef bought most of what Murad saw in the
room under the alias Dr. Paul Vijay. In the next few days, Murad helped
Yousef buy more chemicals from a store in Quezon City. On their way
back, they stopped at the Shangri-la Mall near the Edsa Plaza Hotel,
where Yousef and KSM once stayed. At the mall, they bought four
Casio wristwatches to use as timers.[47]

The two men divided their duties for the next few days: Yousef
made three pipe bombs for the assassination attempt against the pope;
Murad made two nitroglycerin bombs for the airplane bombings.[48]

The story has often been told of how a smoky accident in Yousef's
apartment happened to draw police attention, and though Yousef
escaped, his laptop provided the stunning news that his attacks were
nearly ready for execution. The story is true as far as it goes, but the
Philippine authorities were not quite so asleep at the wheel. The explosion aboard Philippine Airlines flight 434 had placed the police on
heightened alert with the pope's visit just a few weeks away. Yousef had
called the Associated Press, claiming that Abu Sayyaf was responsible,

which suggested Filipino suspects, but Avelino "Sonny" Razon of the Presidential Security Group (PSG) tasked with security for the pope's visit was tipped to watch for Middle Easterners. "The PNP (Philippine National Police) particularly the PSG was on heightened alert because in December 1994, we received reports that a group of Middle Eastern personalities would be coming over to the Philippines to assassinate the Pope," he said.[49]

The PSG had one man in particular under surveillance—Tareq Javed Rana, a Pakistani suspected of supporting international terrorists with drug money. They were on the right track. He was a close associate of Ramzi Yousef. While under surveillance, Rana's house in Parañaque, a suburb of Manila, burned down. An official police report would later say the PSG believed the "conflagration was caused by combustible chemicals such as those used for making an improvised explosive device (IED)."[50] Intelligence sources believe Yousef and his colleagues had actually stayed there and may have caused the fire while building a bomb.

On January 3, just twelve days before the pope's arrival, businessmen George and Salvador Lacson, as well as their friend Peter Smith, an Australian expatriate, notified the police of the sound of explosions and military-type training by what they thought were Middle Eastern men at Matabungkay Beach in Lian, Batangas—about a two-hour drive from Manila. Later, police would identify fifteen foreign nationals— Egyptians, Palestinians, and Pakistanis—and five Filipinos among the group. A team of special police intelligence agents had found a partially burned Bible and pamphlets preaching a radical version of Islam.[51]

By January 6, the police were on red alert. When senior superintendent Aida Fariscal got a call about a fire in the Doña Josefa Apartments a little after 11:00 P.M., she looked out the window of the Western Police District. Although she saw no smoke at the building a few blocks away, she asked her night-duty officer to check it out. Patrolman Ariel Fernandez was gone almost an hour. When he returned, Aida, impatient, grilled him in Tagalog, the native language.

"Ariel, what happened to you? Were you barbecued or did you go out drinking? You took so long. Don't you know I've been waiting?" Aida berated Ariel.[52]

"Ma'am, don't worry. The fire alarm is off. There was no fire," Ariel responded. It's customary to address a superior as "sir" or "ma'am" in the Philippines as a sign of respect, and Ariel was a fledgling compared to Aida, who had developed a reputation as a tough-talking, hard-working officer. She was stubborn, and that always helped her. "So why was there a fire?" she asked.

"Ma'am, those Pakistanis in room 603 were playing with firecrackers."

"The New Year is over," she said. New Year's in the Philippines is like the Fourth of July in the United States. Nearly every Filipino family stages its own fireworks display. "It's over; it's almost the Feast of Three Kings. How were they playing with firecrackers?"

"Ma'am, the Pakistani showed us. He said they spilled the powder at the sink, and then they lit a match. That caused a big explosion with lots of black smoke. They couldn't stop the smoke so they opened the window. That's what the tenants there noticed. That's why they called us here."

"And then what happened?"

"When we arrived, the Pakistani"—whom they would later find out was Murad—"was at the edge of the stairs on the ground floor. The other guy"—Ramzi Yousef—"was leaning against the ledge of the security guard at the lobby. The fireman asked them, 'So what happened to your room? There's a reported fire alarm.' 'Well, don't worry, we were just playing with firecrackers,' they said. So everyone got into the elevator"—their apartment was on the top floor of the building. "When we got inside the apartment, 603, ma'am, we smelled the powder. But the powder wasn't black; it looked like salt. It was white. The firemen saw it—spread over everywhere. Then we inspected the room with the firemen and the tenants. Inside the bedroom. They kept saying, 'Well, nothing happened. Nothing burned.' The firemen weren't suspicious, so they said, 'Okay, everybody, go home. There's no fire after all, no fire, so let's go home.' So we left," Ariel said.

"I didn't have to think," Aida recalled to me seven years after that incident. "I told Ariel immediately, 'Wait for me. I'm going to get dressed. I don't believe they were playing with firecrackers. We're going to find ourselves a bomb and some terrorists.' "

I marveled at the details she remembered. We were sitting in a restaurant in the Malate district, now converted from the red-light twenty-four-hour entertainment houses to a very respectable restaurant row. Aida is a character: she was wearing shiny camouflage pants, hoop earrings, and bright pink lipstick. Retired from the force and a grandmother now, she asked that we pick a table with our backs to the walls "for security reasons." Old habits die hard. After that night in 1995, she had asked for and was assigned a security guard because she feared for her safety. "Ramzi Yousef is a powerful man," she said at the time. Seven years later, Aida retained her idiosyncrasies: a strange mixture of bombast, vulnerability, and strength. I could see she was bitter; she had an axe to grind. After all, if it wasn't for her initiative, the terrorists would have escaped. Yet she was overlooked in the promotions and accolades by what she saw as a male bureaucracy.

Certainly, things might have turned out differently if she hadn't gone back to the apartment. Perhaps the pope would have been assassinated. Less than two weeks after that night, they and three others were scheduled to board several airplanes each, to the United States, to set bombs that would explode somewhere over the ocean. Documents in Yousef's laptop outlined attacks against eleven planes, although KSM would later tell his U.S. interrogators that they targeted twelve planes. It was supposed to be "48 hours of terror." If they had succeeded, U.S. prosecutors say, they would have killed more than four thousand people and shut down the airline industry.[53] Yousef called it Operation Bojinka—code for "big bang"—al-Qaeda's most imaginative plot at that time.[54]

Aida Fariscal stopped it by being persistent and stubborn. "I got dressed." She explained, "I was living in the police station at that time, and I couldn't go dressed the way I was. I had on a flowered dress and my rubber slippers." She changed to her uniform and walked to the Doña Josefa. She asked Ariel and another officer, Reynaldo Tizon, to come along as backup. She almost forgot to bring her gun, but she thought to call the guard at Doña Josefa, Roman Mariano, to ask him not to let his tenants leave. He replied they were already gone. She told him: "Mariano, we're coming back. Act like you don't know us. Get the keys from the front desk. When you see Ariel arrive, just walk ahead to the room. Don't let on we know each other because you're not supposed to open the apartment."

Aida had no search warrant, and it was the middle of the night. "I gave him good advice," she told me, "and this is verbatim what I told him: 'Those who live there, they're the ones who the newspapers are talking about who are about to do something evil to that Very Important Person who will visit our country in a week's time. Your building is going to be pulverized. That's why you need to take care of us, and don't tell the front desk.' " When they arrived at Doña Josefa, Aida and

Ariel walked in. Roman Mariano saw them, got the key, and walked toward the elevator. All three waited; no one spoke. When they got upstairs, Roman led the way to the apartment and opened the door. Aida walked in. "Now I finally saw what Ariel saw, but he didn't have imagination. Me, I have a fertile imagination."

The one-bedroom apartment stunned her. The first thing she saw were cabinet dividers. On the lower shelves were four unopened boxes of portable gas stoves. She remembered the markings: General Electric. Above that were what looked like several large bundles of industrial-size cotton balls. Beyond the divider was a round marble table with a pouch that contained loops of electrical wiring: green, yellow, blue, and red. In the corner of the room sat large, opened cardboard boxes. Inside, she saw large bottles—"like the large mineral water that you turn upside down. I saw reading from the brand of the packages they were chemicals: sulfuric, chloric, whatever. The brand is from Germany. My heart was beating fast now, and my imagination was running away. I asked myself, 'Who sold this to the Philippines? How did these chemicals get here? They're so big!' And then I asked Mariano, 'Where is the telephone?' "

Aida crossed to the other side and saw a cabinet with a mirror. On the cabinet, she saw two Bibles. Lodged into the mirror's frame, she saw a picture of the pope—"the kind you can buy on the sidewalk," she said. Also on the cabinet was hair-coloring dye as well as two rosaries, including the large brown ones normally carried by priests. Several contact lens cases were scattered on the ledge. Aida crossed into the bedroom and saw more cotton balls. These looked used. "They had a yellowish color," she said, "like they had been dipped in some of the chemicals I saw there."

Just then the telephone rang. She jumped with fright. "They want to know if there's anyone here," she realized. "I told everyone, 'Get out. No one run, no loud noises. Let's just go.' You remember the movie with Sylvester Stallone—*The Specialist*?" she asked me. "The telephone rang, and then when they picked up, it triggered an explosion that split the building in two."

I marveled at Aida's reasoning—the mixture of real-life police savvy that came from experience and the dash of Hollywood all too prevalent in the Philippines. That's what makes this country unique: Filipinos take Hollywood seriously. There's a saying that's become popular: the Philippines spent 250 years in a convent and 50 years in Hollywood. Aida was the product of her culture: extremely religious and extremely romantic. Whatever the reason, her caution was good. FBI agents would later tell the Philippine police that the chemicals in the room were so combustible and unstable that a lit match or sparks from two objects rubbing together would have taken the building down.

Aida, Tizon, Ariel, and Mariano got in the elevator. She asked Mariano to stand lookout and let her know if the two tenants returned. She positioned Tizon across the street. She thought he was too new and a bit of a coward. She asked Ariel to stay with her while she called her superiors for backup and to let them know what they had found. She was just dialing the number when Mariano began to signal frantically. She pushed Ariel to act, and he stopped the man—handsome, she said, about mid-twenties—at the foot of the stairs. Aida put down the phone when she heard the two men arguing. She tried to break them up.

"Good evening, Sir. I'm the superior officer of this young officer. We've been waiting a while for you to report what happened in your room," Aida said.

"I was going to do that. That's why I came back, but this little policeman is telling me that we are making bombs," he responded.

Ariel chimed in, "It's really true. You are really manufacturing bombs." In Tagalog, Aida told Ariel to be quiet and began to read Murad his rights. When Tizon crossed from the other side of the street, Aida went back to the front desk: she had to let her commanding officers know, and she remembered they needed a search warrant. While she was making the call, she heard a gunshot. Ariel was taking aim at Murad, who was running away. Tizon was chasing him, but Murad had too much of a head start—until he tripped on the exposed roots of one of the trees uprooted by a recent typhoon. When they finally caught him, they used rope from a clothesline to tie his hands since none of the policemen had handcuffs.

Getting Murad back to the precinct was a comedy of sorts. Aida and her men didn't have a squad car, so she tried to commandeer a jeepney—the World War II–era jeeps that had been converted to colorful public transportation. The driver didn't stop. Finally, she was able to get a minivan taxi. At the station, Murad offered Aida $2,000 to let him go. That's more money than any Philippine police officer made in a year. Aida turned him down. She booked him as a Pakistani national under the name he gave: Saeed Ahmed.

Aida went back to apartment 603 around 2:30 A.M. to wait for the bomb squad. Police teams began arriving at 4:00 A.M. The bomb squads and security teams, including the PSG, arrived later. Backup teams were stationed outside the Doña Josefa building. Those inside apartment 603 took an inventory of what they found in the room: assorted highly volatile chemicals, chemical glassware, wiring, timers, twelve fake passports, the business card of Mohammed Jamal Khalifa, chemistry books, manuals on manufacturing bombs, and, underneath the kitchen sink, a pipe bomb attached to a Casio wristwatch timer. Perhaps the most important find was Ramzi Yousef's laptop computer and four diskettes. One file, code-named Bojinka, specified all the plans for the 48 hours of terror.

When Murad was arrested, he was turned over to the PSG. For two days, officers of the PSG tried to get information from Murad—with no results. Murad refused to talk. Finally, they decided to turn him over to the Intelligence Command. That was when Boogie Mendoza, as head of the Special Operations Group (SOG), got involved. Murad was brought to Camp Crame inside the high walls of the PNP intelligence compound. Mendoza began interrogating him about 5:00 P.M. on January 8. It would take nearly ten hours before the first breakthrough.

Boogie Mendoza is known as a skilled interrogator. It is, in some circles of the Philippine police, considered a fine art compared to the more brutal version of getting information—physical torture. Mendoza prides himself on never needing to lay a hand on his prisoner. The challenge is to find the prisoner's weakness; it is a test of wills. Murad was inside a bare room at the intelligence compound. He had had little sleep in the past forty-eight hours. Mendoza tried to create a bond of sorts with him. At least, he didn't touch him.

"I was able to break him—as the saying goes—in the briefing or interrogation when I was able to spot his principal weakness, and [his] weakness is the hatred . . . against the Israeli Jews and American imperialist," said Mendoza.

He began to try to figure out what Murad wanted. He told Murad he had friends at the Red Cross who might be able to help, trying to see if that card of humanitarian concern would help. Then he saw a weakness: Murad kept asking what would happen to him. He was afraid he would be turned over to the FBI or to Israel's Mossad. At about three in the morning, after nearly ten hours in the interrogation room, Mendoza stood up to leave.

"I can't spend much more time with you," Mendoza said. "I'm leaving for the United States and if you have nothing to tell me, others will come in and talk to you. Maybe some people around you will kill you."

"No, wait, you can't do that," Murad said.

"Why not?"

"Because I'm a very important person."

"Why are you important?" Mendoza asked.

"I think you will be interested in the World Trade Center story," Murad answered.

Murad began to tell a riveting tale. He gave Mendoza his real name and that of his companion, Abdul Basit Mahmood Abdul Karim, a twenty-six-year-old Pakistani who used eight different aliases in the Philippines. Abdul Basit had at least fourteen other aliases he used around the world, including Ramzi Ahmed Yousef—the name he had used to enter the United States on September 1, 1992. A little more than five months later, on February 26, Yousef had organized and led the first bombing of the World Trade Center in New York.

Murad confessed he was the one who actually did "structural studies" of the twin towers but that Ramzi Yousef "was responsible in the bombing of [the] World Trade Center." Murad had "suggested to [Yousef] the World Trade Center to be the best target for bombing because it is one of the tallest building and famous commercial center in the world."[55]

During an interrogation session on January 7, Murad was forthright.

"What is your plan in the United States?"

"Killing Americans," said Murad.

"Why? Why?"

"This is my—the best thing. I enjoy it."

"What is your plan in America?"

"Killing the people there. Teach them . . ."

"How will you kill the people?

"I know how to kill the people," Murad said. "There is . . ."

"How?"

"You can kill them by gas. You can kill them by gun. You can kill them by knife. You can kill them by explosion. There's many kinds," said Murad.

Murad would be in the custody of Philippine officials for nearly three months. Initially, the Philippines kept his arrest quiet and shared little information with their U.S. counterparts, but that changed when the police lifted Yousef's fingerprint from apartment 603. When he was turned over to the FBI, Murad waived his rights and confessed.

Yousef may have been involved in one other terrorist attack in the United States that U.S. authorities claim was the work of home-grown militants: the Oklahoma City bombing on April 19, 1995, which killed 168 people and injured 600 others. Since that bombing, there have been numerous claims that Ramzi Yousef met and trained Terry Nichols in the Philippines in December 1994. Yousef allegedly gave Nichols the technical expertise he and army pal Timothy McVeigh needed to bring down the Alfred P. Murrah building. I have not yet seen enough hard evidence of this rumor, but circumstantial evidence is interesting, and the rumor keeps surfacing.

Terry Nichols was married to a Filipina, Marife Torres, whom he met through a mail-order agency in the Philippines in 1989. The "mail-order brides" for many years were the modern-day versions of Cinderella and her Prince Charming, another sign of the poverty in the country and a means by which some Filipinas escape it. In 1990, Terry Nichols traveled to Cebu City, where Marife and her family lived, to marry the seventeen year old. She joined him in the United States soon after. Over the next few years, Nichols made several trips to the Philippines, his last one about five months before the Oklahoma City bombing; he arrived in Cebu on November 23, 1994. Marife was already in Cebu because she was attending classes at Southwest College, a university Ramzi Yousef visited in early 1994 and where he spent time with many friends. Ramzi Yousef arrived in Cebu on December 11 in the midst of the fourth test for his new bombs. Both men were in Cebu from December 11 until the beginning of January.

The first person to argue that they had met was Stephen Jones, the chief defense lawyer of Timothy McVeigh.[56] Jones said Edwin Angeles, one of the Abu Sayyaf founders turned double agent, claimed to have been at several meetings with Yousef and an American he knew only as "the Farmer." The earliest meetings allegedly took place at a Del Monte canning plant in Davao City in the southern Philippines in late 1992 and early 1993, just prior to the first World Trade Center bombing. The last ones, Angeles said, took place at his house in December 1994.[57] During those meetings, Jones said, Yousef, Nichols, and Angeles, among others, discussed bomb plots, the making and handling of bombs, and how and where they could get firearms and ammunition. Angeles drew a sketch of "the Farmer"; he looked like Nichols.[58]

It is no longer possible to verify this with Angeles: he was murdered by gunmen on January 15, 1999. According to Jones, there is a videotaped police interrogation of Angeles giving these details and referring to "the Farmer" and another American named John Lepney. He sent me a copy of the tape. There, sitting on a chair was Angeles responding to his interrogator in Tagalog, but the audio quality was so bad it's difficult to discern exactly what he was saying. No one else during the court trial saw this tape. Trial judge Richard P. Matsch refused to admit it into evidence.

There is one other piece of the puzzle. When the bomb went off in Oklahoma City, Abdul Hakim Murad was sitting at the Metropolitan Correctional Center in New York City, waiting for his own trial for his part in the Bojinka plot in the Philippines. When he heard about the bombing on the radio, he told his guard that the "Liberation Army"— the fictitious group created by Yousef to claim responsibility for the 1993 World Trade Center bombing—was responsible. He later confirmed it in writing.[59] The judge also refused to admit that as evidence in the trial of Timothy McVeigh.

Murad's claim that Yousef was responsible for the Oklahoma City bombing arose before either Timothy McVeigh or Terry Nichols was publicly identified as a suspect.

As for the Abu Sayyaf, after the arrest of their major backers, the group launched an attack so violent that officials in the Philippines thought it must be in retaliation for the arrest of Murad. One of the first glimpses of trouble came a little before dawn on April 4, 1995, when a group of nuns traveling 16 kilometers from the town of Ipil stopped to get a snack. Ipil sits at a crucial juncture of the two provinces of the Zamboanga peninsula—Zamboanga del Norte and Zamboanga del Sur. Most of its 70,000 residents are Catholic.

While there, the nuns saw about two-hundred armed men, some in combat fatigues, others in jeans. Most had crew-cuts. They could almost pass for soldiers, but on their feet, they wore *tsinelas*, thin, cheap rubber slippers often worn by the poor. The nuns didn't look closely enough at those details. They took them for soldiers.[60]

It was good the nuns stopped to eat because the truckload of armed men moved ahead of them. They belonged to the Abu Sayyaf.

Bishop Federico Escaler was having lunch with a different group of nuns at his home about a block away from the town market. When they heard firing, the bishop tried to reassure his companions. "It's just firecrackers," he told them. And then in close range, they heard the unmistakable sound of a bazooka. Bishop Escaler jumped up, told the nuns to go indoors, and asked his aide to call the Southern Command, the main military headquarters, through a two-way radio.

"There's shooting. We need help," his aide told the radio operator. The Southern Command, the military's base in Mindanao, is about 100 kilometers away in Zamboanga City. As Bishop Escaler slammed out, he heard a languid response: "You've got to be kidding. We don't have any reports of that," answered the military operator.

In the streets, it was bedlam. The marauders were shooting randomly, looting banks, and burning buildings, without challenge. Acrid black fumes made breathing difficult. People were running, trying to get away. But they couldn't flee fast enough.

Bishop Escaler passed the police station, parts of the building still burning and spewing black smoke. In front were two corpses still in uniform. He stopped and blessed them. The town police chief had just taken his post that day; he too was among the dead.

Panting, with gunshots ringing through the air, Bishop Escaler began inching forward. In front of the barbershop were more charred bodies. He looked closer and recognized them.

People were screaming around him: some in fear, others because they were wounded. Still others were taking whatever they could carry and running away from the town center. Escaler turned a corner and saw a man in fatigues still shooting even as he picked up a young girl who ran toward him. He saw him hold her in front of him and realized they were taking hostages.

How could they get away with this? he wondered. Why weren't they being stopped? An army brigade based in Ipil did make an attempt to help. Led by Colonel Roberto Santiago, fourteen soldiers ran out to try to stop the attack. When they reached the town center, they pulled back, overwhelmed by the number of armed men and the cries of the hostages they held in front of them. All told, the attackers took about thirty hostages—men, women, and children. Many would die as the attackers retreated.

Helicopter gunships arrived around four o'clock in the afternoon, but it was too late. The damage had been done. The helicopters hovered over the ruins of the town. Fifty-three people were dead.

It was, according to Rafael Alunan III, the interior secretary who supervised the National Police, "the opening shot in the war to establish an Islamic state in Mindanao." [61]

Murad was extradited to the United States on April 12, 1995. Ramzi Yousef fled the Philippines a day after the apartment fire at Doña Josefa. But evidence from his laptop computer gave U.S. and Filipino investigators many leads that, along with an informant, led to Yousef's arrest in Pakistan on February 7, one month later.

Wali Khan Amin Shah was arrested on January 11 but escaped two days later. He fled to Langkawi island in Malaysia and would have gotten off free if not for an identifiable injury he got in Afghanistan: his ring, middle, and pointing fingers of his left hand were cut off. [62] Someone in Langkawi noticed his hand and alerted the authorities. He was arrested in February and rendered to the United States on December 2, 1995. [63]

All three would be tried and convicted in a U.S. court in 1996. The FBI and CIA closed its case. Filipino authorities heaved a sigh of relief. Both countries called it a great victory against terrorism. But they celebrated victory too quickly. "You broke one cell, but actually since you've broken that, you've already eased off. So that gave them room to form other cells," said Philippine immigration commissioner Andrea Domingo. [64]

In 1995, al-Qaeda sent new operatives to the Philippines to run terror plots against the United States. This time the strategy was different: al-Qaeda began infiltrating and co-opting home-grown organizations and weaving together a far more complex and insidious terror network called the Jemaah Islamiyah. "The cell in 1995 expanded," said Boogie Mendoza, "it grew bigger. It was able to sustain the business interests and transactions, and most importantly, it developed the so-called counter cells in Malaysia, Indonesia and Singapore."

Two men, who escaped in 1995, would play a crucial role in that evolution: Khalid Shaikh Mohammed, the self-confessed mastermind behind the September 11 attacks, and Riduan bin Isamuddin (aka Hambali) who helped Wali Khan escape from his Philippine prison in 1995, gave him shelter in Malaysia, and disappeared into the background after his arrest.[65] What both men did after 1995 was to meld quietly into the background and quietly build al-Qaeda's multilayered underground network in Southeast Asia.

CHAPTER 3

THE ASIAN
OSAMA BIN LADEN

What makes Southeast Asia such fertile ground for al-Qaeda is its large Muslim population within a political landscape that is much more open and fractured than the Arab Middle East. Many people trace the rise of terrorism here to the "Asian Osama bin Laden," an Indonesian cleric named Abu Bakar Ba'asyir. Indeed, he is the most widely followed extremist cleric in the region, with a magnetic personality and fanatical following. Yet even his story shows that the tradition of Muslim extremism and armed struggle is older and deeper than any single living leader.

Ba'asyir is a teacher and a preacher, a man who founded a school that is popular among a large number of Muslim parents for its rigor and standards. He has also become a symbol of Muslim resistance to autocratic rule for Indonesians who are not themselves fighters or extremists, a man who is fighting for Islam. He is the product of a modern separatist tradition that stems back nearly sixty years.

In 1948, as a charismatic young Indonesian named Sukarno was fighting for independence against Dutch rule, another little-known Islamic militia unaligned with Sukarno arose in separate opposition to the Dutch. Called the Darul Islam rebellions, they were led by Kartosuwirjo,[1] who like most Indonesians only had one name. Active in Muslim nationalist policies under the Dutch East Indies, he announced the establishment of the Islamic Army of Indonesia (Tentara Islam Indonesia, or TII) in 1948, and on August 7, 1949, after Sukarno had overthrown the Dutch, Kartosuwirjo officially proclaimed the Islamic State of Indonesia (Negara Islam Indonesia, or NII) in opposition to Sukarno's forces, a fight that would continue for the next thirteen years. Kartosuwirjo, based in West Java, called his territory Darul Islam, "Abode of Islam." To extend his reach, he joined forces with another militia commander named Kahar Muzakkar, whose militia controlled the northern part of Sulawesi. They had also fought against Dutch rule and after independence had been denied positions in the new Indonesian army, so they too began a new rebellion against the central government. Both Kartosuwirjo and Kahar Muzakkar were defeated by Sukarno's forces by the mid-1960s. Muzakkar was shot by the military in 1965; Kartosuwirjo was arrested in 1966.

In Indonesia, 1965 was a watershed year. Sukarno's regime, maintained by the military and the communist party, was unraveling. On September 30, 1965, six senior generals were assassinated by middle-ranking officers in the military, who claimed the senior officers were planning a coup. A little-known officer, Major General Suharto, led the army's response to the alleged plot. Through an intricate web of machinations, he would use the period of instability to consolidate his power. Suharto claimed the murders were the beginning of a communist plot hatched by the Indonesian Communist Party (PKI) with the support of China and Mao Tse-tung. He unleashed a wave of massacres that still haunts the Indonesian psyche today. It is still unclear how many people were killed: the estimates vary from 100,000 to 1 million. Bands of young men backed by the army killed anyone they thought to be a PKI supporter. Journalist Aristides Katoppo saw "bodies . . . bobbing up in the rivers, and . . . I learned that these were villages which were supposed to belong to the Communists' peasants' groups."[2] Much of the killing happened in Bali. Most victims were Chinese—allegedly because China was accused of backing the coup, but in fact many of the victims were innocent traders whose economic success and ethnic origin made them scapegoats. "It's unbelievable that the rest of the world didn't know," said Katoppo. "It was not a secret."

A CIA document compares it to the worst mass murders around the world: "In terms of numbers killed, the anti-PKI massacres in Indonesia rank as one of the worst mass murders of the twentieth-century, along with the Soviet purges of the 1930s, the Nazi mass murders during the Second World War and the Maoist bloodbath of the early 1950s."[3] In fact, the numbers were not near Stalin's nor Mao's dizzying heights, but they were certainly in the range of the Tutsi massacre in Rwanda. Later, Hollywood would call it "the year of living dangerously." Scholars still disagree over the exact chain of events behind "the bloody coup of 1965," but what is certain is that about six months later, Indonesia had its first transfer of power in the post-Dutch era when taciturn, folksy Suharto deposed Sukarno, who by then had developed a reputation for lavish tastes and excess.

Suharto's first goal was to take care of the economy. In the late 1960s, inflation was 1,000 percent a year, and interest on Indonesia's foreign debt exceeded total export revenues. With the help of Western-educated technocrats, Suharto diversified and modernized the economy, pumping oil revenues from the 1970s into agriculture, infrastructure, and education. For twenty-five years, the Indonesian economy grew at an average annual rate of nearly 7 percent. Clinics, schools, and services spread out across much of the countryside— 17,000 islands home to a diverse people, with more than 300 ethnic groups speaking an estimated 583 languages and dialects.

To the nearly 56 million Muslims then, Suharto was harsh. He created a rigid political system whose goal was to eliminate opposition before it even became public, all done carefully behind the scenes. Publicly, he gave his country a semblance of democracy, with elections every six years, but they were carefully controlled. To eliminate the chaos of the early years, only three political parties were recognized: the ruling government party of Golkar, the Muslim United Development Party (the PPP), and the nationalist and Christian Indonesian Democratic Party (PDI). Every politician was handpicked, every legislator screened. Running for office required a security check and approval by the government. Experts on Indonesia described Suharto as the puppet master in Indonesia's traditional Wayang shadow puppet play: the events we perceive—what the audience sees—are just the shadows made by the puppets manipulated by the puppet master, a variation of Aristotle's myth of the cave.

In the mid-1970s, with dissatisfaction growing, Suharto himself helped to rekindle Muslim extremism thanks to twisted political logic worthy of Machiavelli. Suharto feared that the PPP, the one permitted Muslim party, would gain a large number of votes in the upcoming 1977 elections since it was one of the few ways to show dissatisfaction with his rule. To preempt that possibility, General Ali Moertopo, in charge of covert operations under Suharto, rallied old Darul Islam members into a new group that was basically his creation, the Komando Jihad. The military told Darul Islam members that with the fall of Vietnam in 1975, they feared a communist threat and they needed the help of militia members. In effect, he was siphoning off votes from a legal party to a new, more radical movement. But the Komando Jihad was set up to take a fall: he created them in order to crush them. In the election year, 1977, the government arrested 185 people it accused of trying to set up an Islamic state in Indonesia.[4] The elaborate conspiracy and dragnet continued for several years, into the next election season in 1982. The two leaders of Komando Jihad, Haji Danu Mohamad Hasan and Haji Ismail Pranoto (or Hispran), were brought into court in 1983. Hasan claimed he had been recruited by military intelligence as early as 1971 and that he and his forces were operating under military instructions. Although they had allegedly stopped clandestine work in 1977, Hasan was not arrested until 1981, to intimidate political Islam in time for the 1982 general elections.[5]

Hispran was arrested earlier, on January 8, 1977, charged with trying to overthrow the government. His lawyers tried—unsuccessfully—to call General Ali Moertopo as a witness during the trial a little more than a year later. Next to be arrested were Abu Bakar Ba'asyir and his associate, Abdullah Sungkar, on November 10, 1978. The man who would become known as the Asian Osama bin Laden was thus neither a founder of Darul Islam nor even the leader of its revived organization.

Both of Yemeni descent, Ba'asyir and Sungkar's major claim to fame is that they had founded an Islamic boarding school, or *pesantren*, in 1971. It would become a nexus for the ideology of radical Islam. Al Mukmin school in Pondok Ngruki, Central Java, would teach many of the men who would later be arrested and linked to al-Qaeda. The government claimed that Sungkar and Ba'asyir swore an oath of loyalty to Darul Islam in 1976. Sungkar, the indictment says, became the military governor of the so-called Indonesian Islamic State soon after and that the two men then began recruiting Indonesians into a group they were calling the Jemaah Islamiyah, which means "Islamic Community." The two men were sentenced to nine years in prison for subversion. In late 1982, their sentences were reduced on appeal to the time they had already served, and they were released. They went home to Pondok Ngruki and for the next two years built up the underground network

Jemaah Islamiyah, which they hoped would soon encompass much of Muslim Indonesia and push for Islamic sharia law within its borders.

The university town of Yogyakarta, a drive of about an hour and a half from Pondok Ngruki, near Solo, had become the center of an Islamic resurgence, partly sparked by the Iranian revolution, partly sparked by the repression of political debate under Suharto. "All other channels of expression were closed," explains analyst Dewi Fortuna Anwar. "So Islam really grew under Suharto—not the political Islam—but the social Islam."

In 1983, after they returned to Pondok Ngruki, Abu Bakar Ba'asyir began to set up a network of small cells, bringing together others imprisoned under Suharto[6] and creating the *usroh*, study groups. It was a recruitment method that would be copied in other countries in the region. Members swore an oath of obedience to Abu Bakar Ba'asyir and were told to create small groups of eight to fifteen people in their villages with the goal of living according to Islamic sharia law. In Indonesia, Malaysia, and Singapore, members were told to shun infidels and their non-Muslim organizations. The criminal laws enforced by a non-Muslim government were considered heathen and not to be obeyed.[7] They also collected the Muslim tithes to help fellow Muslims, with 30 percent of the collection given to Ba'asyir. It was not simply a shakedown; it was also motivation. "Some people had the notion they could raise funds to support this group through basically committing crimes against non-Muslims," said Sidney Jones, a longtime Indonesia watcher and the Jakarta head of Brussels-based think tank Crisis Group Indonesia. She got firsthand information from some of the members recruited by Ba'asyir. "So there were robberies and, in some cases, murders committed in the name of raising funds or strengthening this particular group."[8]

Ba'asyir's preaching was electrifying to his followers, calling for political revolution.[9] "Brothers and sisters, according to the example of the Prophet Mohammed, Islam must be wedded to the government, to the nation. It must take in the law of the State. This was the example of the Prophet. It must not be a purely personal matter. Don't follow the police. Don't follow the nation. Don't separate Islam from the nation. That is wrong. According to the Prophet Mohammed, Muslims must adhere to Sharia law. Sharia law is more important than life itself. Sharia is priceless as compared to life itself. Life without Sharia is nothing." That is why Muslims need jihad: "Because of this conviction, they struggle, and this they can begin very simply—to follow the laws of Allah: education, recitation of the Koran, worship and so forth, until the highest form of struggle, namely Jihad, a war to oppose nonbelievers who are in the process of standing against Islam."

He divides the world into the believers (true Muslims) and nonbelievers, the *kafirs*, or infidels: "Allah has divided humanity into two segments, namely the followers of Allah, and those who follow Satan. The party of God, and the party of Satan." He goes a step further in instilling paranoia and distrust among religions. "We reject all of your teachings that are associated with social issues, economics or beliefs. Between you and us, there will forever be a ravine of hate, and we will be enemies until you follow Allah's law."

By 1984, antigovernment activity by Muslim militant groups had intensified, including bombings and acts of violence linked to the Ngruki network. This was partly in reaction to the government's renewed crackdown on the Muslim opposition, triggered by the riots in Tanjung Priok in September 1984, when army troops opened fire on Muslim protestors and killed dozens. Still, until this point, Jemaah Islamiyah was a home-grown movement that developed according to a radical interpretation of Islam and political oppression in Indonesia.[10]

That changed when Ba'asyir and Sungkar were notified they were about to lose their appeal and would again be jailed. In 1985, they decided to flee to neighboring Malaysia, which had become a melting pot of Muslim dissidents from around the world—a crucible that connected Southeast Asia's Muslims to a global jihad. In Malaysia, Ba'asyir and Sungkar rubbed elbows with other Muslim militants with their own causes and broadened the scope of their jihad, giving them common cause with Muslims in Egypt, Chechnya, and the Philippines. It was Sungkar who took the next step: he traveled to Afghanistan to meet with Osama bin Laden.[11] Al-Qaeda co-opted the cofounders of Jemaah Islamiyah by providing extensive training and finance. Sungkar and Ba'asyir soon created an intricate network that spanned Southeast Asia and Australia, using alumni from the school in Pondok Ngruki as operatives, fund-raisers, and recruiters. They sent members to Afghanistan and to the southern Philippines for military training. They also helped al-Qaeda build training camps in Southeast Asia. Their core group included family, friends, and students all revolving around Pondok Ngruki. "All of the people who have been arrested in connection with al-Qaeda who are Indonesian nationals or who are suspected of having some communication with al-Qaeda go back to a very small group of people centered in central Java in Pondok Ngruki," says Sidney Jones.[12] It was a pattern: Ramzi Yousef recruited his cell members from his family and high school in Kuwait City.

Because they fled Suharto's repression, Sungkar and Ba'asyir set up Jemaah Islamiyah's first base of operations in Malaysia, but the fall of Suharto in 1998 opened new pastures for Jemaah Islamiyah and al-Qaeda. Sungkar and Ba'asyir returned to Indonesia in 1999 and moved the center of their operations back to the school at Pondok Ngruki. Sungkar would fall ill and die soon after their return, pushing Ba'asyir to the position of emir of Jemaah Islamiyah.

It was an incredibly different Indonesia: a new democracy in the midst of redefining an entire political system. Fundamental beliefs and traditions, as well as law and order, were shaky at best. The military would slowly be pushed to reform itself, seeing its seats in the top legislative body dwindle until its political role would be all but extinguished. The equivalent of Singapore and Malaysia's Internal Security Act—Indonesia's subversion law, under which hundreds, including Ba'asyir and Sungkar, were arrested and detained without trial under Suharto—was abolished. Perhaps most important, Islamic political parties—and openly campaigning to establish Islamic sharia law—now became legal.

It was the new democratic freedoms that allowed Abu Bakar Ba'asyir to live and operate freely in Indonesia for nearly a year and a half, despite the fact that he had been pinpointed as the leader of al-Qaeda's network in the region by captured terrorists from Singapore, Malaysia, and the Philippines.

Soon after Ba'asyir's return, he formed—and was elected chairman of—a new militant umbrella organization, the Indonesian Mujahideen Council (MMI), considered the public face of the underground Jemaah Islamiyah. High-ranking Indonesian intelligence officials told me that in that momentous year Ba'asyir also sent a letter to dozens of hard-line and moderate Muslim clerics in Malaysia and Indonesia offering them a chance to meet Osama bin Laden, who was asking them to "prepare for a jihad against Americans." (Ba'asyir denies having sent any such letter.)

Al-Qaeda may yet obtain a legal foothold in Indonesia's political system. "Through the MMI, we have seen that al-Qaeda and Jemaah Islamiyah are penetrating the mainstream political parties of Indonesia," said terrorism expert Rohan Gunaratna, "and this is a real danger."[13]

When my friends ask me what it was like to live in Indonesia between 1996 to 2001, I tell them to picture a frog. Fill a large pot with tapwater; then put the frog in it. Now put the pot with the frog on top of a burner and turn up the heat. Slowly, the temperature rises. The frog, which can jump out of the pot at any time, gets so acclimated that it doesn't feel the gradual changes in temperature. Soon the water is boiling, but the frog is still in the pot. That's what it's like. You get so used to obscure, bizarre, violent situations that you fail to gauge when they actually become life-threatening. When extraordinary events happen every day, the extraordinary becomes ordinary. For a five-year period beginning in 1996, every year was a "year of living dangerously," filled with riots and violence in a constantly shifting political landscape. After all, beginning in 1997, Indonesia had four different presidents in four years.

By 1996, the Indonesian Democratic Party (PDI), the smallest of the three political parties, had found a standard-bearer who captured the imagination of Indonesians—Megawati Sukarnoputri, the demure daughter of Indonesia's first president, Sukarno. Although she herself was far from being a revolutionary out to challenge Suharto, her name and lineage was enough to promise a groundswell of support for what was once the smallest political party, now seen as the only credible opposition and a potential threat to Suharto in the 1997 general elections. Suharto and his generals decided to preempt any possible challenge by replacing her as the leader of PDI. When they tried to engineer her ouster from the PDI party congress held in the northern city of Medan, about two hundred of her student supporters refused to leave the party headquarters in Jakarta. They kept vigil, publicly challenging Suharto for weeks, until July 27. The military barely waited until the leaders of the Association of Southeast Asian Nations (ASEAN) concluded a meeting in Jakarta before moving against the students.

Around dawn on July 27, I got a call from one of the students inside the PDI headquarters. "Come quick," I was told. The crackdown had not begun, but they wanted journalists there as protection. My crew and I rushed to the colonial-style mansion that served as PDI party headquarters, in central Jakarta on the edge of Jakarta's most prestigious residential area. When I got there, I saw two military trucks parked on the side roads. There were lots of people milling around outside so I walked toward the trucks. When I turned the corner, I saw several men with military haircuts putting on red T-shirts, the party color of PDI. When I walked back, riot police had started forming lines to hold people back. They allowed a group of these men wearing red T-shirts to come in and gather in front of the house. The men in red began throwing rocks, bricks—anything they could get their hands on. We were told these men were the members of PDI who had ousted Megawati, but it seemed unlikely. After about an hour and a half, the men really began to attack, and that was when all pretense of an internal party dispute ended. Baton-wielding riot police came close on their heels, followed by the sound of gunshots. Then it was mayhem. Students clambered out the back of the building, bringing the violence out on the streets and triggering the worst riots Jakarta had seen in twenty years. Ten thousand people rampaged down one of the main roads and set fire to buildings owned by the ethnic Chinese. It was a harbinger of worse things to come.

The woman at the center of it all, Megawati, is a quiet, middle-aged housewife, seemingly stunned when she was pushed to the opposition's center. Although she joined the PDI in 1983, she did little to mark herself as a potential leader. "She had not been an outstanding parliamentarian," said Dewi Anwar. "There had not been great speeches or any great bills that she introduced. In fact, she had not been seen as the most politicized of the children of Sukarno. Her younger sisters are much more vocal than her, but after this confusion of the PDI—when the military and the government took it upon themselves to oust Megawati—ironically, Megawati's stature has increased. Because while in the past, she was probably seen as a nonentity, the fact that the government has seen her as a credible threat, for whatever reasons, has in fact given her that stature that probably the government did not want her to possess in the very beginning." [14]

Megawati once told me her guiding political philosophy: "You're too impatient, Maria. What I learned from my father is patience. We are not Westerners. The time has to be right." [15] She actually had more in common with Suharto than she did with her student supporters. Repeatedly, she told me that she did not consider herself an opposition leader. "PDI is not an opposition party," she said. "It's the government who treats us like opposition, but I don't agree with this."[16] She believed in an old, elite power politics: she played by those rules and was alarmed when Suharto began turning against her. "We regret that we live in a very divisive society," said Megawati. "We are living in a glass house where everybody has their own room. They cannot say hello to each other because they are separated by glass walls, but they can see each other. We are Indonesians who believe in the principle of working together. That's why I believe in following the consensus."

Megawati was no revolutionary until she was pushed against the wall. Even then, her rhetoric remained guarded, emphasizing concerns about the rule of law, still hoping for change from within the establishment. Powered by the more radical position of her student supporters, she began warning of the risks of open conflict. "They are staging a silent protest," she told me a month after the PDI riots. "It's not vocal because it's not allowed. This silent protest is very dangerous because when it comes to the surface, it will be like an eruption from a volcano."[17] The volcano erupted, but it would take several years before Megawati gained power.

On May 21, 1998, Suharto ended his rule after anarchy reigned in Jakarta. Fueled by the 1997 financial crisis, the riots began in the northern city of Medan, partly as a response to steep fuel price increases of more than 70 percent. In less than eleven months, more than fourteen million Indonesians lost their jobs. As had happened in 1965, the riots targeted the ethnic Chinese community, perceived by many to have a larger share of the wealth than others. The mayhem spread to Jakarta after the military killed four students from Trisakti University on May 12. That triggered the May riots, with mobs rampaging for nearly five days, killing more than 1,217 people. The official estimate of property damage was around $500 million, but that was considered extremely conservative given that more than 6,000 buildings had been damaged or destroyed. The official tally was 2,547 shophouses, 1,819 stores, 1,026 private homes, 535 bank offices, 383 office buildings, 40 shopping malls, 15 markets, 12 hotels, 11 police stations, 9 gas stations, and 2 churches. In addition, 1,100 cars were burned as well as 800 motorcycles and 66 buses.[18]

A year later Suharto, still defiant and insistent that he had taken the right actions for his nation, told me he would never leave Indonesia. "I didn't make any mistakes," said Suharto. "Why should I leave? I was born here. I will die here. There are many people who insult me. Go ahead, insult me. Whoever insults me, they will take on my sins."[19] Suharto insisted on following Indonesia's Constitution, handing power to his vice president, Bacharuddin Jusuf (BJ) Habibie.

Habibie had already developed a reputation as a crazy, madcap scientist with a high-tech dream for Indonesia—that by embracing high-tech projects Indonesia would join the league of major industrial powers. No one in Indonesia thought Habibie would last: his supporters felt he was too close to Suharto and was too much of a symbol of the past; his enemies thought he was too much of a maverick, too difficult to control, too crazy. His every move was criticized—down to whether he was "presidential" enough in his mannerisms. The verdict, of course, was that he wasn't. Much as Indonesians had hated Suharto's authoritarian ways, they wanted their leader to maintain the illusion of absolute authority.

According to Javanese myths, a true leader with *wayhu*, meaning "divine revelation," creates order in the universe. The royal sultans of Solo were named Pakubuwono, which literally translated means "the nail of the universe." Take out the nail and the world unravels. Habibie was no nail. I think history will be kinder than journalists have been to this enthusiastic man with boundless energy, who accomplished more in his sixteen months in office than anyone could ever have expected—passing more than twelve hundred laws, releasing political prisoners, and strengthening political institutions. "The changes are very fast," Habibie told me, gesturing emphatically. "They are not only day to day, but second to second."[20]

Every time I visited Habibie in his office, I was struck by how his staff wanted to hold on to the rules of the past in the absence of any defined rules for the present. The last time I interviewed him, protocol officers told me while we were setting up that they thought my skirt was too short. They reminded me I was speaking with a Muslim leader, and that I should accord him the proper respect. Also, since I was a woman, I should avoid touching him. They asked if I could keep my notebook on top of my lap so my legs would be covered. I could tell the officers had a checklist they were following. Yet after the interview, when our photographer, Anastasia Vrachnos, told Habibie it was my birthday, the president spontaneously jumped up and began gleefully singing "Happy Birthday." I was stunned when all his aides followed. I stood up too. Then he began clapping his hands to keep beat—and so did everyone else. I looked around the room and smiled. At the end of the song, President Habibie kissed me on the cheek and I kissed him on the other cheek. When I pulled away, I was horrified to see that I had left a lipstick mark on him so I excused myself, reached over and wiped the lipstick off his cheek. I thought that was a faux pas because of the silence in the room. The awkwardness didn't last long because, again, Habibie jumped in, asking what I planned to do for my birthday. He gestured to an assistant who ran to a side room to get presents for me: three books—an authorized biography of Habibie; a history of Indonesia; and the one Habibie was most proud of, a book showcasing his photographs of . . . clouds. That was Habibie for me—the scientist and the dreamer.

Habibie chose respected political analyst and foreign affairs specialist Dewi Fortuna Anwar as his presidential spokeswoman. It was largely because of the ideas of these two pivotal figures that Indonesia offered a vote for autonomy to its twenty-seventh province, East Timor, where rebels had been fighting for independence for nearly a quarter century. When East Timor voted for independence, rampant violence ensued, killing over 1,000. Two months later, on October 20, 1999, the top legislative body, the People's Consultative Assembly, met for more than sixteen hours to debate East Timor and Habibie's rule. First, Indonesia officially endorsed East Timor's vote for independence and set the tiny nation free. Then, in a vote to accept or reject a Habibie speech defending his sixteen months in office, 52.5 percent of the lawmakers rejected the speech, in effect giving him a no-confidence vote. In the following elections, Megawati Sukarnoputri, who ranked as Indonesia's most popular politician, lost to Abdurrahman Wahid, a half-blind Muslim cleric who heads the Nahdlatul Ulama, the world's largest Muslim organization.

Part of the reason Megawati lost was that she did not have the support of the PPP, the Muslim party, and the Central Axis, headed by another key Muslim leader, Amien Rais. Muslim leaders like Hamzah Haz opposed her because they did not believe a woman should lead a Muslim nation. The next day, however, Megawati easily won as vice president against Hamzah Haz.

In less than a year, the People's Consultative Assembly would have a no-confidence vote for Wahid, and so finally, on August 1, 2001, Megawati became Indonesia's president. Hamzah Haz became her vice president. Three years into the new democracy, life had not gotten better. Law and order barely existed in certain parts of the country, and Indonesians were caught in a political and economic malaise. With real power up for grabs, politicians were constantly jostling for power. Hamzah Haz, the leader of Indonesia's largest Muslim political party, was eager to ride the wave of Muslim fundamentalism both before and after 9/11 and reap votes for the 2004 elections. He openly backed suspected terrorists, at one point inviting the country's Islamic extremist A-list, which includes Abu Bakar Ba'asyir, to his house for dinner. "There are no terrorists here," said Haz. "I guarantee that. If they exist, don't arrest any Muslim clerics, arrest me."[21]

When Jaffar Umar Thalib, the head of Laskar Jihad, was arrested, Haz visited him in prison "to offer sympathy" as a "Muslim brother." He also visited Ba'asyir's school in Pondok Ngruki and said, "There's no terrorist network in Indonesia, particularly in this school."[22]

The slim sixty-five-year-old Islamic cleric often wears white robes and a white cap. His thick gold-rimmed eyeglasses frame gentle but probing eyes, his narrow face punctuated by a white, neatly trimmed beard tinged with yellow. Abu Bakar Ba'asyir is extremely confident in his beliefs, and his words are backed by the power of his certainty. During one interview with CNN, he carried the Koran, loosely held in his lap, his arms hugging Islam's sacred book while the cameras and lights were on. At one point, he invited our entire crew to discover the teachings of Islam. In some ways, he reminded me of Christian missionaries who fanned out across Indonesia's eastern islands—kind, inquisitive, and perpetually worried about the souls of others.

"All I do is teach Islam the way it really is," he told me, "the way it is written in the Koran and Al-Sunnah. I don't dare do less . . . or more. I teach Islam so that Muslims are truly committed to the religion. Don't relax. Commit to sharia law. I am sure that the one truth in this world is Islam, and we invite the nonbelievers to join us. The one thing that can save us is Islam."[23] He then explained the concept of jihad that has been passed on to thousands of students at Pondok Ngruki: "I teach the defense of Islam, that at this point, we can see is weak. Namely, jihad. Defend Islam with words as well as actions. If Islam is attacked with words, with arguments, then we must defend it with arguments. We must not be emotional. If they attack with words, we cannot retaliate by hitting them. But if Islam is attacked physically, with weapons, we must defend Islam with weapons. It must be said if Islam is attacked with weapons, there are only two responses: we either win or we die. That is what it means to rise up and defend Islam. That is what, according to infidels and Jews, they see as violence. But if they murder people, they don't consider it violence. But if Muslims defend their religion, they call it violence."

The school he cofounded at Pondok Ngruki has about 2,000 students. Indonesians send their children there because it's known for its strict discipline and its connections to schools in Pakistan and the Middle East: most of its alumni receive scholarships for further religious study abroad. It also reflects Ba'asyri's radical ideology. Pictures of AK-47s line the corridors along with signs that proclaim "America and Jewish [sic] are terrorists" and "No Prestige Without Jihad." When our team visited, my producer, Kathy Quiano, found a handsome eighteen-year-old named Lutfie with a neatly trimmed goatee inside the mosque, praying. He was finishing his last year of school. In his hands, he held a Koran with the word jihad traced in pencil on the side of its pages. Lutfie's family is from Ambon, where wars between Muslims and Christians have destroyed cities and chased hundreds of thousands out. Lutfie was learning about jihad and terrorism: "There is terrorism that is bad, and there is terrorism that is good," he said. "If a police terrorizes a thief, is that bad? There are people who terrorize criminals. Now what I think is terrorism that's good, I think you should see it for yourself. A cleric who's only a teacher is accused of being a terrorist, I think you won't accept that."

The last time I sat with Ba'asyir was four days after the Bali bombings, exactly four days before he would finally be arrested. It was the last sit-down interview he would give to a Western television reporter, and he used it to fuel the conspiracy theories that laid the blame for the Bali blasts at the feet of the CIA. "The violent incidents that have been happening in this country recently have been engineered by foreigners. In this regard, I suspect America—as masterminded by Israel. Israel is Islam's strongest enemy. America is being used by Israel in order to—in this case—attack Islam. And I am one of those people who can be considered as a fighter for Islam, fighting for sharia law. Israel does not like this. Because of that, I have become a target. Perhaps they want to arrest me or kill me." Calm and candid, he outlined his theories in front of a sizable entourage. They sat on chairs, on the floor. Some kneeled behind him as he attacked the Indonesian government and the United States and defended Osama bin Laden.

"The so-called terrorists America is pursuing are actually Islamic heroes," Ba'asyir said. "So America's definition of terrorists describes those mujahideen who defend Islam. That is what they call terrorism, but there are real terrorists in this world: that is America and Jews. They are the real terrorists." He cited U.S. actions in Afghanistan, Sudan, Somalia, Iraq. "That is proof that America is a terrorist. Proof that Jews are terrorists is also very clear. They colonize Palestinian land, murder the Palestinian people, and destroy Palestinian homes." These actions have united the Muslim brotherhood against "the real terrorists. The struggle to evict Jewish infidels that are colonizing Palestinian lands and people—we too as Muslims feel colonized. We cannot pretend not to know. They are our family. That is what it means to be a Muslim. If there is one Muslim who is struck by disaster, we all feel the effects."

Lutfie had been more succinct: "In Islam, if one person falls ill, we all fall ill. If one of us is hurt, we all feel the pain." That central belief has been used by Ba'asyir—and Osama bin Laden—to link Muslim frustrations around the world. There is a thin line between moderate and radical, and often the most effective weapon used by radical Islam to push moderates over the line are the actions and foreign policies of the United States. "The U.S. professes itself to be a champion of democracy, but when it comes to external policy, we know very well that the U.S. went to bed with a lot of authoritarian leaders, including in Indonesia, in the Philippines, in Iraq and so on. . . . Mostly, what angers a lot of Muslims—in fact, I would argue the only meeting point for many Islamic countries, which are extremely diverse—is the Israeli-Palestinian issue. There is a lot of anger—what is seen as a double standard of the U.S. in regard to Israel on the one hand and Palestine on the other," said moderate analyst and former presidential spokeswoman Dewi Anwar.

Lutfie responded vaguely to questions about what he is learning in Pondok Ngruki. "I just study the Koran, that's it." On America, he said he knows only what he sees on television. "The only thing I've heard is it wants to attack Iraq, yeah, someone who wants to attack another for no reason," he said after a repeated line of questioning. What he was most adamant about was the innocence of his teacher, Ba'asyir, whom he says he treats like his father. "If you have a member of the family, like your father—what if your father is being accused of being a murderer or whatever? Will you accept that or not? How would you feel? The same as I do maybe. Because those slanderous statements, according to Allah's rule, they were made by infidels. Good is being terrorized by evil. When we preach, there are obstacles in our way, and this is one of them. Muslims who are imprisoned do not lose anything. If they die, then they become martyrs," said Lutfie.

Ba'asyir's ideas and words set off chain reactions far beyond the boundaries of the schools he set up. Thirty-nine-year-old Kasman drives a *bajaj*, a motorcycle attached to a sidecar that's used as public transportation in Jakarta's streets. Indonesians like him are the ones Ba'asyir appeals to. Kasman considers himself a moderate Muslim, but he also, like many other Indonesians, believes Osama bin Laden is not a terrorist. "Osama bin Laden is a Muslim," said Kasman. "Because he's a fellow Muslim, we must defend him. He is innocent."[24]

Kasman makes less than three dollars a day driving his *bajaj*—not enough to feed his four children. He and his wife have seen each other rarely over the past two years: she lost her job after the Asian financial crisis in 1997 and was forced to find a job overseas as a domestic helper in Saudi Arabia. She sends money home to her family. Kasman says economically, his family is worse off than they were during Suharto's time, but he says life is better now because at least human rights abuses by the police and military have tapered off against poor people like him. "As one of the little people"—what Indonesians call the *orang kecil*—"it was hard to be honest during the Suharto era. If we had a business, it felt like you're always being chased, being scared of authorities," said Kasman. "Having a business was hard. Now there is a little bit more freedom, even though it's still hard. At least there's no one scaring you."

Although he likes Americans and sympathizes with the victims of 9/11, Kasman believes the West is guilty of a double standard, particularly when it comes to terrorism. "The Muslims are always blamed," he said. "In Indonesia and in Iraq, it is the Muslim people. They say and do nothing about Israel and Kuwait," he says, focusing on the sufferings of the Palestinian people and Iraqis. He believes the CIA set up the Bali blasts: "Even though I'm naïve, my personal understanding is that the mastermind may be from America itself. It may not necessarily be by the American people, but it may be by the American government because America once accused Indonesia as being a nest for terrorists. So to prove its allegations in Indonesia, the Bali bombings were a means of providing evidence. That is the mastermind coming from America." Kasman said he believes the government did not have enough evidence to arrest Ba'asyir. "It confuses me—why? Because he is a Muslim leader, and then suddenly he is captured and arrested, and even though it's not clear what his crime is, they still arrest him?"

Ba'asyir vehemently denies any ties to terrorism. He continues to deny any connection to Jemaah Islamiyah or al-Qaeda. He even claims they are products of Western conspiracy: "Jemaah Islamiyah, I am sure is a manipulation, a fiction that was created to arrest people. Such as al-Qaeda. There is no such thing as al-Qaeda. It can be understood that al-Qaeda, the invention of al-Qaeda, and Jemaah Islamiyah are against Islam. This shows that America is attacking Islam." Ba'asyir adds, "Their aim is to weaken Islam in Indonesia and in so doing weaken the government so that they can control and dictate to this government. In addition to weakening Islam, they also have economic goals."

These arguments have widespread appeal among Muslims. That is part of the reason that the Indonesian government has been treading lightly, arresting Ba'asyir after Bali but refusing to completely crack down on Jemaah Islamiyah. To counter, some intelligence officials have leaked documents and information to journalists, but Indonesians view leaked intelligence documents with suspicion. In one interview, for example, I confronted Ba'asyir with a report of the interrogation of a captured JI leader who said Ba'asyir ordered him to hatch a plot to assassinate Megawati while she was still vice president. I waited while my question was translated for Ba'asyir, and I watched his face set slightly. I heard a murmur go through his aides. He maintained eye contact with me and then responded in low tones, "That's a lie. That's an engineering committed by . . . I accuse America and Israel. Assassinating Megawati has never crossed my mind, especially because Megawati is a Muslim woman. How can a Muslim kill his fellow Muslim? That's a sinful deed."

What do you do when you know someone is outright lying? Normally, you confront the person, but if you're a television reporter doing an interview and the cameras are rolling, you nod your head. Sources in the police and military—competing institutions that rarely agreed— were not the only ones who verified the information. It was verified by three different countries: Indonesia, Singapore, and the Philippines. It had taken me two months to pull this together from six trusted sources. All six worked independently of each other, and they all arrived at the same conclusion.

One major point is working against President Megawati's government: she is a woman. Ba'asyir only articulated what many Muslims in Indonesia believe, "A nation led by a woman won't be successful. That's what the Prophet said, and this becomes my opinion. The Indonesian nation, as long as it's led by a woman, won't be successful. So let's wait and prove it. It's just that a woman should be put in the right place. To be successful, Megawati should take an appropriate place for herself. Don't be in the top position. She must occupy a leadership position that's in accordance with her nature as a woman, like the minister for women's affairs or something like that. Don't be the country's top leader because she will never succeed."

One of the Indonesian intelligence agents who interrogated Ba'asyir the first time he was called for questioning in January 2002 gave me an insight into Ba'asyir's confidence and showed me how difficult it would be to win the war on terror. He said Ba'asyir admitted attending key planning meetings in Malaysia and to knowing the men who had been arrested in Malaysia and Singapore, but he denied carrying out any terrorist plans. The agent told me Ba'asyir compared himself to a craftsman. He said, "I make many knives, and I sell many knives, but I'm not responsible for what happens to them." [25]

Less than a week after the Bali bombings, Abu Bakar Ba'asyir was arrested under unclear circumstances, fueling criticism that the cleric was arrested to pacify Indonesia's Western allies. A day or so before, Ba'asyir had been hospitalized, and he was literally taken from his hospital bed. Dozens of his supporters rallied around him, and there were some scenes of violence, but they were quickly controlled by authorities. With time, his supporters visibly dwindled.

More than six months later, on April 23, 2003, Abu Bakar Ba'asyir, wearing white flowing robes, walked confidently into a Jakarta courtroom, the first day of his trial, while hundreds of his followers shouted, "Allahu Akbar! [God is great!]." He sat, smiling and relaxed, while Indonesian prosecutors read out a twenty-five-page indictment charging him with treason: of setting up the terror network Jemaah Islamiyah with the intent to overthrow the government; of authorizing a series of church bombings in Indonesia in 2000; of plotting to bomb American and other Western interests in Singapore; of attempting to assassinate Vice President Megawati Sukarnoputri. The court procedure was televised nationwide in Indonesia, the first time the government ever presented its evidence publicly to its people and labeled Ba'asyir a terrorist.

After the prosecutors were finished, Ba'asyir said, "I do not accept the charges. These are lies from America."

CHAPTER 4

TERROR HQ

Zacarias Moussaoui is widely known in the United States as the "twentieth hijacker," the man who was supposed to be on the flight that crashed in Pennsylvania but instead was in detention in the Midwest on immigration charges. This label, according to new intelligence, is probably wrong. Ramzi bin al-Shibh, now in custody, who tried on five separate occasions to obtain a visa to travel to the United States, has confessed that he was the true twentieth hijacker. It seems increasingly likely that Moussaoui was instead part of a second wave of strikes aimed at the United States, say U.S. intelligence sources. The explanation behind this intelligence involves the story of Ba'asyir's deputy and al-Qaeda's main operative in Southeast Asia, Riduan bin Isamuddin, a man better known simply as Hambali, and his adopted country, Malaysia. There, Hambali set up a meeting place for some of al-Qaeda's senior leaders in 2000, the first planning session for the attack on the USS *Cole* in Yemen and the attacks that would shake the world two years later on 9/11.

Malaysia is often cited as a model for Southeast Asia—a largely Muslim country that has embraced development. If you want to experience a modern, tolerant, progressive Islam, the kind Western policymakers and government officials dream about, visit this small nation of 23 million people. In this multicultural society, women wearing the Muslim headdress walk the streets next to girls in tight T-shirts and miniskirts, while the call to prayer from the minarets blends easily with the hip-hop music blaring from the jukebox on the sidewalk. Neither pork nor alcohol is banned.

Malaysia aims for superlatives. It has the world's largest cave passage, the world's largest natural rock chamber, the longest cave system in Southeast Asia, the world's tallest flagpole, the largest flag in the world, the tallest buildings in the world, the longest building in the world, Asia's largest mall. For a while, it pushed its people to achieve record-breaking feats: to be the biggest, the best, the first, and if they can't be included in the *Guinness Book of World Records*, Malaysia created its own coffee-table book published in 1997 "to inspire greatness within all Malaysians." That national obsession led to the setting of such dubious records as the highest backward climb up a staircase (2,058 steps), the longest variety show (thirteen hours), and the largest number of heads shampooed in one day at a shopping mall (1,068). During the height of Asia's boom times in the early to mid-1990s, when Malaysia hit growth rates of nearly 9 percent for a decade, the government set out to build megaprojects: Putrajaya, an ultramodern government center that cost about $8 billion, and, next to it, Cyberjaya, created to entice multinational companies to bring their headquarters here. All this is connected to the gleaming, brand-new Kuala Lumpur International Airport, a dream collectively known as the Multimedia Super Corridor. The fact that investors did not flock in, and Cyberjaya is a publicly funded dot-bomb, does not lessen Malaysia's belief in progress.

Malaysia's prime minister, Mahathir Mohamad, now Asia's longest-serving leader, is a visionary, a cheerleader for his people. Born on December 20, 1925, he was educated in his home state of Kedah until he went to medical school in Singapore. When he graduated, he joined the Malaysian government as a medical officer before setting up his own practice; eventually, he went into politics full time. On July 16, 1981, he became Malaysia's fourth prime minister. Dr. Mahathir is a home-grown leader who understands the problems of his people, often criticized in the West as an authoritarian leader with a patchy human rights record. Now he jokes that the West is adopting much of his philosophy in its war on terror: he operated the way he did because his nation had its own unique problems—which the United States just couldn't understand until it began to face similar problems. Unlike many others in Southeast Asia, instead of blindly following the West or muttering against it quietly, he has publicly questioned its leadership and refused to swallow its prescriptions. During the Asian financial crisis, he stood up to the International Monetary Fund, the only leader with the self-confidence to come up with his own solution and set the value of his currency instead of allowing it to float against the dollar. He argues that no one knows his country, his people, and his region better than he does. And he is often right.

For years, his favorite phrase, *"Malaysia Boleh"*—Malaysia Can Do It—was on everyone's lips. Mahathir said his megaprojects were "good for the ego" of a developing nation. "It is important because small people always like to appear tall," he said. "If you can't get tall enough, you put a box under you."[1] But Malaysia is also a lesson about what happens when your dreams come crashing down. After the Asian financial crisis left his country and his government overextended, Mahathir lashed out. First there was denial, then anger, then paranoia. He blamed the West, then George Soros, and then currency speculators for pulling out the foundation of his country's growth. He began to speak darkly of a conspiracy to bring down Malaysia.

My first real brush with Malaysia censorship pressure was during the 1997 fires euphemistically termed "the haze" in Southeast Asia—fires that were so prevalent during that dry season that they showed up on satellite photographs. I crisscrossed Indonesia, Malaysia, and Singapore reporting on the effects of forest fires in Indonesia on its neighboring countries, creating a thick brown-black mixture of smoke, fog, and haze that prevented residents from seeing the sun for months. Malaysia's information minister called me in for a dressing down, emphasizing that my reporting was having a negative impact on tourism. He kept telling me that CNN shouldn't keep wrongfully highlighting the haze. It was a surreal experience. Outside his window, the haze had rolled in, and it was difficult to see the outlines of city buildings. I continued reporting.

On December 18, 2002, I walked into the majestic Putrajaya complex for a conversation with Mahathir. He had said this was the final year of his reign (he had announced he would step down in October 2003), but he remained proud and defensive, criticizing the Western press and their governments for exacerbating Malaysia's problems. His office is inside Malaysia's twenty-first-century government center, a grand but empty structure with high-security corridors separated by doors that open with futuristic sensors. My heels echoed, and when I stopped to brush my pass over the sensor, the click releasing the door to the next corridor seemed exaggeratedly loud. When I got to his office, the doors opened to an impressive view of the mosque in Putrajaya. Dr. Mahathir was sitting behind his huge desk to my left. He was wearing a gray safari suit and the lapel name pin all government bureaucrats wear in Malaysia. Dr. Mahathir insists all are equal, and he too wore the pin. It simply said, "Mahathir Mohamad." He didn't stand up when I came in. He stared at me while his aide offered me a seat. It was the coldest reception I had received from anyone in years. He coughed repeatedly and didn't look well. Perhaps it was because it was in the middle of Ramadan, the fasting month. He seemed tired, but it didn't stop him from criticizing CNN.

"Of course, CNN here in Malaysia has always been very biased. It's not only you. The reporting has always been very biased against Malaysia. They have never said nice things about us. Even there in their own statements, they still mention where the press is controlled by the government, and yet they are being printed here. I mean, at least tell the truth."

I defended CNN's coverage, saying that he could hold me personally accountable. He was quick and biting, but he was listening. That meeting lasted nearly three hours. Two months later, he granted me a rare, hour-long interview on camera; he was much more upbeat. "The Muslims in many countries and their governments appear to consider Malaysia as a kind of model for Muslim countries which they would like to emulate.[2] All Muslim countries would like to become developed countries, but they have so many obstacles. They are not able to overcome the structure of their governments, whereas in Malaysia, we have been able to develop the country—to use the democratic system without sliding to anarchy." He was also clearer on the enemy: those "who are orthodox, conservative—who believe that worldly development is not what the religion wants us to seek."

For many years Malaysia had a policy of allowing all Muslims to enter without a visa, making it a frequent meeting point for Muslims dissatisfied with their own governments. Many of Mahathir's enemies had come from other countries. Like every Muslim leader around the world, Mahathir has had firsthand experience with fundamentalism and extremism. Increasingly over the years, a political movement to introduce Islamic sharia law has been gaining ground. It was partly fueled by Abu Bakar Ba'asyir during his brief exile in Malaysia, but other Indonesian clerics have stayed much longer, and they have built a network, the Jemaah Islamiyah, that is working for the overthrow of Malaysia's secular government as part of a vision of turning most of

Southeast Asia, and even part of Australia, into one giant Islamic state. Malaysia and Indonesia, as the region's two Muslim nations, are prime targets, and over the past three decades, they responded differently to the threat. Indonesia, with a much larger Muslim population, tried to stamp out radical Islam under Suharto. Dr. Mahathir, on the other hand, allowed Islam to flourish. There has been an increasing Islamization of his country, and yet a debate flourishes over whether he and his government are "Muslim enough." Malaysia's defense minister, Najib Tun Abdul Razak, explains that the radicals "have given a new twist to the interpretation of Islam as well as their attitude towards the government in Malaysia. They have this erroneous belief that we are not Islamic—or not Islamic enough—for their liking. So therefore, we have to be overthrown either by the ballot box or, if that is not possible, then through violent means."[3]

More and more women are wearing the *tudong*, the local version of the chador, either because they want to or because they are encountering increasing pressure to do so from their husbands and employers. The major opposition political party is the highly orthodox Parti Islam SeMalaysia (PAS), which already controls the governments of two of Malaysia's thirteen provinces. In those provinces, PAS has alarmed the Chinese and Indian minorities by attempts to introduce a Taliban-like form of government and Islamic sharia law.

In the wake of the Asian financial crisis, many Malaysians expressed their disgust and dissatisfaction by voting against Mahathir's party in the 1999 elections, swelling the ranks of PAS. PAS more than tripled the number of seats it held in the national Parliament, to 27 out of 193, and picked up the second of its two provinces. Since then, PAS has tried to implement controversial Islamic laws, which has alarmed many Malaysians. In 2002 in the newly Islamic province of Terrenganu, the PAS government tried to rule that a raped woman who can't prove she'd been raped would automatically be guilty of illicit sex. If she were married, the penalty would be death by stoning. If single, she would get 100 lashes of the cane and a year in jail. A massive protest by women's groups pushed the law into insignificance.

Several weeks later, PAS tried again, this time to introduce a sharia criminal offenses act that included punishments ranging from death to amputation and flogging for crimes such as theft, adultery, drinking alcohol, and renouncing the Muslim faith. Mahathir decided to hit back. Deputy Prime Minister Abdullah Badawi, who also serves as Malaysia's home minister, ordered the police force to ignore the law. The federal government told district police chiefs to uphold criminal laws only in line with the federal constitution. Dr. Mahathir, on a visit to Terrenganu, thundered that people who attempt to enforce such laws "have deviated from Islam and should be condemned to hell."[4]

Like Indonesia and the Philippines, Malaysia has a Muslim extremist movement that operates at many levels, not just in the electoral arena. In August 2001, the government announced it had arrested twenty-five members of Kumpulan Mujahidin Malaysia (KMM) under the Internal Security Act, a draconian law long criticized by human rights activists because it allows detention without trial. In the war on terror, the act has allowed the government to act swiftly to dismantle the network. Several PAS members and supporters were among those arrested, including Nik Adli Nik Aziz, the son of PAS spiritual leader Nik Aziz Nik Mat.

As chief minister of the province of Kelantan, the soft-spoken Nik Aziz Nik Mat is Prime Minister Mahathir's chief opponent. When his son was arrested, Aziz immediately said it was politically motivated: "I can think of no other reason why the government arrested my son but to undermine the PAS party."[5] Many believed him—at least until the evidence started filtering out.

It was only after the September 11 attacks that it became clear that there was an entrenched al-Qaeda network in Malaysia. There were two clear strands: an al-Qaeda cell using the country as a key transit point and staging area for attacks in the region and beyond and a home-grown extremist movement that had been co-opted into al-Qaeda's global jihad. KMM's members, in effect, had become the foot soldiers for al-Qaeda's plots.

Police sources say they had solid evidence of KMM's plans before they arrested Nik Adli Nik Aziz. On May 18, 2001, members of KMM attempted to rob a bank. The job was botched. The bank's security guard shot three armed men, two of whom died. Based on the third man's interrogation, Malaysia's Special Branch, its security agency, got its first leads.

"They managed to arrest one of these people. I think he told every-thing—almost to the point of boasting what they want to do,"

Mahathir told me. "That's how we discovered the network, which was before the eleventh of September."[6] "The robbery provided us the lead as it involved two graduates from the University of Arkansas and University of Karachi. The police follow-up was swift," said a police source. In June, police arrested nine more KMM members from several cities, including Kuala Lumpur. In one safehouse in Puchong, police seized firearms and ammunition. Many of the KMM's members had been to Afghanistan for training. They were plotting to overthrow Mahathir's government, planning assassinations, and sending fighters to fuel Indonesia's Muslim-Christian conflict in the Maluku islands.

Two members, who happened to be brothers, exemplify the reach of KMM in Malaysia and Indonesia and the interconnected, twisted ties that bind these militants together into Jemaah Islamiyah, al-Qaeda's network in the region.

On August 1, 2001, twenty-six-year-old Malaysian Taufik Abdul Halim was at the Atrium Mall in Jakarta, Indonesia, when the bomb he was carrying exploded prematurely. He was arrested by the Indonesian police, who notified Malaysia. Halim proved to be a member of Malaysia's KMM working on a mission for Jemaah Islamiyah, or JI. He was sentenced to death in an Indonesian court, a sentence later commuted to life imprisonment, and he gave his interrogators a great deal of information.

Taufik had trained in religious schools in Pakistan from 1993 to 1996, interrupted by a stint in Afghanistan from 1994 to 1995. In June 2000, he and nine other Malaysian recruits had met at the Kuala Lumpur airport. The group went to Sabah (the Malaysian side of Borneo), traveled by land to a seedy port on the southern tip of Sabah, and then crossed by boat to the Indonesian side of Borneo despite having no passports. They continued by boat and plane to northern Maluku, where Christian-Muslim violence had occasionally flared. For three months, they stayed there, but there was little conflict. Finally, they went on to Ambon, where fighting was ongoing. In court, Taufik said he and his colleagues helped defend villages there—only one of many Muslim fighters fueling the jihad in Ambon. The bomb he was carrying when captured in 2001 was given to him by Imam Samudra, the JI operative later named as field commander for the Bali blasts in October 2002.

Taufik's brother, Zulkifli bin Abdul Hir, was arrested separately in Malaysia and accused of killing a Christian member of Parliament, Dr. Joe Fernandez. Malaysian authorities say it was a KMM plot, but the Special Branch believes Zulkifli is also a principal leader of Jemaah Islamiyah. Clearly both brothers were members of KMM and worked on KMM's own plots under the broader umbrella organization Jemaah Islamiyah.

Unlike the Philippine and Indonesian extremist groups, KMM is relatively young. It was founded by another Afghan war veteran, Zainon Ismail, on October 12, 1995.[7] Forty-five of the KMM's estimated sixty-eight original members trained in al-Qaeda camps in Afghanistan,[8] including Nik Adli Nik Aziz, who took over the leadership of KMM in 1999. Thirty-four years old, Nik Adli returned to Malaysia and founded his own school, backed by his father's PAS, outside Kelantan's capital, Kota Bharu. His father says he led a quiet life as an Arabic teacher in the school. Located next to his home, the school is a bastion of Islamic fundamentalism. It teaches its 1,400 students an uncompromising view of Islam that includes the idea that jihad is every Muslim's responsibility.

One man deserves credit for enfolding Malaysia's terror group under JI's and al-Qaeda's umbrella: the Indonesian cleric and deputy of Ba'asyir known as Hambali. In 1997, Malaysia's Special Branch says an Indonesian cleric wearing a *kopiah*, or skullcap, and flowing Arab dress began leading meetings with Nik Adli and other PAS members involved in the KMM. They discussed the idea of setting up an Islamic state and the responsibilities of every Muslim to his faith. "They were told that the only way to set up an Islamic state was to overthrow the Malaysian government by force," said the investigator. "The infidels have no place in an Islamic state." The meetings continued until October 2000. That cleric became the spiritual leader of KMM. He was already the leader of Mantiqi 1, Jemaah Islamiyah's terrorist cell covering Malaysia and Singapore.[9] He was also operations chief, in charge of all terrorist plots.[10] By 2001, he was the highest ranking non-Arab al-Qaeda leader (part of its leadership council), maintaining an apartment in Karachi, Pakistan, and helping set up the 9/11 attacks along with a second wave.[11]

Born Encep Nurjaman in 1964 or 1965, Hambali grew up in the

sleepy little village of Sukamanah in West Java, Indonesia. He studied the Koran at a school founded by his great-grandfather in the tiny town of Ciganjur. The head of the school now is thirty-five-year-old Muhammad Wawan Ridwan, a religious teacher who went to school with Hambali.

"When we heard reports about him on the news, we were confused and surprised," he claims. "Usually, people who are following hard-line Islam like to preach this and that, like to tell us to achieve certain targets for this school, for example. But he was nothing like that. On the other hand, he said something about not being able to totally follow the Koran."[12]

The houses of the residents are a short walk from the school and its mosque. For many, there is no road access; they take footpaths weaving through ponds and woods.

The home of Hambali's family is made of concrete. His family wasn't poor; one of his relations owned a computer store near the house. Neither were they rich. "Contrary to the way they portray him in the news today, he was just a quiet kid," says Wawan. "I was far naughtier than him. He studied and went straight home. Not like me. After school, I'd sometimes get into a fight, or I'd play around the school before going home."

Hambali's twenty-four-year-old cousin, Dani Ahmad Roswandi, was tired of answering questions about his notorious cousin. "He's a normal guy," said Dani. "I can say nothing extraordinary about him." His family refuses to believe the man known as Hambali is actually their relation. "The person who has been widely reported and talked about is Hambali, and our family does not know any Hambali," says Dani.

Hambali's parents were respected religious teachers.[13] His father died in mid-2000; his mother, Eni Mariani, still lives in their house. She describes Hambali, the eldest of thirteen children, as a particularly devout youth. "He was very religious, but also very quiet, aloof and reserved."[14]

Hambali isn't the only one from his neighborhood whose imagination was captured by Islam. His aunt remains a fixture there: it's her voice heard through the loudspeaker calling the women of the village to a Koran reading session. Wawan, for his part, refuses to condemn the acts of terrorism and call to jihad of the man known as Hambali. "I believe there are different ways in spreading the word of Islam," said Wawan. "I can't say which one is wrong or which one is right because the goal is the same. My way is through education—through higher education which allows people to learn at their individual pace. I don't disapprove of other ways because there are times when Allah himself is heavy-handed."

During the childhood of Wawan and Hambali, under the rule of Indonesia's President Suharto, thoughts like these, spoken aloud, could have gotten them jailed. Back in the early 1980s, long before Suharto fell, neighbors in Sukamanah say the devout Hambali may have become involved in the new network of local Muslim extremist groups. It's uncertain whether he met Ba'asyir, one of the founders of the network then, but he certainly met him soon after.[15]

In 1985, Hambali left his village for Malaysia to look for a job. Many Indonesians often left home to work as migrant workers in search of a better life. "He was jobless for two years before leaving for Malaysia. So as far as I know, he left to work in Malaysia," says Wawan. He returned only once—about a decade later—shortly after the al-Qaeda cell in Manila was busted. "When he came home that one time, he said that he worked as a merchant, that's all," said Dani.

He didn't stay in Malaysia long, and he didn't leave for a job. From 1987 until 1990, Hambali answered the call for the modern jihad by going to Afghanistan. He later told supporters that he had met with Osama bin Laden several times while fighting as a mujahideen guerrilla against the Soviets. When he returned to Malaysia in 1990, he married a Malaysian-Chinese woman named Noralwizah Lee. Four years later, the two of them appeared on the board of directors of al-Qaeda's front company, Konsojaya, which funded the first al-Qaeda cell in the region. Philippine investigators say their phone wiretaps showed frequent calls made between Hambali's Konsojaya office and the Manila office of Osama bin Laden's brother-in-law Mohammed Jamal Khalifa. The man who would become al-Qaeda's number three, Khalid Shaikh Mohammed (KSM), began visiting Malaysia starting in 1994 and tapped Hambali, whom he first met in Afghanistan, as his operative.[16] He gave the seed money of about 95,000 ringgits, or about $33,000, to Hambali to launch Jemaah Islamiyah's local operations there.[17] In 1996, KSM traveled to the border between Malaysia and Singapore to "personally observe Hambali's recruitment operations."[18] KSM described Hambali, who first worked for him as part of al-Qaeda's media committee, as "extremely charismatic and popular."[19] Hambali, said KSM, had no trouble finding operatives for any special operation, and the recruits he found were "loyal and well-prepared."[20]

Hambali's secret lay in the meticulous groundwork he set in place beginning in the early 1990s in Sungai Manggis, a small village about an hour's drive south of Kuala Lumpur. For nearly a decade, this quiet "Terror HQ" neighborhood of tin-roofed, clapboard houses was the base for Malaysia's Jemaah Islamiyah. Hambali lived in one of the houses owned by the family of a long-standing civil servant named Mior Mohammed Bin Yuhana. When the police told him that he was renting a house to notorious terrorists, he says he was "upset. Not really shocked. Feeling disgusted." He had had no reason to suspect them. "They practice according to what the Koran says, and I was liking them very much, their children. We meet together. We talk together. Only when the happening, the stories of the bombing in Bandung . . . make me feel the saddest in my life." The Bandung bombing was part of an ambitious JI plot in 2000 to deliver thirty-eight bombs to priests and churches in Indonesia. The bombs in Bandung exploded prematurely, killing three of the bombers.

Mior was arrested and held by the Malaysian police for fifty-seven days but finally released. Hambali had lived with his wife, Noralwizah Lee, and her mother, for about $25 a month, in a small, wooden one-bedroom house with white peeling paint. "Very simple man," said Mior. "Very soft-spoken and humble. Very talkative. Hambali would go around meeting people in a very cordial way."

Next door to Hambali lived Abu Bakar Ba'asyir. A red and brown house that forms the far perimeter of the lot, it was the largest among the group. Ba'asyir led the prayer sessions that Mior attended.

Mior was cautious in answering questions about what exactly Abu Bakar said in these meetings: "His preachings? Be a good Muslim. And obey God's law. And follow what the Koran says. That's to the extent that I know. What he did behind, I don't know either." Others who attended were more forthright. Mohammed Sobri, a former soldier in the Malaysian army, arrested and detained for seventy-three days by the Malaysian Special Branch, says that the Terror HQ preachers opened his eyes to Muslim suffering and the need to respond. Sobri was particularly impressed by Hambali: "This may be because he had fought in Afghanistan and had met Osama. He talked about Palestine and Chechnya and Bosnia with real firsthand information."[21]

Ba'asyir and Hambali were joined by a fiery orator, another Indonesian who was imprisoned under Suharto—Mohammed Iqbal bin Abdul Rahman, better known as Abu Jibril. He lived a few houses from Hambali and was the first of the group to move to Sungai Manggis. Abu Jibril met Ba'asyir in prison and fled to Malaysia a year earlier. He also was an Afghan war veteran. In 1986, he began renting a house from Mior. His wife, Fatimah Zaharan, still lives in Sungai Manggis and was also arrested and questioned by the Special Branch. She staunchly denies her husband is a terrorist but acknowledges he spread the idea of jihad: "It's all from the book. If the book says it is necessary to have a holy war, then he will teach that. He never preached a word outside the holy Koran."[22] Jihad was Abu Jibril's specialty, and within the organization, it was his responsibility to turn that belief into action.

The final key figure who lived in Sungai Manggis was Imam Samudra, the man who became the field commander for the Bali blasts in 2002 and two years earlier gave a bomb to Taufik Abdul Halim.

By the mid-1990s, the Jemaah Islamiyah's structure was coalescing, following al-Qaeda's organization.[23] Its operational base was in Malaysia, and its emir was Abu Bakar Ba'asyir. Hambali was his deputy. One Special Branch officer compared it to the mafia: "If Ba'asyir is the godfather, Hambali is his consigliere." Like al-Qaeda, the policymaking body of Jemaah Islamiyah is known as the regional *shura*, or leadership council. It is headed by Hambali. Five divisions report to him: Missionary, Training and Jihad, Economics, Front Organizations, and International Affairs. The men he chose as his deputy for each played key roles in setting up the network.

The Missionary division broadens Jemaah Islamiyah's recruitment base from small, private Koran study groups to full-fledged schools, using Abu Bakar Ba'asyir's Pondok Ngruki school in Indonesia as a model. One of its graduates, known as Mukhlas, would become the principal for another school, the Lukmanul Hakim in Johor Bahru, Malaysia; he, along with a student and one faculty member, would be implicated in the Bali bombings. For a time, after Hambali fled to Pakistan in mid-2001, Mukhlas took over the leadership of the Malaysian and Singaporean cells.[24]

Mukhlas's school was supposedly shut by Malaysian authorities at the end of 2002 after a ten-year run. As Defense Minister Najib Tun Abdul Razak explained, "They're not teaching religion, but they are exploiting

religion. They are inculcating a culture of hatred. And this is too dangerous a development to be left unattended."[25] Dismantling this division of
Jemaah Islamiyah is crucial, say Malaysian officials, because this provides
years of indoctrination for new recruits. "We have to deal with the
pipelines, so to speak. It is not sufficient to take pure security measures
like arresting people. You have to win the hearts and minds of these people. So therefore the nearest task, as far as we are concerned, is to win the
ideological battle. And one of the ways in which we can do this is to take
over religious education in this country by the central government."

But has the government been successful? At Mukhlas's school, on a
visit in January 2003, my crew and I found an open side entrance. We
found classrooms with little dust and a clean mosque—signs the facilities for the school were still in use. While my crew began shooting, I
walked down a winding path to another group of buildings in the back.
It was so quiet I could hear the wind whistling. I thought it strange that
such well-maintained buildings would be abandoned. Then in the distance I saw a young man. My surprise was mirrored in his eyes. Immediately, I waved and smiled. Taken aback, he smiled back. Within minutes,
an older man with a goatee came walking toward me. "You no good. I no
like. You go." By his last word, he was yelling. He turned around and left.
After a few minutes, he came driving out on a motorcycle. He stopped
again at the open side gate and told us to leave. He was wearing a faded
yellow Poso T-shirt, after the town in Indonesia that had become a destination for Jemaah Islamiyah's fighters looking for a jihad. Poso is also
where authorities discovered an al-Qaeda training camp and is the base
of Jemaah Islamiyah's armed group, the Laskar Jundullah.

That's where Jemaah Islamiyah's second division comes in: training
and jihad, which focuses on creating an army unit and on funneling
members to Afghanistan, the Philippines, and Ambon. Abu Jibril, the
principal recruiter, was a key leader and Hambali's deputy for this unit.
Arrested in June 2001 in Malaysia's first wave of arrests, he traveled
throughout the region, urging recruits to go to their baptism of fire[26] in
Poso and Ambon. Jemaah Islamiyah created propaganda videotapes like
those of al-Qaeda.

In one popular tape, Abu Jibril stood outside a mosque preaching
to about three dozen armed followers. He was building to an emotional
crescendo: "Oh God, help us to destroy the infidels who have killed our
children."

"*Allahu Akbar!* [God is great!]," swells from the crowd. Then Abu Jibril holds up a Koran in his left hand: "The Koran is to build our people," he says in a quavering voice. Then he brings up his right hand, holding a battered pistol. "The gun is to destroy the obstacles that stand in our way. We cannot separate them!" he yells. (In yet another sign of the interpersonal links which bind this group, Abu Jibril's brother, Irfan S. Awwas, is a key founder and now the chairman of MMI, Jemaah Islamiyah's legal front in Indonesia.)

The third division collects Muslim tithes and channels money through various companies. Hambali's deputy in charge of funding is Malaysian Faiz bin Abu Bakar Bafana. Originally a Singaporean national, Faiz is one of the wealthier and better-educated JI members. Trained as a civil engineer, his neatly trimmed beard, thin-line moustache, and wire-rimmed glasses give him the look of a scholar. In 1984, he left his job in Singapore and moved to Kuala Lumpur, where he owned and managed his own construction company.[27] Two years later, he joined a Koran study group run by Jemaah Islamiyah. In 1987, he swore an oath of loyalty to the group. In early 1991, Faiz went to Afghanistan for military training, and in 1998 he spent a week in further training at Camp Abubakar in the Philippines.

By 1996, Jemaah Islamiyah had divided the region into four territorial groups called *mantiqis:* Mantiqi 1 covered Malaysia, Singapore, and southern Thailand; Mantiqi 2 covered all of Indonesia, except Sulawesi and Kalimantan; Mantiqi 3 covered the Philippines, Brunei, the east Malaysian states of Sarawak and Sabah, and Sulawesi and Kalimantan in Indonesia; and finally, Mantiqi 4 covered Indonesia's Irian Jaya and Australia. Each of these groups set up its own versions of the five JI divisions.

In 1996, Abu Bakar Ba'asyir appointed Hambali the leader of Mantiqi 1, and Hambali then chose Faiz to head his Economic division. According to a classified regional intelligence report, Faiz named seven companies serving as front organizations for his group, including a construction firm, a printing press, an auditing firm, a meat supplier, and a textile company.[28] Yet as of this writing, not one JI or al-Qaeda business in Malaysia had been shut down by authorities. To make matters worse, Jemaah Islamiyah has recruited army officers and government civil servants, some of whom channeled government contracts to their front companies—so, ironically, government money has been paid to organizations trying to topple the government. At least two such cases have surfaced: a sympathetic senior Water Supply Department engineer awarded a government contract to install water pipes in Selangor to one front company, and a school headmaster helped award a stationery supply contract to another. In these two instances, the civil servants were arrested and are now in prison.[29]

Faiz also uses Jemaah Islamiyah's companies to employ members of the organization. In November 1995, a newly-recruited Indonesian, Fathur Roman al-Ghozi, was given a job in Faiz's construction company after returning from training in Afghanistan. Three years later, al-Ghozi would meet Faiz again; he was now Faiz's guide to get to the MILF training camps in the southern Philippines. By 2001, al-Ghozi had become Faiz's agent, one of the key plotters behind an ambitious suicide-truck-bombing plot in Singapore.

Little is known about the fourth division of the regional *shura* which reports to Hambali: known among members as Al Ehsan, or front organizations, it is allegedly headed by Abdul Razak Baharudin.[30] He oversees various nongovernmental organizations that funnel money to the group, much as does Faiz. Only one nongovernmental organization has been publicly identified as under his control, a supposed charity set up in 1998, which operated openly in a shop in Selangor, Malaysia. It solicited donations to help Muslims in need, but the money it collected—37,000 ringgit ($9,737) in 1999 and 77,000 ringgit ($20,263) the next year—was used to fund the travel and training of JI members to Afghanistan, the southern Philippines, and Ambon, Indonesia.[31] Money that Malaysian Muslims donated to help stop conflict actually fueled Muslim-Christian violence in the hands of Jemaah Islamiyah.

The fifth division of the regional *shura*, International Affairs, focuses on al-Qaeda's direct activities in Malaysia and shows how Jemaah Islamiyah supported al-Qaeda's plots and goals, with membership in the two organizations freely intermingling. Hambali's deputy for this division is Yazid Sufaat, a U.S.-educated biochemist and former Malaysian army captain. When he was arrested by the Special Branch on December 9, 2001, Sufaat would tie together many of the now notorious al-Qaeda operatives linked to the September 11 attacks.

The focal point was Sufaat's three-room condominium at Evergreen Park, a weekend retreat next to an eighteen-hole golf course and a country club. It was there that Hambali hosted a key three-day al-Qaeda planning meeting on January 5, 2000, which revived the 9/11 plot he was involved with in 1995. The meeting took place just days after a failed al-Qaeda attempt to bomb the naval vessel USS *Sullivan* in Yemen. Tawfiq bin Attash, a.k.a. Khallad, a bin Laden lieutenant and key plotter for marine attacks, flew to Malaysia to attend. Some Malaysian intelligence officers believed KSM was also at that meeting, but subsequent interrogations of KSM showed he was not present. There they planned the bombing of the USS *Cole* in Yemen, which happened ten months later, and delivered the funds for that strike. More important, it was a key planning session for September 11. Among the attendees were Ramzi bin al-Shibh, who along with KSM would admit to planning the attacks, and two of the hijackers on the plane that crashed into the Pentagon: Khalid al-Midhar and Nawaf al-Hazmi.

Through this intricate, circuitous route, the "twentieth hijacker," Zacarias Moussaoui, reenters our picture. In September and again in October 2000, Hambali would ask Sufaat to host Moussaoui in the Evergreen Park condominium. Sufaat showed him around the area and helped him set up e-mail accounts. He also gave Moussaoui a letter to help him enter the United States. It appointed him the title of U.S. marketing agent for a small Malaysian computer software company called Infocus Tech. At Malaysia's Registrar of Companies, Sufaat, who signed the letter as the company's managing director, isn't listed in any capacity. It's his wife, Dursina Sejahratul, who turns out to be a substantial shareholder of Infocus Tech. That letter was found with Moussaoui when he was arrested in the United States.

At the time, he was the only person facing public prosecution in the United States for the September 11 attacks, and the thirty-five-year-old Moussaoui admitted he was a member of al-Qaeda but denied any involvement in the September 11 attacks. In fact, he said he "was part of another operation to occur outside the United States after September 11 involving different members of al-Qaeda."[32] The cell he has had the most contact with is Jemaah Islamiyah in Southeast Asia, leading investigators there to believe the "second wave" of attacks would originate and hit American interests in the region.

KSM—Moussaoui's old boss and al-Quaeda's former military chief now in U.S. custody—verifies Moussaoui's statement, according to sources who have seen the interrogation reports, except for one point.[33] KSM said Moussaoui was not part of the September 11 hijackers but was in the United States for a "second wave" attack to take place inside America.

It's clear al-Qaeda had other ambitious plots it was developing simultaneously with the 9/11 attack. In 2000, KSM sent Moussaoui to Malaysia and placed him under the supervision of Hambali. "Hambali arranged for Moussaoui to visit the flying school in Malacca" (the Malaysian Flying Academy) "to see whether he could train to fly the wide-bodied aircraft," said terrorism expert Rohan Gunaratna. "But Moussaoui was very disappointed after visiting the flying school because he could not get the right type of simulator training."[34] The picture painted of Moussaoui in court documents and video conference depositions is of an aggressive, yet whimsical and obstinate man.

While in Malaysia, "Moussaoui demonstrated paranoid behavior."[35] Another Hambali deputy, Faiz bin Abu Bakar Bafana,[36] talked about how Moussaoui believed Faiz's home was bugged so he insisted on going outside to talk of sensitive plans, yet he talked freely inside Faiz's house about "a 'dream' he had to fly an airplane into the White House." During the time they worked with him, Faiz and Hambali found Moussaoui's behavior to be so erratic and fragmented, they called him "cuckoo."[37]

KSM confirmed that, telling his interrogators that Hambali sent another trusted operative, Mukhlas, to meet with him to lodge a complaint about Moussaoui. KSM also gave other alarming details about Sufaat, who was doing far more ambitious work for al-Qaeda. The 1987 biochemistry graduate of Cal State Sacramento was developing biological weapons for al-Qaeda. A regional intelligence officer verified that, telling me Sufaat used a company he owned, Green Laboratory Medicine, to try to purchase anthrax. This, speculates KSM, may be why Moussaoui was interested in learning how to fly crop dusters. Fortunately, Sufaat could not buy the right strain of anthrax that could be dispersed as a weapon.

But Moussaoui and Sufaat did succeed in doing one thing together. KSM said Moussaoui used the money he was given for flight training to buy ammonium nitrate, a fertilizer easily turned into explosives. (The bombs used in both the 1993 World Trade Center attack and in the Oklahoma City bombing two years later were made from ammonium nitrate.) Sufaat used the same company, Green Laboratory Medicine, to purchase 4 tons of ammonium nitrate for a suicide truck-bombing plot in Singapore set to attack seven targets simultaneously, including the U.S. Embassy and other Western institutions, perhaps intended to signal the beginning of "the second wave."

CHAPTER 5

BLACK NINJAS AND JIHAD IN AMBON

"From 6 o'clock every evening until dawn the next day, everyone here lives in a state of fear."[1] Black-clad men wearing black masks, armed with knives, swords, and sickles, were attacking their victims in the middle of the night. These were not armed robbers, in it for the money. Their gory tasks often lasted for hours, and they were designed to sow terror. They dragged their targets out of their homes and killed them outdoors before mutilating and dismembering the bodies. A lucky few escaped, like one man who told me, "I woke up to find a sickle at my neck. I tried to push it away, but they threw me down and kicked me. I screamed, and they ran away."[2] Others who lived in more remote areas were not as lucky. In the morning, residents woke up to find body parts dangling from nearby trees, and in several instances, human limbs were left lying in mosques, now defiled by blood. The word whispered with fear in the villages was *ninjas*. "It's an analogy to the ninjas on TV," said Kusnadi, a local anthropologist. "They see what's on TV, and since it's similar to what's happening here, the people began calling them ninjas—a person who wears black clothes and a mask."[3]

Indonesia, 1998. For four months, from July to October, 182 people were brutally killed and dismembered in a brazen and successful attempt to terrorize residents in the town of Banyuwangi, a stronghold of mysticism where sorcery and black magic are as much a part of life as Islam, creating a unique religious blend easily stirred into violence. Events here and in East Timor in 1999 (where ninjas again began reappearing) show how the government and military manipulate its people, a weak point later exploited by al-Qaeda. Residents said there were four distinct stages and targets. First, the killers chose villagers who practiced black magic. "In the beginning, those killings were done by local people,"[4] said Abdurahman Hasan, the chairman of the local branch of the Nahdlatul Ulama, the NU, the largest Muslim organization in the world. "The second stage was when the killings were no longer done by locals but by paid assassins, gangsters from outside, and their targets were not the black magic practitioners but those who practiced white magic—the people you went to for help. They also became targets. Then mosque leaders, public figures, and finally, the last one, the targets were Muslim leaders in boarding schools. The ninjas are skilled professionals," said Hasan.

Fifty-year-old Baehaqiy Aliy survived an attack with the help of his neighbors. It was just after dark, and the gaunt Islamic teacher was going through the Koran with a group of students in a sparsely furnished wooden house surrounded by dense trees, far enough from the main road that it felt isolated. "After we started reciting the Koran, we heard a shout. I didn't pay attention to the shouting because usually it's only the neighborhood kids playing outside, but the shouting continued. So I decided to find out what was happening. When I got outside, suddenly, the kids began shouting, 'There are masks, there are masks!' I saw movement to my side. I ran toward the main road, but those masks began running after me. I only saw shadows." Aliy showed me where it happened, and I could see how remote the area was. As we walked the path through the woods, all I could hear was the heavy sound of crickets. "Those masks were not captured in the end. And they slammed their swords on these windows." He showed me the gash marks made by his attackers. "These are the marks—one, two, three, four. Smashed. When they hit it at first, nothing happened, but then they hit repeatedly until the glass on the window shattered." A vigilante group from the neighborhood helped save him. When the attackers saw the group approaching from the west, they ran away.

Muslims in the area felt under siege, and they responded in kind, turning the violence into a battle for their religion. By the end of September, there was an average of three killings a day, and the killings—and paranoia—were spreading from Banyuwangi to neighboring cities. By mid-October, vigilante mobs had become as dangerous as the killers themselves, lynching at least thirty-five suspected ninjas. On October 18, in East Java's second largest city, Malang, a mob converged on two suspected ninjas and beat one to death. The police picked up the second man, but before they could get him to the police station, the mob attacked again. The police stood by while the mob killed the second man, mutilated his body, and decapitated him. They shoved a spike into the severed head and tied the headless body feet first to a motorbike. Like a motorcycle gang, they paraded through Malang's streets: one man displaying the severed head, the motorcycle at the rear dragging the bleeding body. The police were on the side of the Muslim vigilantes. "We give information to the people who do the neighborhood watch," said Major Soebroto, the deputy police chief of Jember, East Java. "Be vigilant and stop the killings, but do it according to the law."[5]

Members of the military and police claimed the "ninjas" were engaged in revenge killings, dating back to the bloodbath of 1965, when members of the Communist Party were massacred in East Java. Allegedly, some officers said, relatives were seeking vengeance. But the true cause seemed closer at hand.

Over two thirds of those murdered were members of the Muslim NU Party, many of whom were mainstream Muslim clerics and boarding school teachers. The NU was expected to be a potent political force in Indonesia's upcoming first general elections. "What happened in Banyuwangi and other cities, the target really is NU—whether by coincidence or intentionally," said Abdurahman Hasan. "Maybe it's connected to the general elections. Maybe there are people who want to keep the status quo—who don't want any changes. They want the general elections to be postponed." A retired military intelligence officer was the first to state publicly that he believed his old intelligence agency was behind the Banyuwangi killings. A former instructor in the agency's school for intelligence techniques, Rudolf Baringbing said, "Only fools would believe that these killings were purely criminal acts."[6] He pointed out that although hundreds had been arrested, no clear explanation or scenario had been given by law enforcement agencies. The national leader of NU, and the presidential candidate of its political party, half-blind Muslim cleric Abdurrahman Wahid, noted that "every power holder, including Suharto, uses witchcraft as his or her weapon. It's a political tool."[7]

Earlier that year, in May, riots in Jakarta targeting the ethnic Chinese had helped end the thirty-two-year rule of Suharto. Now the victims were Muslim clerics. Over the next months, a familiar pattern would emerge in conflicts that sprouted across the Indonesian archipelago: accusations that the military instigated communal violence through a proxy group, then a security force would mobilize a rival militia. Indonesia's newfound freedom from authoritarian rule had opened a Pandora's box, releasing long-suppressed tensions and jealousies which often erupted into violence. In Jakarta, there were fierce neighborhood battles, often ending in riots and looting. In Poso, religious tensions flared into open warfare between Muslims and Christians. In West Kalimantan, ethnic rivalries between the Dayaks, the old head-hunters of Borneo, and the Madurese spurred weeks of brutal beheadings. (In one instance, I walked onto a field where boys were playing soccer—except the ball they were using was the decapitated head of an old man.) In Aceh, the nearly three-decades old Free Aceh Movement, known by its Indonesian acronym GAM, prepared to renew its fight for a separate state, fuelled by the success of the independence movement in East Timor.

What the domestic players did not count on were the outsiders who took advantage of this tumultuous transition period. The propaganda tapes in Osama bin Laden's collection, which I had watched in Atlanta in 2002, were not just propaganda at a distance; al-Qaeda actively recruited Muslim fighters to join these battles. Jemaah Islamiyah established training camps for Muslim fighters in those areas. But the place where al-Qaeda was most successful in creating its own battlefield in Indonesia—what officials called the "new Afghanistan"—was in Ambon in the Maluku islands.

Ambon is both a city and a province in the Maluku islands, once known as the Spice Islands when the Dutch ruled the East Indies. After Indonesia became independent, it was a prime tourist destination for decades. The city of Ambon, nearly half Muslim and half Christian, was touted as Indonesia's shining example of racial harmony. Under Suharto, as in most other parts of Indonesia, communal violence occurred sporadically, but authorities always clamped down quickly. Public discussion of the sensitive issues of race, religion, and ethnicity was forbidden. People used the acronym SARA as the code word for them. After Suharto fell in 1998, violence flared out of control. Muslims in Jakarta began to form jihadi groups to "help their brothers in Ambon." It did not help that some foreign Christian evangelical organizations referred to the violence against Muslims as a "religious cleansing."[8] It was only a matter of time before al-Qaeda stepped in.

My first trip to Ambon was in February 1999, a little more than a month into the conflict. Ambon's airports had been shut down, and I had been forced to report from Jakarta about how the fires that engulfed Ambon were so large they were picked up by satellite photographs. Finally, travel resumed. When we got to Ambon, many parts of the city were already gutted and burned. The population was divided into Muslims, who carried a white flag, and Christians, who carried a red flag.[9] Journalists were automatically labeled as one or the other, making it difficult to get access to both sides. Many neighborhoods were being divided between red and white, and crossing those lines could cost your life. I stayed at the Hotel Ambon Manise, a three-star hotel on the border of the divided areas in the village of Batu Merah—what I call ground zero. This is where the violence had begun on January 19, 1999.

As in all other matters in Ambon, there is a Christian and a Muslim version.[10] The first involved three men: a Christian mini-bus driver named Jacob Leuhery, known as Yopy, and two Muslims named Usman and Salim. January 19 was the end of the Muslim holy month of fasting, Ramadan. Yopy was just starting his shift at his bus terminal when Usman and Salim tried to extort money from him. He told them he was just starting his shift and had none to give. Later in his shift, he returned to the terminal, and the two came back and demanded money again. When he replied he had not had any passengers, one of the Muslims took out a knife and threatened to slash Yopy's neck. Yopy escaped, ran to his home nearby, and got his own knife. In response, a Muslim mob, about 700 strong, allegedly at the instigation of the two Muslims, attacked Yopy's home. Both Yopy and Salim would later be arrested by the police.

The second version says that Yopy had earlier borrowed the minivan for a private charter, and the conductor, a Muslim from the terminal, was asked by the Muslim owner to get the money for the hire from Yopy, who allegedly refused to pay and threatened the Muslim conductor. With the help of Christian passengers, Yopy allegedly assaulted the conductor, who ran to the town to get Muslim reinforcements.[11]

By February, none of this really mattered. The battle lines were set. The only way my team could get around Ambon was to split into two cars—one Muslim and one Christian. The feeling of anarchy was palpable, and I didn't think we could trust the security forces to keep us safe.

I hired two off-duty Indonesians, a Muslim soldier and a Christian policeman, each with a submachine gun. When we needed to pass through a Christian checkpoint, the Christian car would lead the convoy and negotiate for the entry of our Muslim car; vice versa for a Muslim checkpoint. It took a lot of quick talking and quick thinking, but I wanted to be able to get both sides. This strategy was barely possible in February; things would only get worse.

We drove through wide stretches of gutted buildings, some embers still burning. Our first stop was a small mosque near the ocean to talk to refugees. Inside the white-tiled mosque, several dozen Muslims were on the floor, some sleeping, while children were playing outside. My Christian policeman was nervous and decided to stay with our drivers by the cars. The Muslim soldier followed my team inside. As long as Nuraki, our male Muslim producer, was speaking, we seemed fine, but when he introduced me as the reporter and I mentioned my name, the mood of the group turned harsh, and they moved in close. There was no love lost here for Christians named Maria and Americans from CNN. "You can't come here," one man yelled. "Americans support Israel. You are against Muslims." I tried to counter that I wasn't against Muslims, that I lived in Jakarta, and that it was important we get their experiences, their side of the story. Suddenly our soldier motioned we should leave, and Nuraki edged up to me and in English whispered to me that he thought he saw a man at the edge of the crowd pull out a knife. I tried to reason with the men: "Please tell us what happened. Say it to the camera. We're not taking sides." No one was listening, and our soldier was getting palpably nervous. One man lunged at me, pulling my bag. Our soldier stepped in and pushed him away. It was time to go.

I decided to stay in larger public areas nearer the center of town to get the Muslim side of the story. We had the phone number of the Muslim leader of the refugees at the Al-Fatah mosque, Yusuf Ely, so we called him to establish a time for an interview.[12]

I walked around the mosque while the crew was setting up. By the latest count, there were 3,750 refugees here, and according to Yusuf, more than 30,000 Muslim refugees were inside other mosques around Ambon. It was stiflingly hot. Families had picked up as many of their belongings as they could carry, and they lay strewn on the floor. I stopped and talked to several people. Many of them had watched someone they loved die; others had fled the burning of their homes. They were frightened and angry. Although he spoke in broken English, Yusuf wanted to let the world know of the calamity. "This is the biggest riot in the whole of Indonesia," he said vehemently. "You can see for yourself. In terms of tragedies, it ranks as third in the Muslim world— Kosovo, Yugoslavia and Ambon." In fact, before the conflict was over, more people would die in Ambon than in either of those high-profile conflicts.

"Muslims are killed by the Christians for no reason. You see, we have one month of what we call *buka puasa*, the fasting month, and then we enter *Idul Fitri*, our holy day when we break the fast. It's impossible for Muslims to attack during that time. That is against our religion and customs," said Yusuf. "We were attacked by the Christians. One Muslim student wanted to go to prayers, and they cut him into eight pieces. Very brutally." He talked about the task force the Muslims had set up and how the provincial governor's pleas to Jakarta for more security forces had largely gone unanswered. "The military must come here and do the military procedure," he said. "If someone [breaks] the law, shoot them. Kill them. Then make other people have no bravery to make same fault like that. It means it gives lesson for others to not do that again. The situation will be peace again, and especially the Muslim people never, never attack the Christians. Never. We only, every day, every minutes, every seconds, killed by the Christian people." Yusuf Ely's words would be played over television stations in Jakarta and would act as a clarion call for Muslims.

The same claims were being made by the Christians. The next day, we started at dawn for Christian areas. As we were going through a Christian checkpoint, things seemed tense. Some of the young men there were wearing black armbands. When we asked why, they said they were going to the funeral of a friend who had been killed the day before. I asked if we could go. They went off to talk between themselves, then returned and said we should follow them. Some got in a car. Two others rode in our cars—one in each. We were driving through winding roads up a mountain when our Muslim car in front swerved off to the side and stopped in front of a house. We got out, and our two guides began speaking vociferously to each other. Other Christians came out of the house. They didn't want to take our Muslim crew members to the funeral. Nuraki and I tried to convince them that if we didn't, then we wouldn't be able to do our jobs properly. At one point while they were arguing with each other, I saw a young man off to the side, his arm in a sling, his eyes red and puffy. I asked our producer Nuraki to ask around about him. It turned out that twenty-six-year-old Nyong was the friend of Helmy Tomasila, whose funeral we were attending. Nyong was with Helmy when he was killed a day earlier, and he had just gotten out of the hospital. I pulled my cameraman over and started to interview him. The antipathy died as everyone stopped to listen. They saw our Muslim crew members working and assigned two Christians to protect them while we attended the funeral. Nyong, a muscular young man wearing jeans and a black T-shirt, the sleeves slit to make room for his bandage, told his story. He was so full of guilt for surviving while Helmy didn't that he burst into tears.[13]

"We were going to get gas for the motorcycle," he said, rubbing his hand over his eyes. "We didn't think there would be any danger. The security forces said it was all right, but when we reached Waihaong"—a Muslim neighborhood—"a crowd stopped us." They were armed with homemade weapons and machetes. "They asked me to get off. Around twenty people were there. I was wondering where the police were. This group tried to take me inside Waihaong, but I stopped and asked them, 'What did I do?' That's when security people started to come toward us. Because I can do a little martial arts, I kicked. A knife was coming toward me. I kicked it away, but they're fast. I ran away, but they knifed me here, in the back." He pulled up his shirt to show a bandage. "I ran and ran. I felt pain because I was bleeding. Lots of blood. I felt dizzy. The police opened fire at them. One of the policemen picked me up and pulled me away." He said when the policeman dropped him at the side of the road, he pulled the knife from his back, but when he did that, another policeman hit him. "He beat me here"—showing his black and blue marks—"because they thought the knife belonged to me and I was about to use it." Nyong broke down and cried. He didn't learn that Helmy had been killed until after he woke up in the hospital.

From the crowd that had gathered I began to piece together what had happened. When Nyong was pulled away from the motorcycle, another mob had formed around Helmy, who was later found with his throat slashed by a machete. "Those people are animals," said Nyong. "I'm furious and want to go after them." That sentiment was echoed by the young men in the crowd. Nyong repeated that he was disappointed that security forces were so slow in responding, but few could complain directly out of fear of repercussions.

We walked together to the funeral on the other side of the mountain and arrived there just as the coffin was being lowered into the ground. Helmy's sister, a slim, young girl in black, her veil thrown aside, threw herself on top of the coffin, which was being showered with flowers by relatives around the bier. She was sobbing uncontrollably. "Helmy, get up!" she implored. "Helmy, the food's on the table. Helmy, you have to eat. Helmy, go home. Have something to eat. Helmy, it's Christmas. Helmy, get up!" I had to turn away from pain so harsh it distorted reality.

The Ambon violence was started by the defense authority, but it took on a life of its own. Security forces in Jakarta lost control of their troops in Ambon. The military is predominantly Muslim, the police predominantly Christian. Both began to participate. "The security apparatus are now fighting with each other," said Munir, a human rights worker. "Either by inciting the people to continue fighting or by taking active part—by fighting themselves. They are now part of the conflict. It is one big human rights violation. According to our records, around 70 percent of the people who died in Ambon not because of the conflict itself but because of the repressive pattern of the security forces." This was a familiar complaint: Indonesian security forces were neither trained nor equipped to deal with rampaging mobs. They either stood back or opened fire. The very people who were supposed to maintain law and order themselves lapsed into anarchy.

When I got back to Jakarta, I began to fear that Ambon would ignite the entire country, with Muslim Indonesia turning on its Christian minority. There was a series of key protests beginning on March 3, 1999. In the center of Jakarta around its National Monument, I walked through a crowd of more than 10,000 people demonstrating, Muslims calling for a jihad. Twenty-two-year-old Dian, a slim, vocal young man, spoke for his friends, who had just signed up to volunteer to fight in Ambon. "It's my responsibility as a Muslim," he told me.[14] "We can't just sit and accept our brothers' deaths in Ambon. It's our right to defend them. We want to do jihad! Whoever wants to send us there, we're ready. By God's will, we're ready." Rumors magnified by Indonesia's often inaccurate media stirred the anger of Muslims in Jakarta. A false report by a local newspaper that four Muslims praying inside a mosque had been killed by soldiers sparked fears of government repression. "We see indications of taking sides," twenty-five-year-old demonstrator Porkas Halomoan said. "Like the shooting of people who just did their morning prayers. We didn't see it ourselves, but we heard that news."

Soon after, the military set up an information center in Jakarta to try to stem false rumors, but not fast enough to stop local papers from reporting thirteen more Muslims killed—deaths that had never happened. Soon, authorities stopped keeping accurate records of the death toll; they were afraid of how it would be used. Police reports would count the dead at about 1,000 after four years of fighting, whereas human rights groups estimated 9,000 to 10,000. I kept a running tally of deaths confirmed for CNN. From 1999 to mid-2002, we reported more than 10,000 killed.

Those protests were only the first of many, culminating in a massive rally on January 7, 2000, which attracted between 100,000 and 300,000 demonstrators. By that point, fighting had escalated during the Christmas and Ramadan holiday seasons, and the Christians were perceived to be winning the conflict, with hundreds of thousands of Muslim refugees fleeing to southeast Sulawesi. The horrors mounted. In Tobelo on Halmahera island in North Maluku, Christians, many of whom fled their homes, killed between 400 and 800 Muslims and forced another 10,000 to flee the district.[15]

Meanwhile, as a result of an economic downturn, more than 14 million Indonesians had lost their jobs or could not find work as they finished school. It was fertile ground for extremism. "We are supposedly in a period of reform, but it's not changing people's lives," said Ubaydillah Salman, the managing editor of *Sabili*, a popular magazine espousing radical views. "People are frustrated, and they see Islam as the answer to all their problems."[16] Many young men wanted to sign up for jihad. There were new radical militia groups springing up, looking for volunteers. The best known and most notorious was Laskar Jihad, followed closely by the Islamic Defenders' Front, or FPI. U.S. officials have accused both of accepting money and weapons from al-Qaeda, a charge both deny.[17] Both have strong ties to Indonesia's security forces.

Laskar Jihad and FPI made their first public appearances on November 14, 1999, a day that came to be known as Black Friday. They had been asked by Indonesia's security forces supposedly to safeguard the special session of the MPR, the People's Consultative Assembly, which was meeting to decide on major revisions to the political system. They were among some twenty Islamist groups, comprising more than thirty thousand civilian militia, in support of President Habibie and opposed to demonstrating students.[18] As legislators met and passed twelve new laws to revamp the political system, violence outside killed twelve people and injured more than two hundred.

The FPI would appear again two weeks later at riots in Ketapang, when mobs attacked churches and Christian schools in North Jakarta. Six people were hacked to death and ten burned fatally in fires that destroyed four churches and damaged twelve others. Founded on August 17, 1998,[19] FPI had already become notorious for attacking bars and nightclubs in Jakarta, places its members consider immoral, and for threatening to evict foreigners, particularly Americans, from Indonesia, a process known locally as sweeping. FPI leader Habib Muhammad Rizieq bin Hussein Syihab once said, "The sweeping we plan to do is sweeping in an elegant way. We will approach foreigners and ask to look at their passports. If they are Americans, we will ask them nicely to leave Indonesia. We will even drive them to the airport. If we have told them to leave, and they don't, we will not take responsibility if there are lunatics who take matters into their own hands."[20] The FPI shows how a proxy group can be manipulated. Sources within military intelligence said that FPI members often targeted and trashed establishments that failed to pay protection fees to the police. At the time it was most active, the FPI allegedly maintained close ties to both the military and the police, taking advantage of the rivalry between them.[21]

The more dangerous group—and a very public recruiter for the jihad in Ambon—was Laskar Jihad. By all accounts, it was heavily backed politically and financially by members of the military. Western intelligence sources say at least $9.3 million were transferred from the military to Laskar Jihad. Co-opting many of the twenty civilian militias created by the military for the November MPR session as a base, founder Jaffar Umar Thalib opened Laskar Jihad offices in Jakarta, Cirebon, Semarang, Solo, Yogyakarta, Lampung, and Kendari in early March 2000. At its height, Laskar Jihad had branch offices in all twenty-six of Indonesia's provinces. Jaffar called for a big meeting at a huge sports stadium in Jakarta on April 6, 2000. Thousands of Laskar Jihad members carrying machetes, rifles, and grenades and dressed in flowing white Arab-style robes jogged around the indoor track, yelling, *Allahu Akbar!*—God is great. Days later, Laskar Jihad opened a training camp on the island of Bogor.[22] Training was conducted by members of the Indonesian military "in their private capacity, not on behalf of the institution," as one Laskar Jihad leader put it.[23] That camp was soon shut down at the orders of President Wahid but at the same time he tacitly encouraged the group to fight in Ambon, by saying at one appearance that it was up to civic society and local officials to find a solution. Laskar Jihad members were soon regarded as heroes and saviors for Indonesia's Muslims. Jaffar Umar Thalib openly proclaimed that 3,000 of his forces would depart from the second largest city, Surabaya, in East Java, for the Malukus on April 29 and 30, 2000. President Wahid now tried to curb them, yet despite a verbal order on nationwide television, security forces did not stop Laskar Jihad from leaving.

"They announced their intentions to go to the Maluku Islands to fight and kill Christians. The government not only did nothing to prevent it from happening, the police and the military facilitated their travel!"[24] says Robert Gelbard, the U.S. ambassador in Indonesia at that time. Laskar Jihad members arrived in Ambon aboard ships and were allowed in, the regional military commander, Brigadier General Max Tamaela, said, because they had no weapons.[25] Yet weapons soon followed. Juwono Sudarsono, then the minister of defense, complained about "a container loaded with firearms entering the area," about which his soldiers "did nothing . . . They let it enter."[26] The *Jakarta Post*, Indonesia's leading English daily, published a letter on its website claiming that nine containers of weapons had been sent. It gave the name of the ship, the name of the company that sent the containers, and the address to which they were sent in Ambon. "There was film on CNN International showing the army handing over automatic weapons to the Laskar Jihad fighters!" Gelbard snorted.

Laskar Jihad quickly established a base in Ambon and set up training camps. A little more than a month after the militants arrived, on June 21, 2000, the elite Police Mobile Brigade base near downtown Ambon was attacked by Laskar Jihad, working with local Muslims and even some federal soldiers.[27] It was a well-coordinated operation by land and sea. The whole compound, including a police arsenal, hospital, housing complex, and officers' residences, was razed to the ground. The police deputy commander was killed by Muslim rioters, but the real target was the arsenal. The rioters seized more than 1,000 weapons and thousands of rounds of ammunition.

Local and national politicians were caught in a quandary. Playing the Islamic card was like drinking from a poisoned chalice. Muslim politicians who talked about Muslim-Christian reconciliation and dialogue were branded pro-Christian. If they were Christian, they were seen as anti-Muslim. Finally, President Wahid declared a state of civil emergency on June 26, 2000, but even that didn't stop the violence. On July 1, Christian villages were attacked by Muslim fighters in white robes, some wearing military-style uniforms. Fighting raged for six days. At the same time, Muslim militants attacked a nearby university, destroying the gymnasium, library, and all its facilities. In the eyes of Muslims, the school had long been identified with Christians. More than 110 people were killed during the first month of the civil emergency. Christians were ethnically cleansed from the North Maluku capital, Ternate.

Among the majority of Muslims throughout the country, there was a great deal of support for Laskar Jihad. Gelbard notes, "In June 2001, a Balinese general who was commanding the army forces in the Malukus decided to take Laskar Jihad on seriously. There was a firefight. Fifteen of the Laskar Jihad fighters were killed, and there was an uproar in the Parliament resulting in that general being fired!"

With more than 10,000 fighters, Laskar Jihad became the largest and most organized jihadi group in Indonesia, merging radical Islam with intense nationalism, fighting not just in Ambon but also Poso. Leader Jaffar Umar Thalib had apocalyptic ideas, arguing that there was an international campaign to create a Christian republic in the heart of Indonesia: in a radio broadcast throughout Indonesia in May 2002, he called for all-out war.[28] "I order all members of the Laskar Jihad to write their will and testament and prepare themselves to take up the position of martyrs. Get all your weapons out." He warned the provincial and central governments that they should not help the church "carry out an evil and treasonous plot against the Muslim faithful. To all the Muslim faithful, I advise they close ranks and prepare themselves to take part in the people's resistance against the attempted betrayal of the nation and State." He challenged Jews, Christians, and Americans. "We Muslims are inviting the U.S. military to prove its power in Maluku. Let us fight to the finish. Let us prove for the umpteenth time that the Muslim faithful cannot be conquered by over-exaggerated physical power. The second Afghanistan war will take place in Maluku if you are determined to carry out the threat, O America."

An Afghan war veteran, Jaffar had studied in Pakistan for several years before going to Afghanistan in the late 1980s. He admits meeting Osama bin Laden in Pakistan in 1987 while they were getting ready to enter Afghanistan to fight invading Soviet forces. Yet Jaffar dismissed Osama bin Laden's poor grasp of Islam, saying bin Laden "knew nothing about true religion."[29] Jaffar claims that bin Laden sent al-Qaeda operatives to visit Laskar Jihad's headquarters in Ambon in the summer of 2001, promising financial support and training if Laskar Jihad joined al-Qaeda and that he refused the offer. American officials discount his claim. "Laskar Jihad and its leader, Jaffar Umar Thalib, had strong connections to al-Qaeda and maybe still have. We saw them develop," said Gelbard. Jaffar did admit his group's links to Malaysia's KMM, and further developments showed Laskar Jihad has both overt and covert links to Jemaah Islamiyah.

Ambon and, to a lesser extent, Poso were rallying points for many extremist Muslim leaders. Abu Bakar Ba'asyir was one. His Indonesian Mujahideen Council, known by its Indonesian acronym, the MMI, created its own armed force, the Laskar Mujahideen. Another group under the MMI umbrella, Laskar Jundullah, later co-opted by al-Qaeda, sent about fifty recruits to Ambon in February 1999. That force would combine with Ba'asyir's Laskar Mujahideen, growing to about 500 Islamic fighters. These recruits, who stayed for six months to a year, were well trained and concentrated on guerrilla tactics. Their commander until his death in October 2000 was Haris Fadillah, alias Abu Dzar. Another key leader was Jemaah Islamiyah's primary recruiter, Afghan war veteran Abu Jibril, who brought in fighters from Singapore, Malaysia, and other parts of the world. Although there is a long-standing intense personal rivalry between Jaffar Umar Thalib and Abu Jibril,[30] their groups had the same cause and often worked together. At a meeting of

Ba'asyir's MMI in October 2000 in South Sulawesi, Abu Bakar Ba'asyir was elected as the "commander" of the governing council, and the leaders of all three militias were given positions of authority. The MMI thus tacitly took leadership over Laskar Jihad, Laskar Mujahideen, and Laskar Jundullah. Abu Jibril's brother, Irfan S. Awwas, was a key founder of MMI and would later take over as chairman after the arrest of Ba'asyir. MMI was an accepted, established political entity. Yet it was shot through with ties to al-Qaeda. Among its three militias, for example, Laskar Jihad maintained it was the most independent, yet it cooperated with al-Qaeda on projects; Laskar Mujahideen answered to Jemaah Islamiyah; and finally, Laskar Jundullah got part of its funding directly from al-Qaeda through a Saudi charity.

Laskar Jundullah first gained notoriety on October 29, 2000, when it entered several luxury hotels in Solo, Indonesia, "sweeping" for Americans. Laskar Jundullah members also said they wanted to force the replacement of U.S. ambassador Robert Gelbard and demanded that the United States stop attacking Muslim nations and stop its support of Israel against the Palestinians. If these demands were ignored, Laskar Jundullah said it would attack U.S. interests in Indonesia. In December 2002, a McDonald's was bombed in Sulawesi by the group. At one point, Laskar Jundullah had a force of six battalions, for a total of 2,000 Muslims active in Ambon and Poso.[31] The war on terrorism is often a dirty one. On March 13, 2001, the leader of Laskar Jundullah, Agus Dwikarna, was arrested by Philippine authorities as he was trying to board a plane for Thailand, allegedly for possession of explosives.

A civil engineer by training, Agus Dwikarna claimed he was in the Philippines for business reasons. A mild-mannered man who wore an Indonesian batik shirt to his sentencing, at which he was sent to prison for ten to seventeen years, he told me he carried no explosives and that he was set up. "I did nothing wrong," said Agus Dwikarna. "Those things in my bag don't belong to me."[32] The information I've uncovered leads me to believe he is right and that the detonating cord and C4 explosives the police said they found were probably planted on him by airport authorities. As one source told me, "We know he's a terrorist, Maria. Should we just let him go?" Philippine authorities were tipped off about Dwikarna's presence in the country. Indonesian intelligence sources said they were relieved Dwikarna was arrested because they had long known of his associations with terrorists, but they didn't believe they could ever get together enough evidence that would stand up in court. One high-ranking Indonesian intelligence official told me, "Tell your Filipino friends, thank you!"

Dwikarna was the regional head of a Saudi Arabian charity, Al-Haramain Foundation, a conduit for al-Qaeda money into Southeast Asia.[33] Indonesian intelligence officials told me they had arrested foreigners in Sulawesi whom they suspected were al-Qaeda fighters. One pulled out a letter saying he was in Indonesia for charity work; that letter was signed by Agus Dwikarna.

A classified Philippine intelligence document obtained by CNN says, "Agus Dwikarna has direct links to Al-Qaeda thru Omar al-Faruq, Al-Qaeda's senior representative in Southeast Asia, and Ayman al-Zawahiri, Al-Qaeda's no. 2 man."[34] In fact, Southeast Asia had become increasingly important to al-Qaeda. Intelligence documents from three different countries document a June 2000 visit to Indonesia by two of al-Qaeda's top leaders: Egyptian doctor Ayman al-Zawahiri, bin Laden's deputy, and military chief Mohammed Atef, al-Qaeda's military chief. They visited areas plagued by conflict: Ambon, West Papua (formerly known as Irian Jaya), and Aceh, where Muslim hard-liners were fighting for a separate Islamic state: "Both of them were impressed by the lack of security, the support and extent of Muslim population and the obscurity provided by the density of the forests. This visit was part of a wider strategy of shifting the base for Osama Bin Laden's terrorist operations from the subcontinent to Southeast Asia."[35] Their guides, authorities later learned, were Agus Dwikarna and Omar al-Faruq.

A classified U.S. intelligence document I later received outlined Laskar Jundullah's goals and was clearly marked with a warning: that the information within could not be shared with foreign nationals, including Indonesian officials. It's unclear whether the United States ever shared that information with their Indonesian counterparts. It said that shortly before he left Indonesia in early March 2002, Dwikarna held a meeting at his home in South Sulawesi, Indonesia. Among those who attended were Agung Hamid, who would later be implicated in the McDonald's bombing, along with other Indonesian veterans of the Afghan war. They talked about al-Qaeda operatives in Ambon, Bogor, and Jakarta.

It seemed that Dwikarna was having a fight with the al-Qaeda members in Sulawesi. "This disagreement was prompted by several factors, mainly involving differences between Arab Al-Qaeda 'brothers' and Indonesian brothers. The Arabs were viewed as too often interfering in the internal affairs of the Indonesian brothers. The Indonesians also complained that the Arabs did not know, and were apathetic toward, the local situation and political conditions in Indonesia."[36] Indonesians complained about the way the Arabs videotaped training in their camps, only to let those tapes fall "into the hands of US and Indonesian intelligence." They also quarreled over money: the Indonesians wanted more and believed the Arab al-Qaeda members were using the majority of their money to live luxuriously in Jakarta. The document detailed Agus Dwikarna's plans for Laskar Jundullah, exploiting and expanding weaknesses inherent in Indonesian government. In the short term, they had three plans: "The first element is organizing sabotage throughout Indonesia. The second is infiltrating and obtaining support within TNI and Polri" (the military and police). "Third is infiltrating and obtaining support from civil organizations and political parties." Ultimately, Dwikarna wanted to create a fighting force of about 10,000 men, which would try to unite the radical groups within Indonesia and help groups like the Abu Sayyaf in the Philippines. The last part of their long-term plan is particularly insidious: "to take advantage of the confused situation and conditions which exist within the Indonesian Armed Forces (TNI) at the current time"— exploit internal rivalries between the military and police—and take advantage of "increasingly aggravated conflicts between TNI and the Indonesian political elite."

It was already happening in Ambon and with the MMI. Looking ahead to 2004, the danger is clear. Radical groups linked to al-Qaeda will be trying to destabilize Indonesia's first ever direct presidential elections by infiltrating not only the political parties themselves but the very security forces tasked to keep the order.

Violence in Indonesia has hardly been confined to the provinces. In the capital, Jakarta, residents have been assaulted by a myriad of mysterious bombings, most of which remain unsolved. It began on January 1, 1999, on Jalan Sabang, a busy one-way side street behind the CNN office on the main thoroughfare. At about 5:00 A.M., a medium-sized bomb exploded just outside an empty department store. Farther down the street, authorities found two other explosive devices, which had failed to detonate. Walking down the street that morning, I thought about what would have happened if they did. The explosion would have destroyed much of one of Jakarta's oldest streets famous for its open stalls and shops, causing much terror. Jakarta was on edge through most of January as a host of malls, hotels, and downtown office buildings, including the CNN office, received bomb threats. More actual bombings followed. Many initially blamed them on forces in the military sympathetic to Suharto. (Analysts pointed out that many of the bombings followed court appearances of the Suharto family.) In fact, many of them were practice runs by Jemaah Islamiyah, as operatives perfected building and planting explosives.

On October 26, 2000, the U.S. embassy in Jakarta cited "credible threats" and closed its visa and consular services for about a week. As tough-talking Ambassador Gelbard later explained, "The Indonesians were still very traumatized and irate with the United States, whom they perceived to be part of some kind of conspiracy with the United Nations and Australia about East Timor." He became frustrated with the Indonesian government. "When I arrived, having had so many years of experience working on counterterrorism problems, I had been briefed in Washington about the existence already of at least five al-Qaeda front groups, a hajj travel agency, charitable groups and so on." He tried to offer help to Indonesia's first civilian defense minister, Juwono Sudarsono. "I told him about the implantation of these al-Qaeda groups, and I told him we were prepared to offer a serious briefing about their existence and the nature of the threat. No reaction at all. At a later point, I went back to see him, offered the same kind of briefings to him again. No interest. And this was the kind of problem I experienced throughout the Indonesian government—as part of either denial or a profound distrust of the United States. Or a combination of both. In any event, we found that even as terrorist groups in Indonesia were making themselves quite evident through their actions, and even announcing their intentions, there was a very conscious effort on the part of the government to ignore their actions and refuse to take any kind of measures against them . . . their failure to move only allowed these groups to grow and consolidate themselves."

Embassy officials developed information that al-Qaeda had the embassy under surveillance, but "the police refused to provide the additional security that we needed. . . . After exhausting what I felt were all possible remedies . . . I felt compelled to close down the embassy to outsiders." It caused a diplomatic furor. The foreign ministry claimed closing the embassy was sullying Indonesia's image. Gelbard scoffed at those claims, saying he was merely a tool used by Wahid's political enemies. He was certain about the information his staff had developed, and he wanted more support from the State Department—"in particular for support at a high level to demonstrate that it was not just an issue of me, since I was, by this time, being heavily scapegoated in Indonesia. Regrettably too, my State Department contact told me in a telephone conversation that he had strongly recommended against any of my recommendations because he felt our analysis was simply wrong; he felt there was no threat to the embassy at all. At that point, I felt very much alone."

Gelbard and his team, though, were right. The man who did the surveillance of the embassy and ran the operation was al-Qaeda operative Omar al-Faruq, a Kuwaiti national sent to Southeast Asia by al-Qaeda's operations chief, Abu Zubaida, in 1995. Arrested by Indonesian authorities on June 5, 2002, al-Faruq was sent to Bagram Airbase in Afghanistan and is now in U.S. custody. He told U.S. interrogators that he "had cased the US embassy in Jakarta to develop a plan to destroy the embassy with a large car bomb."[37] In August 2001, the CIA found diagrams and blueprints detailing the U.S. embassy and its security in the possession of a terrorist suspect in the Middle East. "Our information was absolutely confirmed," said Gelbard. "We learned from multiple sources from outside Indonesia that an al-Qaeda hit team was coming into Indonesia, I believe from Yemen, to try to blow up the embassy, and that the information they were using was based on the surveillance that indeed had taken place back in October, November of 2000."

The plot was foiled, but the six-member Yemeni hit team escaped. U.S. intelligence discovered they had fled to the island of Surabaya. Gelbard asked Indonesian intelligence to arrest them, but military intelligence insisted that only the local police could make the arrest. Although the United States had already flown in two CIA officials and a plane to take the al-Qaeda operatives to the United States, the Yemenis were tipped off, and they fled the country altogether. Small wonder that Indonesia was fast developing a reputation as a potential safe haven for al-Qaeda.

The story of Omar al-Faruq shows how al-Qaeda and Jemaah

Islamiyah worked together. Trained in Afghan camps for three years beginning in 1992, he was dispatched to the Philippines in 1995 along with an al-Qaeda camp commander.[38] Their job was to set up training camps for JI and al-Qaeda members at Camp Abubakar. Al-Faruq also wanted to get commercial flight training in the Philippines but was unable to do so.[39] Meantime, at the MILF camp, al-Faruq became the liaison between the Arabs and MILF chief, Hashim Salamat.[40]

After the fall of Suharto in 1998, al-Faruq was told to move to Indonesia, where he became a sleeper agent, covertly helping Jemaah Islamiyah and other al-Qaeda operatives. He took the name Mahmud bin Ahmad Assegaf and married twenty-four-year-old Mira Agustina. She still insists her husband was nothing but a merchant who traded in pearls and wood. "In 1998, I received his proposals," says the shy woman who was covered from head to toe in a burka. She had not yet even met him. "I was still in school so I didn't reply seriously. Mahmud proposed three times, but I didn't respond. In July 1999, I went home during a school holiday, and I was introduced to him. I prayed and asked for Allah's protection, and that very same day, we were married."[41] He proposed, she said, through her father, Haris Fadillah, a.k.a. Abu Dazar, the commander of Laskar Mujahideen in Ambon until he was killed in the fighting in October 2000. He is also a JI operative, which she denies. "That only hurts me more," said Mira. "My father worked hard as an *ojek*"—pedicab—"driver, as a newspaper vendor, as a ticket collector on a public bus. His last job is as a debt collector."

Omar al-Faruq has told his interrogators that his wife was directly involved in the family's true business. She kept the books for al-Qaeda money funneled through the Saudi charity Al-Haramain. Al-Faruq also confessed that his wife was present at a meeting in May 1999 attended by her father, at which a plot was hatched to kill Megawati Sukarnoputri, then Indonesia's vice president. Money for the assassination changed hands.[42] One attendee went to Malaysia and the Philippines to buy guns, but he later claimed he couldn't get the weapons back to Indonesia. (Jemaah Islamiyah now alleges he stole the money.) Mira Agustina took notes from their meeting and translated them into Arabic, according to her husband. Al-Faruq would attempt and fail to assassinate Megawati once more. "I am deeply hurt and shocked" by her husband's claims, Mira says. "I feel like the most violated person on earth. If they were true, automatically, it means that I have been lied to all of this time, but I just cannot be sure now that they are true, and that my husband is responsible for all that."

Indonesian and American intelligence reports concur that al-Faruq was the main force behind Laskar Jundullah, helping to establish training camps in Ambon and Poso to prepare local mujahideens for "al-Qaeda's terrorist acts in Southeast Asia."[43] After the group's leader, Agus Dwikarna, was arrested, al-Faruq "appointed" Yasin Syawal to take his place, suggesting that al-Qaeda had control over the organization. (Syawal trained in Afghanistan with his friend Hambali and had a more personal connection to Jemaah Islamiyah's founders: he is the son-in-law of Abdullah Sungkar.)

Al-Faruq has also given details about how al-Qaeda money flows, pinpointing a key link with a Saudi Arabian charity.[44] Information gleaned from Omar al-Faruq—corroborated by other al-Qaeda operatives in U.S. custody, U.S. officials say—was largely responsible for the United States raising its terror alert level to its highest level one day before the first anniversary of the September 11 attacks. Al-Faruq, working with Hambali, was tasked by al-Qaeda "to plan large-scale attacks against US interests in Indonesia, Malaysia, Philippines, Singapore, Thailand, Taiwan, Vietnam, and Cambodia. In particular, al-Faruq prepared a plan to conduct simultaneous car/truck bomb attacks against U.S. embassies in the region to take place on or about 11 September 2002."[45] Al-Faruq told the CIA that although he was arrested, "other operatives would assume responsibilities to carry out operations as planned." Al-Faruq also talked about plans to bomb a U.S. naval ship in May 2002, but he couldn't get the suicide bombers he needed.

Al-Faruq confirmed what I had started piecing together about the mysterious bombings in Indonesia. He said that beginning in mid-1999, he organized a series of bombings across the country, sanctioned and approved by Abu Bakar Ba'asyir, and carried out by operatives of Jemaah Islamiyah and al-Qaeda. It started on April 19, 1999, at the Istiqlal mosque in Jakarta, Indonesia's largest mosque. A medium-sized bomb exploded on the ground floor, blowing out the glass in the row of offices used by Islamic groups on that floor, leveling several rooms, and injuring five people. Muslims were understandably furious. Al-Faruq says the attack was ordered by Ba'asyir, who wanted Muslims to blame Christians in the hopes of triggering counterattacks. Ba'asyir has repeatedly denied all of al-Faruq's claims.

The next JI bombing attack was on August 1, 2000, at the Philippine ambassador's house on the stately, wide street where most of Jakarta's diplomats lived. It was done by Fathur Roman al-Ghozi, on orders from Hambali.[46] He was helped by an armed wing of Malaysia's KMM.

The next attacks were more ambitious: JI operatives working with al-Qaeda in an attempt to plant thirty-eight bombs on Christmas Eve, targeting priests and churches in eleven cities. Many of these operatives would go on to carry out the Bali bombings two years later. The explosives used were the same: carbon, potassium, sulfur with TNT. Most came as packages covered in gift wrapping paper. Twenty of the bombs sent Christmas Eve exploded, most within thirty minutes of each other in ten cities, killing nineteen people and wounding more than 120 others. Six days after those bombings, five nearly simultaneous explosions hit the Philippine capital, Manila, killing twenty-two people. Based on the interrogation reports of JI and al-Qaeda members now in custody, it is clear how these operations were carried out.

The operations chief for the region and actual operative was Hambali, assisted by Faiz bin Abu Bakar Bafana. Plans for the Indonesian operations were finalized in Kuala Lumpur, Malaysia, in October 2000. Four senior JI members were named field coordinators: Hambali for Jakarta; Yazid Sufaat, the former army captain from Malaysia (now in custody there), was assigned the northern Sumatran city of Medan; Imam Samudra, who would become the field commander for the Bali attacks two years later, was in charge of Batam; and Enjang Bastaman, alias Jabir, was given Bandung, about three hours away from the capital, Jakarta.

After that meeting, Hambali asked Faiz to go to Solo, Indonesia, in November 2000.[47] At a small hotel in Pasar Klewer in Solo, Faiz met with Abu Bakar Ba'asyir, Hambali, and Zulkifli Marzuki, the JI secretary. Hambali discussed three main issues: Ba'asyir's request for Jemaah Islamiyah to contribute $4,000 to the Pondok Ngruki high school; attacks on American interests in Singapore; and "a plan to launch bomb attacks on the Christians in Indonesian provinces on Christmas Eve 2000 on the grounds that since the Muslims were attacked by the Christians in Ambon" at the end of Ramadan "in 1999, it would be better for Muslims to launch the attack first before being attacked by the Christians" in 2000.[48] Faiz said everything discussed that day "had the approval and blessing of Jemaah Islamiyah leader, Abu Bakar Ba'asyir."

The explosives used for the Indonesia attacks were reportedly purchased by Faiz and Hambali for about $47,000 during a trip to Manila in December. They were met by Fathur Roman al-Ghozi and MILF member Hatem Mukhlis Yunos, who were in charge of the Philippine operations.[49]

Later in December, in Kuala Lumpur, at another meeting, Hambali asked Faiz to gather data on U.S. military targets in Singapore for yet another attack. Faiz responded by asking his brother to do surveillance work on U.S. naval ships in Singapore.[50]

One week before the bombings, a final planning meeting took place at the Hotel Alia in Jakarta.[51] The operation that resulted on Christmas Eve was not perfect; many of the bombs failed to go off, and some went off prematurely. Jemaah Islamiyah viewed the operations as largely a success, with one major exception. One of its more capable operatives, and Hambali's close friend, was delivering a bomb in Bandung when it exploded and killed him. The bombs were built to be detonated by cell phones, and Jabir used his cell phone for one bomb but forgot to change the card inside his phone. Someone, perhaps another plotter, called the phone, prematurely triggering the explosion.

A day later, Hambali met Zulkifli Marzuki at the Kuala Lumpur airport to evaluate their operations and discuss the effects of Jabir's death on Jemaah Islamiyah.[52] Another meeting at a front company was held to analyze the premature explosion and discuss how to prevent it from happening again. The next day, Hambali met with Faiz. "With tears in his eyes, he told me that his close friend Jabir died in the explosion in Bandung," Faiz told his interrogators.[53]

Between the December 24 Indonesian bombings and the December 30 Manila strikes, Jemaah Islamiyah had proved it could carry out simultaneous attacks in twelve different cities in two countries. It had sown terror and ratcheted up conflict between Muslims and Christians, playing both sides off each other. The possibility of a Muslim revolution was—and is—still very much within the terrorists' reach.

CHAPTER 6

GANGSTERS IN
THE PHILIPPINES

Understanding the complex weave of terrorism, extremism, and local ethnic conflicts in Southeast Asia requires both a top-down view of al-Qaeda and a bottom-up view of local conflicts that al-Qaeda has been able to exploit. In Indonesia, local conflicts began with ethnic divisions or ancient political vengeance. In the Philippines, as this and the next chapter show, there are separatist groups that are often lumped together but in fact can vary from mafia-like shakedown artists to true Muslim extremists.

There's a small elevator that opens to the VIP departure lounge of Manila's international airport. Early on June 10, 2002, it was the focus of more than two dozen journalists, photographers, and television cameras, waiting for forty-three-year-old American Gracia Burnham to arrive—her first public appearance after more than a year of being held hostage in the southern Philippines by the Abu Sayyaf. CNN was carrying it live so I was there, talking about what Gracia Burnham had lived through when the elevator doors opened. I stopped for a second when I saw her. It was less than three days since she had been pulled out of the jungle, a bullet piercing her leg during the military rescue. She was in a wheelchair, her right leg in a cast held aloft in front of her by a pillow. Her short brownish-blonde hair had been curled. She had on a red T-shirt and wore a hint of blush and lipstick. It was a stark contrast from the photographs and videotapes released by the Abu Sayyaf during the year she spent as a hostage in the jungles of the southern Philippines, her hair flat and dank, her lips compressed in a thin line, the edges of her eyes pointing downward. Today, she seemed like a different person. She was back in civilization.

She smiled tentatively at everyone in the room as she was wheeled behind the table by an embassy official, and the microphone was adjusted. From her lap, she picked up a legal notepad and looked directly at the journalists facing her while U.S. ambassador Francis Ricciardone introduced her. I caught her eye and smiled. In the year I was reporting on her captivity and her release, I had grown to admire this woman. Immediately after she was rescued, she insisted on meeting the children of Ediborah Yap, a Filipina nurse who had been held captive with her and who did not survive the military rescue. Gracia said she wanted to talk to Ediborah's children about their mother—to tell them about their mother's courage and her love for them. She didn't speak to the press for a weekend, despite the frenzy that surrounded every rumor of every move she made. She saw a limited few: her close friends from the fifteen years she lived in the Philippines and fellow hostages who were released before her. Everything she did was aimed at helping others who had lived through similar trials rejoice that they had survived or reconcile to their loss. That morning, she would speak for only a few minutes and then would board her plane for the United States.

She was calm, seemingly at peace; she looked beatific. Her first words were about her husband, Martin, a pilot for a Christian missionary group, the New Tribes Mission. The two had been celebrating their eighteenth wedding anniversary, a one-day vacation surprise from Gracia, when they were kidnapped from the Dos Palmas beach resort in Palawan. She started her statement with a firm voice. "Good morning. Martin and I had so many dear friends here in the Philippines. You know who you are. Our friends in Malaybalay, in Brookes Point, in Darapida, in Manila. We love you so very much, and we thank you for the precious memories that you gave us during our fifteen years here." She took a short pause, and a parade of emotions gushed out in one sentence. "Martin loved this country with all his heart." Her voice broke, and I thought she was going to cry, but she pulled herself together and went on, stumbling slightly. "We want to thank each and every one of you for every time you remembered us in prayer. We needed every single prayer you prayed for us during our ordeal in the jungle."[1]

Her voice broke again, and I realized this woman's faith must have been essential for her survival—perhaps the bedrock of her courage and of the grace with which she was now handling the many competing claims and pressures she faced. I had reported on many of these hostage releases in the past two years: there were always tearful reunions and often angry and bitter accusations—particularly from the foreigners—at the country and the military that allowed their kidnappers free rein. The military dismissed them as Stockholm syndrome, saying the victims had begun to identify with the kidnappers. Certainly, in more than 200 kidnappings since 2000, nearly every foreign hostage had appealed *against* any military rescue, Gracia and Martin among them—which is why Gracia's next words surprised many of the journalists: "We especially want to thank the military men, the Filipinos and the Americans, who risked and even gave their lives in order to rescue us. May God bless these men in their ongoing efforts." Already speculation was rampant that the Philippine military, trained by their American counterparts, had botched the rescue.

She paused nearly imperceptibly before making her next statements, her voice getting stronger as she gave her full support to the Philippine government. "During our ordeal, we were repeatedly lied to by the Abu Sayyaf, and they are not men of honor. They should be treated as common criminals. We support all efforts of the government in bringing these men to justice." Again, her voice broke when she said, "I return to the States this morning to rejoin my children and to put my life together. Part of my heart will always stay with the Filipino people." Now she choked back tears and smiled as the embassy official wheeled her away.

Her short prepared speech was heartwrenching, especially because she refused to let herself break down. She had spent 376 days—one year and eleven days—as a hostage of the Abu Sayyaf, and on the day she was rescued, the day of freedom she had dreamed of, her husband, Martin, was killed—shot not by the Abu Sayyaf but by bullets of the Filipino soldiers who came to their rescue. Gracia was going home to her three children alone. The third hostage had been Ediborah Yap, kidnapped a few days after the American couple. Gracia was the sole survivor.

In the book Gracia would publish about a year later, *In the Presence of My Enemies*, she wrote, "The soldiers were clearly upset, realizing that in their rescue attempt, they had shot all three hostages. . . . Eventually, the lieutenant in charge came over to talk with me. 'Mrs. Burnham, I know that you're probably very angry with us,' he said. 'But we were just doing our jobs.' " Gracia told him, "I know. We never forgot who the bad guys were and who the good guys were. I don't think of you as the bad guys."[2]

Although Gracia also wrote about how the Abu Sayyaf received food and bought their ammunition from the Philippine military—from the very soldiers chasing them—she displayed little anger in her book and in person, repeating her first public statements after her release. "Well, I think we have to just keep in mind that the reason we were there was the Abu Sayyaf took us hostage. They were the bad guys. It wasn't the Philippine military that were the bad guys," Gracia would tell CNN. "Yeah, it's unfortunate that Martin died in a gun battle like we thought he would, but that wasn't the fault of the Philippine military. It was the fault of the Abu Sayyaf. They were the bad guys."[3] She described her captors as "just a group of guys. They never seemed to have a plan. They weren't well organized. They called it their struggle. They were trying to get their homeland back . . . so they declared jihad."

Abu Sayyaf's jihad was imported from al-Qaeda. In fact, Osama bin Laden's brother-in-law Mohammed Jamal Khalifa recruited Abu Sayyaf's Filipino founder, Abdurajak "Jack" Janjalani, and sent him on trips to Mecca, Syria, and on to Afghanistan and Pakistan.[4]

Everything came together in the summer of 1991 in Peshawar, Pakistan, the capital of the Afghan resistance and the destination for tens of thousands of Muslims who joined the holy war. The magnet was a Pushtun warlord, Abdul Rasul Sayyaf, a legendary Afghan mujahideen and founder of the Afghan Islamic movement—the man Janjalani would name his group after, Abu Sayyaf.

Sayyaf is a big man: about six feet three, probably about two hundred and fifty pounds. He has fair skin and a thick beard. He usually wears a white skullcap or a large turban and the traditional Afghan tunic with loose pants. Schooled in Cairo, fluent in Arabic, Sayyaf took money from the Saudi and American governments and put together an army, a newspaper, a political party, a refugee camp, and a school called Dawa'a al-Jihad (which means "convert and struggle"), which became known as a notorious meeting place for terrorists. In many ways, Sayyaf gave bin

Laden the prototype for the organization of al-Qaeda. It was in his base in Afghanistan that bin Laden trained and set up his own brigade of Arab fighters, marking his transition from a financier to terrorist.

In 1991, Pakistani and Filipino investigators claim bin Laden personally met Janjalani and introduced him to Ramzi Yousef, who also attended Sayyaf's school.[5] Other key figures were there: Yousef's uncle, KSM, was Sayyaf's secretary, and Wali Khan Amin Shah was working for the charity International Islamic Relief Organization (IIRO), the same group Khalifa would set up in Manila. Khalifa himself was also in Peshawar and, under orders from bin Laden, offered funding and support to Janjalani to develop a group that would aim to create an Islamic state in the southern Philippines.[6]

Janjalani and Yousef became good friends—attending parties, meetings, and teaching camps in Peshawar. When Janjalani returned to the Philippines in the summer of 1991, Yousef went with him—allegedly introducing himself to members of the group later called the Abu Sayyaf as bin Laden's representative.[7]

By 1994, all these men were in the Philippines and Abu Sayyaf had long been up and running, part of the reason terrorist incidents had increased dramatically, as chronicled in Boogie Mendoza's intelligence report. Its close links to al-Qaeda were part of the reason that the Abu Sayyaf was added to the U.S. list of foreign terrorist organizations and that, after the strikes in Afghanistan, the United States opened a second front against them, sending in more than 1,200 American troops and special forces in February 2002. At the height of its appeal in 2001, Abu Sayyaf had about 4,000 members, but today that is down to fewer than 1,000,[8] most based in Jolo, Sulu, where U.S. troops are scheduled to arrive for the next round of training exercises with their Filipino counterparts.

Although al-Qaeda funded and trained many of Abu Sayyaf's fighters and (as noted earlier) directed some of its bombings, the group has a life of its own that is very different from the disciplined, large-scale planning of top al-Qaeda men. In its first four years until 1995, police say the Abu Sayyaf carried out more than one hundred terrorist crimes, many of which targeted foreigners. Kidnapping for ransom became a reliable cottage industry for them. In 1993, Abu Sayyaf kidnapped sixty-one-year-old American Charles Walton, a Christian missionary for the Summer Institute of Linguistics, which aims to translate the Bible into local dialects. Unlike the Burnhams, he was freed after twenty-three days. The following year, the group kidnapped three Spanish nuns and, later, a Spanish priest. They also engaged in vicious violence. In April 1995, the Abu Sayyaf carried out the attack on the predominantly Christian town of Ipil in Mindanao, partly in retaliation for the arrest of Yousef and his cell members, razing the town center and killing fifty-three civilians and soldiers.

The year 1998 was pivotal: the military and police caught up with Abu Sayyaf's founder and leader, Abdurajak Janjalani. He died during a shootout in Lamitan, Basilan, taking with him much of the ideological glue of fundamentalism, which gave a political and moral cause to his group. Philippine authorities say that's when the Abu Sayyaf splintered into as many as five distinct subgroups that, over the next few years, would become little better than gangsters known for their viciousness and brutal beheadings. The main group based in Basilan was led by Janjalani's younger brother, Khadaffy, who was trained in Libya. The other farther south in Jolo, Sulu was headed by Ghalib Andang, also known as Commander Robot.

Officials in Manila dismissed Abu Sayyaf as a criminal gang, but the military insists that its links with al-Qaeda continued. According to confidential reports leaked to the intelligence community, as many as twenty members of Abu Sayyaf were reportedly in the graduating class of a Mazar-e-Sharif camp in 2001—that is, trained by al-Qaeda.[9] Philippine intelligence documents a year earlier asserted "foreign Muslims" were training the group and that Osama bin Laden had ordered more aid, including possibly $3 million, to be delivered to them.[10] In March 2000, four Arabs visited Khadaffy Janjalani's stronghold in Basilan. An intelligence source reported one of the men was addressed as Ibnu bin Laden. While his identity remains unclear, the group allegedly gave the Abu Sayyaf a closed-circuit television security system for their camp.[11]

On March 20, just days after the Arabs left, the Basilan group, led by Abdurajak's younger brother, Khaddafy Janjalani, attacked two elementary schools in Basilan and kidnapped more than fifty people—all Filipinos, mostly teachers and students, one as young as three years old. Shortly after, the Abu Sayyaf made one of its first political demands: in exchange for the hostages, it asked the United States to release three terrorists held in U.S. prisons, including Egyptian Sheikh Omar Abdul

Rahman, the blind cleric, and their former trainer, Ramzi Yousef. The demand was ignored by both the Philippines and the United States.

Most of those Filipinos would be held hostage for nearly a year, and during that time, the Abu Sayyaf committed many atrocities, murdering some, beheading others. There were many stories of courage and endurance, like that of a three-year-old named Crisalyn (her last name is withheld for privacy)[12] and her brothers. Her ten-year-old brother Darryl heard the attackers coming and was able to hide safely from the armed men, but when he saw them leading away his sister, Crisalyn, and their six-year-old brother, Crisanto, he came out of hiding. "I ran after them," said Darryl. "I couldn't let them go without me."[13]

The Abu Sayyaf made their hostages walk eight hours to their mountain camp. For most of that time, Christian Crisalyn was carried by one of her Muslim teachers. Crisalyn celebrated her fourth birthday in that camp before the kidnappers offered to release her because, finally, they said she was "too young." Crisalyn cried and refused to go without her brothers. Darryl told her to be quiet and leave as soon as she could, but surprisingly, a day later, their kidnappers agreed to release the whole family. Decisions of life and death were made on a whim.

Families sent envoys to negotiate ransom and to carry mail, food, and clothes to their loved ones. It spawned and maintained a whole industry of shady middlemen and messengers, most of whom were used repeatedly over the next two years to bring visitors to their camps. Abu Sayyaf's central base is on Basilan's Mohadji mountain. Called Camp Abdurajak,[14] it measures about 20 by 40 miles and is so well hidden that Red Cross workers who have been to the base camp say it is virtually impenetrable. It is one of nine Abu Sayyaf camps in the jungle, and the only way to get there is via a forty-five-minute boat ride from Zamboanga City on the main island of Mindanao. It would eventually be overrun by troops, but in those early days, the Abu Sayyaf was confident of its position, and some of their demands became preposterous. At one point, the group's flashy spokesman, Abu Sabaya, notorious for his sunglasses and bandanna, demanded that a popular Filipino actor who recently converted to Islam, Robin Padilla, come to their camp to negotiate. He got his wish, and Padilla was held for a short while, raising fears that he and his group might themselves be kept for ransom. Negotiating ransom was key. As Gracia Burnham would later say, despite all the talk of religion, their motivation was simple: "The bottom line was money."[15]

The government ordered the military to track down the kidnappers, but as families found out, a military rescue was as dangerous for the hostages as it was for Abu Sayyaf members. Some hostages were used as human shields; others were killed by the Abu Sayyaf as they were fleeing; still others, like Martin and Ediborah, were shot fatally by the military's own bullets. One early military attempt tried to rescue the students and teachers kidnapped on March 20, 2000, by Janjalani's group. When teacher Ruben Democrito was kidnapped, his wife, Leoncia, was seven months pregnant. After more than a month, she and her family began to despair. They were too poor to pay ransom so they agreed a military rescue was their only chance. Her tears stained a letter from Ruben she was holding tightly. In one part, he wrote, "God will make a way for us, for our safe release." Ruben died in the rescue attempt.

In the southern Philippines, rampant poverty, the lack of government services, and the actions of the military—caused by arrogance or incompetence—pushed more civilians to support the Abu Sayyaf. Most Filipinos who live in the Abu Sayyaf strongholds of Basilan and Jolo are too poor to leave. In these remote areas, the rule of law is the rule of the gun, and the government is complicit at local and federal levels. There have been instances of collusion among the Abu Sayyaf, the Philippine military, and local governments. For people who live there, it's difficult to know to whom to turn for help. I found many similarities to situations I lived through in Indonesia in areas suffering from a breakdown of law and order. These are relatively closely knit communities: people know each other and know who are the members and supporters of the Abu Sayyaf. When the children of Abdul Midjal, a staunch Muslim, were kidnapped from their elementary school, he formed a Muslim vigilante group. Unwilling to wait for the government and too poor to pay ransom, Midjal and his men kidnapped the relatives of his children's kidnappers.

Lean and craggy, Midjal turned the Abu Sayyaf's ideology on itself, claiming he and his men were the true Muslim fighters. "We are the ones fighting a jihad now, not the Abu Sayyaf," said Midjal. "They just want to get money to let their organization grow."[16] Midjal's move was supported—and even lauded—by most people in Basilan, including

local government officials, the Catholic hierarchy, and security forces—
"insurance," they called it. Conventional wisdom held that the Abu
Sayyaf would think twice before killing their hostages because now
they had something to lose.

On April 23, 2000, a little more than a month after Janjalani's
group carried out the elementary school kidnappings, the Abu Sayyaf
group based in Jolo, led by Commander Robot, went on a kidnapping
spree of its own that caught the attention of the international press, as
one Filipino bitterly put it, "because they kidnapped white guys." Using
speedboats, the Abu Sayyaf crossed the border into Malaysia and
attacked a diving resort on the island of Sipadan. Shortly before Easter
Sunday dinner, heavily armed men carrying AK-47s and rocket launch-
ers burst into the resort and ordered guests and employees to swim to
two boats anchored nearby. They kidnapped twenty-one people from
seven countries, including Malaysians, French, Germans, Finns, and
South Africans—in all, ten Westerners, nine Malaysians, and two Filipinos. Many were in bathing suits—completely unprepared for the
harsh jungle conditions they would soon be living under. It would take
five months of bargaining, but in the end all but one of the twenty-one
hostages, a Filipino who many believed joined the Abu Sayyaf, would
later be released unharmed—for ransom.[17] In May, even as the Abu
Sayyaf talked to its hostages about its fight for a separate Islamic state,
it demanded $1 million for each Westerner. The fact that that ransom
was paid set a deadly precedent for Martin Burnham and Ediborah Yap.

Throughout the resort hostage ordeal, the Philippine government
maintained that it paid no ransom. That may be technically true, but in
fact it looked the other way while ransom was paid, and it even helped
money change hands. Under pressure from European countries, the
government allowed Libya, which wanted to refurbish its international
image, to help negotiate with the Abu Sayyaf and put together a fund
of up to $25 million, allegedly for "development projects," paid by
Western governments. Two years later, Philippines chief negotiator
Roberto Aventajado told me, "The Philippine government did not pay
any ransom, but of course, there are other governments who consider
life more valuable than money, and to my understanding, the other
European governments actually reimbursed Libya for their expenses—
the Germans, the French, and, I think, even the Finnish."[18]

Aventajado, a cabinet member and trusted friend of Philippine

president Joseph Estrada, said he knew members of the elite Presidential Security Group, or PSG, actually "helped facilitate the delivery." His
Libyan counterpart was a former envoy to the Philippines, Rajab
Azzarouq. It wasn't the first time Azzarouq had dealt with the Abu
Sayyaf. When he was the Libyan ambassador in 1993, he helped negotiate the release of American hostage Charles Walton, but much had
changed between 1993 and 2000. With the death of their ideological
leader, the Abu Sayyaf's greed had grown.

With the implicit support of many Filipinos, the Abu Sayyaf began
making money from everyone—starting with journalists. I saw the
learning curve and the greed of the Abu Sayyaf grow. I wasn't the only
one who watched with horror. Norwegian journalist Pekka Mykannen,
who writes for the Finnish newspaper *Helsingin Sanomat*, studied the
workings of the press under crisis situations for his master's degree. We
often compared notes in the outdoor restaurant on the rooftop of the
hotel journalists used in Zamboanga, the base of the Philippine military's southern command and the jumping-off point for journalists covering the hostage crisis in Basilan. Pekka was brave enough to take our
soul searching public. He agreed to give me an interview on camera so I
could do the story for CNN. "Media is very much responsible for letting
Abu Sayyaf understand what kind of money there is around in Western
countries," Pekka said on the air. "This is a very peculiar case in the history of news making, and journalists have a very strange involvement in
this crisis."[19] What journalists have done—paying significant sums for
access to the terrorists—"has hindered the process of the release of the
hostages, and it has hindered the process of negotiations." Filipino journalists knew what was happening, but they blamed the foreigners.
"Those who do this are foreign journalists," said Ed Lingao, a Filipino
television reporter. "First of all, local journalists don't have that kind of
a budget. Secondly, a lot of local journalists already have contacts
with the Abu Sayyaf. Some have been covering these issues for ten
years, fifteen years—even before the Abu Sayyaf were the Abu Sayyaf."

It started with the first videotape of the hostages shot by a Filipino
journalist trusted by the Abu Sayyaf, Arlyn de la Cruz. That tape
allegedly sold for thousands of dollars to a Western media organization.
"Abu Sayyaf learned that a huge sum of money was paid for this tape,
and it actually took eighteen hours for the Western media to wheel and
deal for this tape before they released it," said Pekka. When the Abu

Sayyaf heard that, they demanded a cut—although it's unclear whether they ever got any of that money. "She's established a relationship with the Abu Sayyaf that has raised quite a few eyebrows, not only within the national leadership but also within the media industry itself," Ed Lingao told me. "When that happens, maybe there's something really wrong."[20]

Then the journalist "tours" of the Abu Sayyaf camps began. With the first group of Filipino journalists to be asked, it started innocently enough, partly because it's understood that Filipino journalists are also poor. One local journalist told the Abu Sayyaf, "We can't afford that, but you should ask the foreigners. They have money." The Filipinos weren't asked to pay blatantly, but when the Abu Sayyaf saw a watch they liked or an instant camera they wanted, they asked for it. When the journalist volunteered it, the Abu Sayyaf who took it would thank him for his "contribution to the cause." One journalist was even politely forced to leave his shoes. At first, none of the journalists publicly admitted this was happening. Instead, they would bring out messages from the kidnappers: "they reject the government negotiator"; "they want the ambassadors from Manila to become negotiators"; and, at one point, "they want Maria Ressa from CNN."

When this message was relayed to me, I was told they would give CNN an exclusive. Having watched them since the early 1990s, I knew it was deceptive. I have visited dozens of rebel camps in several countries, but other "rebellions" weren't simply shakedowns. With the Abu Sayyaf, everyone was tainted. For example, I knew the governor of Basilan was one of the founders of Abu Sayyaf. The "guides" who brought journalists to the rebels charged a fee and kicked some back to the group. If I took the invitation, I would be handing the Abu Sayyaf a valuable commodity: a CNN reporter. I declined and continued reporting from Zamboanga, making occasional trips to Basilan but never to the camps.

Other foreign journalists believed differently, partly because the demand for stories, particularly from the hostages' European nations, was so high. The Abu Sayyaf was blatant: they charged for access to the camps, interviews with Abu Sayyaf leaders, interviews with the hostages. At one point, there was even a cardboard sign explicitly stating the price of each move or interview any journalist could want. One month after the hostages were kidnapped, I heard journalists were paying from $500 to $1,000 for guides and transportation—when it used to cost less than $50. One diplomat associated with the talks said one journalist paid nearly $10,000. "That was giving the Abu Sayyaf money to keep running the show. I think media was basically arming them and making them stronger," said Pekka. "I know we were after very important information about the condition of the hostages. We wanted to show the public and the decision makers how they are doing there, and what kind of group we are dealing with, but on the other hand, media allowed Abu Sayyaf to make it an industry. To have access to this camp—all these various camps—journalists, eager to get their own story on the hostages, were willing to pay."[21]

On June 3, the Abu Sayyaf took the next logical step: kidnapping ten Western journalists, most Germans. They were released ten hours later for a ransom of $25,000, but one German journalist didn't learn his lesson: he returned again to the camp and was actually kidnapped and ransomed a second time. On July 9, three French journalists were kidnapped, additions to the Western hostages with whom the Abu Sayyaf could now bargain: a female reporter and her two crewmen. Slowly, in groups, the Abu Sayyaf began releasing their hostages. By July 17, the military estimated the kidnappers had received $5.5 million, money they used to buy more weapons and ammunition. "The local police commander, Candido Casimiro, said that the price of weapons on Jolo island, where there is plenty available, has gone up 30 percent because of the money available from the Abu Sayyaf," said Pekka. They also enticed new recruits with easy cash: paying an exorbitant 50,000 pesos, or about $1,100, to each of some 2,500 followers.[22] Most were also given new weapons.

By the time the last Western hostages from the Sipadan resort were released on September 9, everyone involved allegedly took a cut: from the middlemen, to security forces and local officials, and even high-ranking government officials, including, allegedly, the Philippine president.[23] All accused dismissed the charges, but allegations surfaced repeatedly against Roberto Aventajado, the chief hostage negotiator, who brushed them aside. He says he believes there's a reason that these charges don't die and that he plans to write a book about his findings.

"Twenty to twenty-five million dollars were actually made available, but to my understanding, only $10 million was used," Aventajado explained. "So there is about $10 to $15 million that has to be accounted for. This is the reason why some people are trying to use me as the scapegoat to account maybe for the balance. For all you know, maybe this balance went to an organization like al-Qaeda. Maybe the U.S. should look into this and trace the paper trail." Aventajado's charge is not far-fetched. A recent FBI report released to the Philippines stated that Osama bin Laden "had been using Muslim terrorists in the Philippines as a source of funds to finance his worldwide terrorist operations."[24] The Sipadan hostage situation was the biggest windfall ever for the Abu Sayyaf, and they received the money by September 2000, eight months after al-Qaeda brought its top operatives to Malaysia to plan the 9/11 and USS *Cole* attacks, right at the time when hundreds of militants across Southeast Asia were moving from training camps to the battlefields of Ambon and plotting terror attacks in the Philippines and Singapore against United States and Western interests.

Locally, millions of dollars in the impoverished economies of Basilan and Jolo turned the Abu Sayyaf into Robin Hoods. In effect, for five months, the Abu Sayyaf succeeded in capturing world attention by hostaging not just the people but their governments. It was the peak of Abu Sayyaf's power: during the five-month Sipadan hostage drama, it dictated terms to the Philippine government, and after the ransom was paid, the Abu Sayyaf contributed more to the local economy than any government program. After such a successful strategy, it would be only a matter of time before the Abu Sayyaf kidnapped again—a lesson they learned: foreigners bring more ransom, and the top prize went for Americans. On the day the last of the Sipadan foreigners were freed, the Janjalani faction, including Abu Sabaya, announced it kidnapped an American and soon demanded a $10 million ransom. However, the American, Jeffrey Schilling, was a black Muslim who allegedly walked into the Abu Sayyaf camps. The Philippine and U.S. governments at first didn't seem sure it was actually a hostage situation, particularly given Schilling's connections to the widow of a former Abu Sayyaf leader. The U.S. government, unlike its European counterparts, refused to negotiate for ransom, and Abu Sabaya was sorely disappointed when little happened for months, and Schilling escaped.

So they tried again. On May 27, 2001, a little more than a year after they had kidnapped the tourists from Sipadan, Khadaffy Janjalani's group used one of the high-speed boats bought by the Sipadan ransom money to get to the southern Philippine island of Palawan, known for its pristine beaches and virgin rain forests. In the middle of the night, armed men stormed the rooms by the ocean of the Dos Palmas resort, pulling out twenty people, including three Americans. While on the boat on the way to their stronghold in Basilan, the Abu Sayyaf asked their hostages to name their ransom price, and the next day, they used a satellite phone to call their relatives and friends for the money. Construction magnate Reghis Romero immediately called a government contact, who spoke with Abu Sabaya. "I know this guy, and he's a good guy. Let him out, since you owe me a favor, remember?" the official said, without explaining the favor. They agreed on a figure, and Abu Sabaya promised Romero's release.[25]

By June 1, the group had landed on the island of Basilan and kidnapped still more hostages from the Golden Harvest plantation. Pursued by the Philippine military, the Abu Sayyaf and their hostages fled to a hospital and church compound in the town of Lamitan, where a day-long siege ended in a fiasco that spotlighted either the incompetence of the Philippine military or collusion and corruption on a massive scale. Until 5:30 P.M. of June 2, the kidnappers and their hostages were surrounded by troops in the walled compound, which had only two points of entry and exit: an alley that led to a small back door and the front gate. During the intense fighting, up to twelve soldiers and civilians were killed; at least one of the Abu Sayyaf members was wounded. Despite the fact that there were at least 1,000 soldiers on Basilan island that day, when the commanding officer called for backup, his superiors, including armed forces chief of staff General Diomedio Villanueva, ignored his request, and no backup arrived. Worse, the soldiers guarding the back door were called off their posts, and shortly before dusk, the kidnappers and their hostages walked out of the compound and disappeared into the jungle.

Several members of a civilian militia group known as the Civilian Volunteer Organization were the only "forces" at the back door. The hostages now included four hospital staff members the Abu Sayyaf thought they might need, including nurse Ediborah Yap. "As we were being taken hostage by the Abu Sayyaf, we heard the words, 'It's OK—it's OK at the back,'" said nurse Sheila Tabunag, who was released five and a half months later.[26] There were no soldiers or police officers at the back. One member of the CVO, Eligio Cordero, explained, "The military told the CVOs and the PNP [police officers] to stay away from the area, but we disobeyed their orders."[27] Some of the militia fired on the group and hit at least one of the Abu Sayyaf members, as well as American hostages Martin Burnham and Guillermo Sobero. Both received minor wounds. "We overheard them saying to each other: 'they said it was clear. Why are they firing!?' "[28] said Eligio's brother, Paterno. The two brothers, along with several Lamitan residents, later testified in front of the Philippine Senate. On August 24, a military fact-finding board nonetheless found "no collusion."

Many residents on Basilan island say they believe the Abu Sayyaf had help from local officials and military officers. Soon after the escape, the gang, angry because they received a far smaller amount of the ransom money than they were promised, went on a killing spree, which began with the beheading of American Guillermo Sobero and continued with revenge attacks over the next two months. More than a dozen Filipinos were beheaded in attacks on two villages—a warning to the military.

The village of Balobo bears the scars. On the evening of August 2, 2001, members of the Abu Sayyaf barged into several homes in Balobo and kidnapped about thirty residents. Glenda Esteban, her husband, Joselito, their eleven-year-old son, Joey, and seven-year-old daughter, Gladys, were captured and forced to march toward the river and on to the jungle. Others were forced to join them: Glenda's two brothers, Alvin and Alex Ramirez, and her uncle, Tereso Ramirez, their neighbor Efren Natalaray and his twenty-six-year-old son, Elmer. By the river, the Abu Sayyaf picked certain people and told them they were "released," but when they pulled away from the group, the Abu Sayyaf had other plans for them—which Glenda later discovered. "What we thought was that if they said 'released,' then they're free," Glenda said. That wasn't the case.

On the first night, Glenda was raped by two members of the Abu Sayyaf, in exchange, she was told, for the life of her son, Joey. "They said that was my payment for my son," said Glenda. "When I told the police, they said it was like I paid ransom." Glenda and Joey were released on August 3, but when they got home, they found more tragic news. "My mother told me, your brother is over there. He's dead. They cut off his head." Glenda began to sob. "So I asked where's my other brother? My mother said, 'No one has seen him.' The next day, they found his body—without a head."

Her neighbors, Efren and Elmer Natalaray, were also kidnapped. "They ordered us to march single file," said Efren. "But when darkness came, I managed to escape. I ran, but my son was left behind." As the Abu Sayyaf and their hostages made their way from the river toward the jungle, the kidnappers picked out ten men, pulled them away from the group, and brought them to the side of the river. Some were forced to wade in. "When they reached the river, they began beheading them," said Efren. "Ten of them in one night. Every five meters, they would behead another one. My son died that night."

Efren's wife, Virginia, was listening to her husband, crying quietly, holding her grandson, four-year-old Jamer. She sobbed as she described what the Abu Sayyaf did to her son. "They pulled off his teeth, cut off his ears," she sobbed. "We were luckier because we were able to find his head because they threw the remains and body parts into the river. There was one whose head was never found, and we had to bury him without his head."

That man was Glenda's forty-four-year-old uncle, Tereso Ramirez. His wife and child were so traumatized they left their home four days after he was murdered and fled to Zamboanga City. "I feel sad, scared, angry," said Glenda. "I keep reliving what happened to us." Still, two family members were spared. Before she was released, she told the Abu Sayyaf her son was sick and needed his father, and her husband, Joselito, along with their daughter, were released a few days later.

Five months after the tragedy, the shock and loss of this village remain palpable. Residents try to get on with their lives, but they are living with unspeakable grief. Every house down the center of the village had been attacked. It was a brutal response to a shakedown that did not pay off as handsomely as expected. Not even the mafia is this nakedly rapacious.

The Abu Sayyaf's indescribable brutality has gouged out a deep well of anger, perpetuating a cycle of violence. Elmer's son, Jamer, was playing at the feet of his grandparents, both of whom tried to stop crying while I interviewed them. "My grandson said he will avenge his father's death when he grows up," said Efren. "What they did to his father, that's what he'll do to them." Jamer says he wants to be a soldier. The irony is that if the charges are true in Lamitan, he will be joining an institution that has been subverted and corrupted and whose actions led to the beheading of his father.

Lamitan would be investigated not just by the military but by the Philippine Senate and its House of Representatives. More than a year after the Lamitan escape, on October 24, 2002, the House of Representatives released its findings. Like the military fact-finding board, it cited serious operational lapses of the armed forces, but the Senate hearings went one step further: it found "strong circumstantial evidence" to support the charges of collusion and recommended court-martial for some of the military officers involved. Yet more than two years after the notorious escape from Lamitan, no member of the military or the local government has been officially charged in court.

Lamitan was the only time in three years that the military had Abu Sayyaf's top leadership, including Khadaffy Janjalani and their hostages, completely surrounded. If the military had maintained the siege, much future heartbreak could have been averted.

All this thuggery might seem far removed from al-Qaeda and a truly religiously inspired terror campaign against America. Yet the connections between Abu Sayyaf and al-Qaeda meant that it was only a matter of time before the United States started paying attention. And, in fact, not all members of the Abu Sayyaf were uninterested in terror for terror's sake.

The hostages heard about the 9/11 attacks from a radio in the jungles of Basilan. It was difficult for them to comprehend what it meant, although they knew it would have repercussions on their situation. "In our minds," said Gracia Burnham, "that was bad for us because the world was going to be against terrorism and they wouldn't want to deal with these men."[29] By November 2001, the Abu Sayyaf's hostages were down to three people: Martin, Gracia, and Ediborah Yap. A single mother, Ediborah was the sole breadwinner for her mother and four children. Before being taken by the Abu Sayyaf, she took care of her family during the day and worked the night shift at Lamitan's hospital. After she was kidnapped, her children dropped out of school. About the same age as Gracia, the two women became friends. Ediborah would be forced to "marry" an Abu Sayyaf member, a euphemism used by the hostages so they could learn to live with rape.

Abu Sayyaf's search for money continued. Sometime after Thanksgiving, Abu Sabaya invited Filipino reporter Arlyn de la Cruz back to the camp to see Martin and Gracia. After the interview, Gracia said that Abu Sabaya suggested, "Arlyn, you can go out and sell this footage to CNN or some network for at least a million dollars—maybe two million. Just send it back to us directly for their ransom, and then we can let them go. You'll get to be famous, we'll get paid—everybody will be happy."[30] In early December, CNN was offered the videotape, but I lauded our management's decision not to buy it. I was glad we did not contribute to the Abu Sayyaf in any way. That interview, according to Gracia, was sold to CBS for $50,000.[31] That matched what I had been hearing in the Philippines.

The true effect of 9/11 was the opposite of Gracia's fears. By February, American troops began arriving in Zamboanga, and over the following weeks, they moved into Basilan. The six-month "training exercise" would last more than six months and bring in more than 1,200 American troops, including 660 U.S. special forces. They were in the Philippines "to train, advise and assist" because it was against the Philippine Constitution for them to engage in actual combat. Despite the semantics, U.S. soldiers were going into the jungles along with Filipino troops. They were using live bullets, aiming at live targets. If the Americans were fired upon, they could fire back. In the midst of a jungle with no other eyewitnesses, does anyone really know who fired first if a bullet goes off? The Americans believed themselves to be getting serious about terrorism in the Philippines. The semantics were important in Manila, where politicians and leftist groups were playing on themes of nationalism to stir protestors against the presence of U.S. troops. Meanwhile, in the southern Philippines, they were welcome. "I want them to come," said Glenda Esteban. "The Philippine military couldn't do it. The Abu Sayyaf always escaped. Maybe they worked together. It's better to have the Americans."

American forces are better trained and better equipped. Yet Filipino forces know the terrain better, and they can withstand local jungle conditions and the exhausting heat better. Despite all allegations against the Philippine military, many of the Filipino soldiers I have met display courage, persistence, and idealism. They work for little pay with patchy support in terms of personnel, and they are saddled with often antiquated equipment. In some instances, units in combat fight without communication. To be sure, there are corrupt elements of the military who need to be weeded out. Captain Harold Cabunoc of the Philippine Scout Rangers is young, idealistic, and realistic. "It's a great honor to serve the Filipino people as a soldier," he said. "When I was young, soldiers were considered heroes. So I also want to become a hero"—and he chuckled—"a living hero, not a dead hero." Perhaps together, these combined forces could rid the southern Philippines of the Abu Sayyaf. By adding a social and economic component to the U.S. presence–a "hearts and minds" campaign—the two military forces have largely succeeded in changing the mood of fear on Basilan and pushing the Abu Sayyaf out—most of them fleeing to nearby Jolo, the proposed site of the next joint exercises.

The U.S. forces also brought a unit whose sole responsibility was the rescue and evacuation of the hostages. That unit would be deployed only to pick up Gracia Burnham on June 7, 2002, the day Filipino troops carried out the rescue attempt code-named Oplan Daybreak. Beginning on May 27, Filipino soldiers had help from sophisticated U.S. surveillance equipment to track the group. There was a short firefight on May 29; then on June 4, soldiers found bloodstained clothes. On Friday morning, a company of Scout Rangers discovered footmarks on a mountain trail. A short while later, they found what was left of the group's meal. "We decided to skip lunch to follow the trail," said Sergeant Rodney Magbanua. "We could sense they were close by. We wanted to end their terror."[32] It rained hard that afternoon. By 1:30, the soldiers found the group. "We fired first," said Sergeant Magbanua. All three hostages were hit. Martin Burnham and Ediborah Yap would die on that mountain.

There were no recriminations, neither personal nor diplomatic. The U.S. government stood behind its allies. "It's clear to us that Mr. Burnham was killed by the Abu Sayyaf, period," said U.S. ambassador Francis Ricciardone just moments after Gracia boarded her plane to the United States. "There's no question in our minds who's responsible. What bullet might have hit him, I don't know. It hardly matters in terms of criminal culpability. . . . There are heroes and there are criminals, and the heroes are the hostages . . . and the Armed Forces, particularly the Scout Rangers." Gracia would say much the same thing in succeeding days and months, though in her book she voices a small regret. "I've learned just how badly the American military wanted to launch a special operation for us! I've been told how they sat around conference tables in Zamboanga City just itching for the opportunity. They would, of course, have done the job far differently. They would have moved into action at, say, two in the morning instead of two in the afternoon, wearing night vision goggles and all the rest to snatch us to safety."[33]

She pointed to another hostage situation, which happened a few months after her return: when rebels took over a school for missionary children in the Ivory Coast in West Africa. Authorities gave U.S. special forces permission to launch a rescue and in a few hours, "the students and faculty were roaring down the highway toward safety, waving the Stars and Stripes out of bus windows. But nothing like that happened in our case," Gracia wrote. "The local authority said no, and the Pentagon felt it could not trample upon an ally's national sovereignty."[34]

Did U.S. officials make their case strongly enough? Did Filipinos listen? I wager that if you tell any Filipino on the street today that letting U.S. troops handle the rescue mission could have saved the lives of Martin Burnham and Ediborah Yap, he or she would agree that they should have been allowed to try. Filipinos have generous hearts, and the hostages' ordeal has made an impact on the national psyche. What has become clear is that the further international politics gets from the people affected on the ground, the less effective it has been in dealing with the problem. The diplomacy has been cloaked in so much double-speak that it has become difficult to address the root problems in a linear manner. It starts with the internal rivalries among the individuals involved, aggravated by the politics of the organizations they represent, the institutions they belong to, and the leaders they report to. Self-interest at every level has obscured and twisted every step of the global war on terror, and these are the cracks al-Qaeda continues to exploit.

CHAPTER 7

THE NEW CALIPHATE

If Abu Sayyaf has been corrupted into a shakedown operation, albeit one with links to al-Qaeda and ambitions to carry out terrorist acts for reasons other than money, another Filipino group has emerged as a much closer associate of al-Qaeda: the MILF. Although the group maintains it has no links to terrorist organizations, the evidence from the intelligence community and testimonies of JI operatives now in custody show institutional links bound together by a common ideology. Much of what follows, culled from intelligence documents and interrogation reports of al-Qaeda and JI operatives from more than half a dozen countries, has never previously been published.

The fact is that under the international radar screen, Hashim Salamat, the chairman of the MILF, has even succeeded where groups like the Taliban and al-Qaeda have failed. He created a nation within a nation: a true Islamic community, governed by a Muslim council, protected by a Muslim army, and living and dying according to Islamic sharia law. The MILF hasn't fully realized its dream of an independent Islamic state, but it controlled a substantial chunk of Mindanao. At its peak, the MILF ran a sprawling base camp covering 10,000 hectares of land, with full jurisdiction over at least seven towns, spanning parts of two provinces of Maguindanao and Lanao del Sur. This was Camp Abubakar. For Hashim Salamat, Jemaah Islamiyah's dream of carving out one giant Islamic state from parts of Southeast Asia and Australia is not farfetched.

Born on July 7, 1942, in Pagalungan, Maguindanao, to a deeply religious family, Hashim Salamat read and memorized verses of the Koran by the time he was six years old. A decade later, he left for Mecca and the hajj. In 1959, he went to Egypt and enrolled at Al-Azhar University in Cairo. That was where he turned from a scholar to a revolutionary: exposed to a litany of Muslim grievances around the world, he developed contacts throughout the world of militant Islam. There he read and was influenced by some of the same radical Islamic thinkers as Osama bin Laden: Syed Qutb of Egypt's Muslim Brotherhood, and Syed Abul Ala Mau'dudi of Pakistan's Jamaat I Islami party. Their work helped convince him to mount an Islamic revolution in his homeland, where the "Bangsamoros"—what he called Filipino Muslims—continue to be oppressed. "Perhaps the Bangsamoro struggle for freedom and self-determination is the longest and bloodiest in the entire history of mankind," said Salamat. "It started in 1521 when Spain invaded the Bangsamoro homeland 29 years after the fall of Andalosia. The Bangsamoro people fought against the Spanish invaders for 377 years and against American intruders for about 40 years and have been fighting Filipino barbarous colonial rule during the past 52 years."[1]

Salamat started by putting together a core group of Filipino Muslim students in Egypt as secretary general of the Organization of Asian Students. The way he charted is familiar, and his rhetoric would later be mirrored by other Islamic clerics in Southeast Asia, including Abu Bakar Ba'asyir. In fact, there is an uncanny similarity in the statements of Salamat, Ba'asyir, and bin Laden: Muslims must base their social and political lives on the Koran; infidels are doing all they can to stop them; and jihad is the way to break through. "The MILF is the realization of the ideas, efforts and sacrifices of Bangsamoro students in the Middle East who banded together and clandestinely organized themselves in 1962," Salamat said, modestly. "Those students were kindled and unified by the common feelings concerning the usurpation of their legitimate and inalienable rights to freedom and self-determination, and that the usurpation of Moro land was a plot against Islam and the Muslim people in the area. Furthermore, it was a wanton design to destroy their identity and to liquidate them. Those students urged their counterparts in the Bangsamoro homeland and the Bangsamoro people in general to return to the fold of Islam and fight against the aggressors. They exhorted them to follow the path of Allah and launch Jihad in the way of Allah." It was he who brought those students together.

When he returned to the Philippines, Salamat founded the Moro National Liberation Front, the MNLF, with Nur Misuari soon after martial law was declared in 1972, but in 1978 Salamat split from the MNLF. Although both were fighting for a separate Islamic state, they differed on just how Islamic it should be. The MNLF was more secular; Salamat's splinter group (later the MILF) wanted a state fully governed by the Koran and Islamic sharia law. "The most distinct difference," said Salamat, "is that the MNLF recognized the Philippine Constitution and works under the Philippine government while the MILF does not recognize the Constitution of the Philippines and fights the government."

In 1980, one year after the Soviet Union decided to invade Afghanistan, Salamat sent about one thousand Filipino-Muslims to Afghanistan to train and fight against the Soviets. The training was, according to one MILF member, part of an agreement forged at the Organization of Islamic Conference (OIC) meetings held in Lahore, Pakistan, in 1979.[2]

Osama bin Laden's rhetoric appealed to Filipinos, enough so that al-Qaeda was able to establish a special Moro subbrigade in Afghanistan in the coming years.[3] He talked about fighting injustice; Filipino Muslims felt they had been robbed of their ancestral lands, their livelihood taken away from them. He talked about Muslim nations rising together: for Filipino Muslims, who had long been marginalized, a minority in a predominantly Catholic nation, they had found an ally. He intertwined his rhetoric with venomous words against the United States, again another message that appealed to Filipinos. After all, the Philippines is America's only former colony, and the Philippine-American War in 1899, while often forgotten in U.S. history books, killed at least 250,000 people.

Bin Laden's words resonated: "We want our land to be freed of the enemies. We want our land to be freed of the Americans. God equipped these living creatures with an instinctive zeal, and they refuse to be intruded upon. For instance, if an armed military man walks into a chicken's home wanting to attack it, the chicken will fight back even if it's only a chicken. We are demanding a right given to all living creatures, not to mention the fact that it is a right for all human beings and a right for Muslims in particular."[4] Bin Laden was setting the stage for a battle between a Muslim David and an American Goliath—extending jihad beyond the boundaries of Afghanistan.

The first group of Filipinos left the Philippines in January 1980; it was made up of about 600 fighters, 200 of them converts to Islam.

Some members of the group pretended to be joining the annual pilgrimage to Mecca while others received fake documents that claimed they were overseas contract workers—Filipinos who live and work outside the Philippines for set employment contracts vetted by the Philippine government. Their destination: Lahore, Pakistan.

There, they met Hashim Salamat and stayed in apartments he arranged for them. After several days, most were transferred to a military camp in Afghanistan. Some of the group stayed in Pakistan and joined madrassas that taught them the concepts of jihad.

Of the 600 or so first Filipino trainees, only about 360 would actually reach a military camp in Afghanistan. There, they would train for a year. According to one of the MILF members, about 180 Filipinos of that first group volunteered to go to the front lines: to join the Afghan guerrillas and fight against the Soviets.[5] After three months, only 70 survived. They would be among the first to return home, bringing back the seeds of radical Islam.

In 1982, the MILF officially split from the MNLF, and this training process was repeated several times. Salamat was by then officially in charge, personally choosing the Filipinos who would go to "undergo training in Afghanistan and leadership seminars in Pakistan." It was a simple selection process: Salamat chose men who had field commander status and had armed followers.

By 1986, Salamat had refined the journey: he first brought his recruits to Manila, where they stayed in a hotel in the Quiapo district (where there's a mosque) for a few days. Papers would be forged giving them visas and passports. From Manila, they flew to Karachi en route to Lahore where Salamat had set up an office. He worked closely with the Jamiatul Faizal University.[6] Some recruits stayed at a mosque inside the university compound and were actually issued student IDs to help them get around.

Typically, the Filipinos stayed in Lahore a few months. There they learned the Wahhabi fundamentalist interpretation of Islam. According to one of the Filipinos, they called it leadership training: focusing on the fundamentals of Islam and psychological warfare.[7] Hashim Salamat was one of three trainers.

After that, they moved to Afghanistan for six months of weapons training. Bin Laden had set up more than a dozen camps. In 1986, the camp the Filipinos were sent to had trainers from different nations, primarily Asian: six Chinese, five Indonesians, Yemenis, Arabians, one Turk, and several other Filipinos.

The MILF grew and stayed on track complete with five- and ten-year plans. By 1995, U.S. estimates placed the MILF's armed members at 35,000 to 45,000 (the government of the Philippines would admit to only 12,500). In 1996, a Bangsamoro Peoples' Consultative Assembly in MILF-held territory gathered about 200,000 people who called for an independent Muslim state.[8] "Like all unjust, oppressive and corrupt governments," Salamat said, "the Manila government will collapse. . . . When this happens, the Bangsamoro Islamic government will automatically arise."[9] It would be the same strategy used by Jemaah Islamiyah throughout the region, but Salamat's call for an Islamic state wasn't taken that seriously in the predominantly Catholic Philippines at the time. In the final stages of the cold war, the fight of the Muslim rebels was thought to be no different from the communist New People's Army—a fight for economic parity rather than a fight for an Islamic way of life.

Astonishingly, the government simultaneously misunderstood and decided to negotiate with them. In the early 1990s, the government allowed the MILF to set up base camps with the idea that it's better to know where they are so the military can keep tabs on the rebels. In Afghanistan, the U.S. government had helped fund mujahideen in the 1980s; in the Philippines, the government licensed a jihad movement on their own turf.

The MILF successfully created a parallel Islamic government in Mindanao.[10] For anyone who wonders what kind of world bin Laden wants to bring about, the answer is here. Intelligence officers say there are at least thirty Regional Islamic Committees scattered throughout Mindanao, Palawan, and the capital, Manila. These committees govern barangays, or villages, and report to the MILF Standing Committee, in effect, the equivalent of a cabinet, which breaks down to nine portfolios, including Finance, Information, Education, Internal Security, and Military Affairs. The Standing Committee reports to the Central Committee or the Jihad Executive Council and MILF chairman, Hashim Salamat.

For civil and criminal acts, the MILF has a separate police force, the Bangsamoro Internal Security Force, which reports to the Committee on Internal Security. This group enforces Islamic laws; those found violating those laws are tried and sentenced in two Islamic Regional

Courts, which report to the Islamic Supreme Court. Punishments range from one hundred lashes for fornication between an unmarried man and woman, to hard labor for those who steal to pay their debts, to capital punishment for murder.[11] In August 1997, two Muslims, thirty-two-year-old Egoy Perez and thirty-year-old Salvador Dimasangca, were charged with car theft, robbery, and the murder of a Christian man. The trial lasted for two months in front of the sharia court. When it ended, the two were sentenced to death. Their public execution by firing squad was witnessed by a thousand people.[12]

Aside from its "religious police," the MILF also has a standing army, the Bangsamoro Islamic Armed Forces (BIAF), which has set up numerous training camps in the MILF's forty-two recognized enclaves in the southern Philippines—what Salamat calls liberated areas. "The liberated areas in the Bangsamoro homeland is [sic] less than one fifth of the previously independent Muslim areas"—those lands claimed by Filipino Muslims—"these areas are mostly in the countryside and highland covered by thick jungles," says Salamat.

Before Philippine troops overran Camp Abubakar in 2000, the MILF operated a military academy that paralleled the Philippine Military Academy, the country's West Point. The two-story building inside the MILF headquarters was simply known as "the academy," and was the hub of military training not only for the MILF but for thousands of Muslim militants across the region and beyond. Those who attended went through a rigorous, disciplined schedule, much like the Afghan training camps after which it was fashioned. In fact, for many years, the academy was headed by Afghan war veterans. When they finished the course, trainees received diplomas certifying their achievements.

Philippine intelligence reports chronicle the MILF's links with international terrorist organizations like Pakistan's Harkat-ul-Unsar, Iranian-sponsored Lebanese Hezbollah, and al-Qaeda. Harkat-ul-Unsar acknowledged sending mujahideen to the Philippines. Declared a terrorist group by the United States, it changed its name to Harkat-ul-Mujahideen then Jaish-e-Mohammed. In all its reincarnations, the group has been solidly linked to al-Qaeda. In fact, Harkat-ul-Unsar signed bin Laden's 1998 fatwah declaring war on Americans. This is the group that kidnapped foreigners from Kashmir in the mid-nineties and hijacked an Indian Airlines flight in 1999 in order to free Omar Sheikh, the man later convicted of murdering *Wall Street Journal* reporter

Daniel Pearl in February 2002. (I was tracking Omar Sheikh in November 2001 and would have met him had CNN not decided the danger was too great.) From 1999 to 2001, I reported from India for several months, tracing the links of the hijackers of the Indian Airlines plane to Omar Sheikh and to al-Qaeda. What I found, surprisingly, led me back to the MILF.

The connections between Salamat's minicaliphate and international terrorists are many. Iran's Hezbollah and al-Qaeda, in Southeast Asia, use the same network to funnel money and create front organizations.[13] It is a network that was largely made operational by the MILF as it gained credibility as a legitimate political organization.

I also believe Hezbollah and al-Qaeda used many of the same people in different plots in Southeast Asia, much like the men who carry guns in the southern Philippines may one day be Abu Sayyaf, the next MILF, the third MNLF. It seems both Hezbollah and al-Qaeda have drawn operatives from the old Darul Islam movement, Jemaah Islamiyah's precursor, in Indonesia. As I was tracking al-Qaeda operatives, I kept running into the name of Indonesian national Pandu Yudhawinata, arrested in the Philippines on October 14, 1999.[14] Pandu was a known Hezbollah operative, trained in Lebanon and Iran. Yet in 1983, he was involved—along with Darul Islam members, some of whom would later join Jemaah Islamiyah—in the bombing of the Borobodur Temple in Yogyakarta, Indonesia.[15] In 1994, he worked with Hezbollah to try—unsuccessfully—to bomb the Israeli embassy in Bangkok, Thailand. During that time, he worked on several plots which were very similar to what some of his friends in Jemaah Islamiyah would later try: conducting surveillance of ships passing in the straits between Singapore and Malaysia, an attempt to bomb a U.S. naval ship, and a potential attack on American targets during the 2000 Olympics in Australia. At about the same time al-Qaeda operatives were casing the U.S. embassy in Jakarta in 1999, Pandu confessed he had been asked to "collect operational intelligence" not only on the U.S. embassy but also on American diplomats living in Jakarta. Pandu said Hezbollah planned to attack Israeli and Jewish targets in Singapore.[16] Pandu said he had been "recruited and worked for the Iranian Intelligence in Malaysia."[17]

Pandu's and Hezbollah's exact links in Southeast Asia to al-Qaeda, the MILF, and Jemaah Islamiyah remain uncertain. However, Pandu was arrested by Philippine authorities because of information procured from phone taps of numbers frequently called by Osama bin Laden's senior lieutenant and al-Qaeda operations chief, Abu Zubaida.[18] Al-Qaeda was in frequent contact with the MILF through its top leaders: chairman, Hashim Salamat; finance committee head, Yusof Alongan; and Manila liaison officer, Abdul Nasser Nooh. Intelligence officers also watched certain Islamic NGOs, used by the MILF, to funnel money for terrorist activities.[19] Not too surprisingly, these NGOs were many of the same ones set up by Osama bin Laden's brother-in-law Mohammed Jamal Khalifa, in 1988—many of them still run by trusted Khalifa men.

Worldwide, the CIA estimates that more than 30 percent of all Islamic NGOs have been unwittingly or knowingly infiltrated by al-Qaeda and other terrorist support groups. In the Philippines, for example, Khalifa was the country director of the International Islamic Relief Organization (IIRO). Boogie Mendoza, who pioneered the research into Khalifa's network in Southeast Asia and its funding of the Abu Sayyaf and the MILF, concluded that under the IIRO's auspices Khalifa founded, bought, or was linked to a number of other innocent-sounding groups, some for fund-raising purposes but others more directly operational.[20] The groups identified by Mendoza included:

- Islamic Worldwide Mission, Inc.: Its head, Mohammad Amin al-Ghaffari, was chosen by Khalifa and was recently deported. One of its stockholders was in constant touch with MILF leader Yusof Alongan.

- Islamic Studies Call and Guidance of the Philippines, Inc.: It actively recruited militants and its leaders were in touch with Yusof Alongan.

- United Overseas Bangsamoro: An MILF fund-raising organization with centers of activity in Riyadh, Saudi Arabia; and Kuala Lumpur, Malaysia.

- JMB Personnel Management Services, Inc: A manpower company that recruited and sent Filipino workers to Saudi Arabia. One of its shareholders was linked to one of the suspects in a terrorist plot against the U.S. embassy in Manila in October 1977.

Mendoza believes the financial network he discovered in 1994 still operates today, with a regional hub in Malaysia. "I think it's still being done," said Mendoza. "The financial machinery is very, very important to the spread of terrorism and its operations. The financial backbone of any terrorism organization is the nerve center of its activity."[21] Mendoza believes its old leaders have just been replaced by new ones. Intelligence services "were able to eliminate old personalities previously engaged in the administration of these networks, but there are new personalities doing the job again."

The intelligence operation that discovered all this, code-named CoPlan Pink Poppy, was launched on October 16, 1998, after the French asked the Philippine government to gather intelligence on Filipinos in phone contact with Abu Zubaida. Before September 11, the French were far more aggressively pursuing al-Qaeda than was the United States, and they were frustrated with the slow pace of Philippine intelligence work. Yet by taking their time, Mendoza and his colleagues unveiled not only the MILF's ongoing cooperation with al-Qaeda but also the extensive nongovernmental organization network that serviced both groups. Three years later, I repeatedly asked why this information was never released to the public, and I was told "it wouldn't stand up in court" because the bulk of evidence came from illegal wiretaps, and politicians "found no real use for it."[22] Pink Poppy ended in 2000 because of a lack of funds, but after 9/11, Philippine intelligence reopened its investigations and built on this existing body of knowledge with Operation Kamikaze.[23]

Still, CoPlan Pink Poppy led to the 1999 arrest of two French Algerians Abdesselem Boulanouar and Zoheir Djalili, which spotlighted another al-Qaeda associate group, Algeria's GSPC, the Salafist Group for Call and Combat. Both French nationals spent time in Camp Abubakar and led investigators to the discovery of Camp Hodeibia. Boulanouar was arrested after he visited Camp Abubakar as he was about to check in on a flight out of the country.[24] He was carrying a training manual he admitted writing for the MILF—a course outline that covered combat, explosives, weapons, jungle survival techniques, communication, military tactics, security, and how to deal with civilians. He also carried documents from Hashim Salamat and other MILF leaders. Philippine authorities were afraid Boulanouar might have come to the Philippines to initiate a worldwide millennium bombing plot, as one report suggested, in reference to the scheme: "The timing of the Ramadan this year presents opportunities for Bin Laden to conduct large-scale attacks. Covert operation is being conducted in cooperation with French, Israeli and U.S. counterparts to determine the connection of the subject to these terrorist plans for the millennium."[25]

Boulanouar was deported to France, where he remains in prison for terrorism-related charges. Philippine investigators now say they were told by their French counterparts that Boulanouar had close ties to Ahmed Ressam, another French Algerian arrested by U.S. authorities for plotting to bomb the Los Angeles Airport at the turn of the millennium. The two men were part of a group led by Fateh Kamel, implicated in a series of robberies in northern France and believed to have been plotting to bomb a meeting of the Group of 7 industrialized nations.[26] "Boulanouar is a very important man," said terrorism expert Rohan Gunaratna. "After he was arrested, the French developed significant information about the linkages that existed between Abu Zubaida and the MILF, and in fact, his arrest very clearly shows to us that the MILF, Al-Qaeda and the GSPC were very closely linked to each other."[27] Intelligence sources echo Gunaratna's analysis. They say they believe Boulanouar was sent to the MILF camps as an agent of Abu Zubaida. "He came to the Philippines basically with the intention of providing further assistance to the MILF at the request of al-Qaeda," explains Gunaratna.

After the bombings of the U.S. embassies in East Africa in 1998, U.S. and Pakistani authorities began cooperating to cut off access to Afghanistan for al-Qaeda operatives, making it more difficult for them to use Pakistan as a transit point to get to the Afghan training camps. At that point, Osama bin Laden and Abu Zubaida made calls to two key allies and asked them to set up alternative training camps: Hasan Hattab, the GSPC leader in Algeria, and Hashim Salamat in the Philippines. A Western intelligence agency monitored calls between Osama bin Laden and Salamat and alerted Philippine authorities.[28] For good measure, Abu Zubaida also called his contact with the MILF, Yusof Alongan. Soon after, the MILF set up Camp Palestine and Camp Vietnam within Abubakar. The GSPC also set up training camps in Algeria.

If 1999 was the year that al-Qaeda made the Philippines one of its primary training grounds, it had laid the groundwork much earlier. In 1994, Abu Zubaida gave fake travel documents to the man he would later call "the senior al-Qaeda rep in Southeast Asia,"[29] Omar al-Faruq. Closely related to al-Qaeda leader Ibn al Shaykh al Libi, al-Faruq trained at the Khalden camp in Afghanistan. He was sent to the Philippines with the commander of that camp and at least two other al-Qaeda operatives. Their mission: "To conduct jihadist training at the Moro Islamic Liberation Front's Camp Abubakar."[30] They weren't just there to improve the curriculum, however. They also wanted to rally together all possible allies. Their first stop was to meet with Abu Sayyaf leader Abdurajak Janjalani to try to convince him to unite his group with the MILF "to create a stronger jihad force." Janjalani rejected the proposal, but he did discuss a plan with the al-Qaeda members for large-scale cyanide poisoning. Janjalani eventually dismissed the plot because he said it would take too much cyanide to be effective.[31] (Though, in typical al-Qaeda fashion, plots with cyanide would continue to recur to the point that I suspect somewhere, somehow, they'll give it a try.)[32] After that, the men went on to Camp Abubakar.

Al-Faruq helped the MILF, but he also traveled to Manila to try to get training as a pilot at about the time Ramzi Yousef's cell was busted.[33] It was a sign that the 1995 plot discovered by Manila police was kept alive by al-Qaeda. Before al-Faruq left for Indonesia in 1998, he also returned at least one more time to the training camps in Afghanistan. When he came back to the Philippines, he brought with him another al-Qaeda operative and the two became "emir and vice-emir," respectively, of the Arab section of the camp, called Camp Vietnam.[34] Before he left for Indonesia, al-Faruq was the chief liaison between MILF chief Salamat and the Arabs in Camp Vietnam.

Al-Faruq had help from Indonesian allies. Camp Hodeibia, the first camp for foreigners within the MILF enclave, was initially created for the Indonesian Islamic Liberation Front, a name given by the MILF to the group later known as Jemaah Islamiyah. The man who first set it up, according to his own confession, was Indonesian Mohammed Nasir bin Abbas, alias Solaiman. He became the head of Jemaah Islamiyah's Mantiqi 3, which covers the southern Philippines and parts of Indonesia. After his arrest in Indonesia in April 2003, he told his Indonesian interrogators he "helped establish Camp Hodeibia in Moro in 1994 by the order of Abdullah Sungkar."[35] (It was Abdullah Sungkar who met with Osama bin Laden in Afghanistan and offered al-Qaeda the loyalty of the network he founded along with Abu Bakar Ba'asyir. Ba'asyir took over as the JI emir after Sungkar's death in 1999.)

Bin Abbas also had links to Afghanistan, where he trained from 1987 until 1991 under Abdul Rasul Sayyaf, the same man who inspired

Janjalani to form the Abu Sayyaf. In 1996, bin Abbas handed the leadership of Camp Hodeibia to Indonesian Umar Patek, who would later be implicated in the Bali bombings. Bin Abbas then began funneling Indonesians to the southern Philippines for training. By 1996, Jemaah Islamiyah had established its barracks, administrative office, mess hall and training center at Camp Hodeibia. Between 1996 and 1998, "over one thousand Indonesian mujahideen were trained at Camp Hudeibia [sic]."[36] Bin Abbas would go back to Camp Hodeibia as its temporary commander two more times, once for two months in 1999 and again for three weeks in 2000. While he was there, Abu Bakar Ba'asyir visited the MILF camps.[37]

In short, thanks to the ease of travel among Southeast Asian archipelagos and a generally shared ideology opposed to secular states, foot soldiers and lieutenants in the jihad movement have connected to each other in fluid and shifting combinations. Camp Hodeibia, Camp Vietnam, and Camp Palestine, all in the Philippines, became virtual universities of international terror. The example of just one Indonesian operative shows how complex and deadly the networks really were (and still are).

In December 1996, shortly before returning to his home in Johor Bahru, bin Abbas, using the alias Solaiman, became the handler for a key JI and al-Qaeda operative, Fathur Roman al-Ghozi. The son of a local politician who had been jailed under Suharto's rule, al-Ghozi was a student at the school Abu Bakar Ba'asyir founded. After that, he went on to finish the equivalent of a university course in Pakistan. That was where two Indonesians asked him if he would be interested in joining a Muslim brotherhood that would go on a jihad to win back what Muslims had lost. With those two recruiters, al-Ghozi attended two years of summer training at the Turhum Camp at the border between Afghanistan and Pakistan. He had two Filipino classmates, both of whom he would later learn were MILF members working with Jemaah Islamiyah. It wasn't until graduation day in 1995 that they told him they had joined Jemaah Islamiyah.[38]

After graduation, al-Ghozi visited his uncle, also a JI member in Malaysia, and he worked in odd-job construction for the man who would later be another handler, Faiz bin Abu Bakar Bafana. He then returned home and visited with relatives for a few months before he got a call from his Indonesian recruiters asking him if he wanted to visit his old Filipino classmates in the southern Philippines. In November 1996, the recruiters came to the home of al-Ghozi's family and introduced him to Solaiman, a.k.a. Mohammed Nasir bin Abbas. Bin Abbas brought al-Ghozi into the Philippines through the back door, traveling by boat from Manado in Indonesia to General Santos City in the Philippines.

At this point, al-Ghozi was assigned to Solaiman's division of Jemaah Islamiyah known as Mantiqi 3; later he would be transferred to the chief, Hambali's Mantiqi 1 (reporting to Faiz bin Abu Bakar Bafana). Meanwhile, he was brought to Camp Abubakar where he taught classes on explosives. Al-Ghozi would prove to be a key figure in various JI plots because he would obtain the explosives for them—at one point for both Mantiqi 1 and 3. That was how he met Mukhlis Yunos, the head of MILF's Special Operations Group (SOG). The two men would work closely together on several operations. When Faiz asked al-Ghozi to buy explosives, he went to Mukhlis, who introduced him to Abu Ali (the alias of Cosain Lapinig Ramos). It was most likely Abu Ali who supplied the explosives that Jemaah Islamiyah used in the December 2000 Christmas bombings in Indonesia.[39]

Abu Ali also had a history with al-Qaeda: he worked closely with bin Laden's brother-in-law Mohammed Jamal Khalifa and with the al-Qaeda front (Malaysian company, Konsojaya) used to fund Ramzi Yousef's cell.[40] Abu Ali would also supply al-Ghozi with 1.2 tons of explosives slated for al-Qaeda's ambitious suicide-truck-bombing plots targeting Western embassies and interests in Singapore.

The actions of these three men show how the interests of the MILF, Jemaah Islamiyah, and al-Qaeda converged. Thus, one Indonesian, recruited by Jemaah Islamiyah members, trained with Filipinos in Pakistan, became a teacher in the Philippines at the MILF camp, and worked with al-Qaeda (among others) to arrange bombings in Indonesia, the Philippines, and Singapore. But that isn't all. While al-Ghozi was in the process of buying the explosives, Mukhlis asked him for financial help for an MILF plot for five simultaneous explosions in Manila. It was intended as retribution for the Philippine military's attack on Camp Abubakar. In principle, it was approved by Faiz in consultation with Hambali, but both men would actually visit Manila on December 16, 2000. They stayed at a Muslim section of Manila at the Noralyn Hotel near the Golden Mosque.[41] Al-Ghozi, with Mukhlis, pitched the plot to Hambali and Faiz.[42] The four men discussed the plot in a combination of Indonesian, Arabic, and English. Al-Ghozi said the priority target was the Manila airport. Mukhlis would be in charge of recruiting the men they would need to carry out the plot there and in four other locations. Hambali personally approved the plan and authorized the final payment of $3,600. He also asked al-Ghozi for a car and a map of the capital.

The next day, Hambali did site surveys of the U.S. and Israeli embassies in Manila, a terror plot he was developing in conjunction with other plans in neighboring countries. The men who would carry it out would most likely be MILF members assembled in part by al-Ghozi and Mukhlis.

Two weeks later on December 30, 2000, just six days after the Christmas bombings in Indonesia masterminded by Hambali, five near-simultaneous explosions went off in the capital. The worst explosion, at a Manila commuter train, killed twenty-two people.

The irony is that on December 6, just days before Hambali arrived in Manila, a Philippine intelligence report warned the MILF might try to bomb targets in Manila, specifically, "massive bombing activities in Metro Manila targeting shopping malls, schools, movie houses, parking lots, major highways/expressways."[43] The information came from documents confiscated from an attack on MILF rebels in November. It warned the attacks would be carried out by the MILF SOG group led by al-Ghozi's contact, Mukhlis Yunos.

Mukhlis is a key JI link in the Philippines. A former religious teacher from Marawi in central Mindanao, he studied Islam in Pakistan and went on to the training camps in Afghanistan.[44] Philippine authorities have linked him and the MILF SOG group he heads to several bombings in the Philippines in 2002 and 2003, including explosions of three of four planted bombs in General Santos City in April 2002 and at the Davao City airport and wharf in March and April 2003. The largest and most destructive of the General Santos City bombs went off during the busy lunch hour rush at the Fitmark shopping mall, killing fifteen and wounding fifty-five others. Investigators said the cell phone that triggered an October 2002 bombing in Zamboanga City, killing an American serviceman was Mukhlis's—the same cell phone frequently contacted by an Iraqi diplomat, Husham Husain, who would be expelled by the Philippines shortly before the United States attacked

Iraq in April 2003. According to Philippine intelligence sources, Husain was trying to recruit members of the Abu Sayyaf and the MILF to attack U.S. interests in the Philippines in retaliation for U.S. actions in Iraq.[45] (In this respect, President Bush's insistence on a connection between Iraq and international terror was true—but only in response to U.S. aggression, not before.)

Philippine authorities would mount an entire operation to try to capture Mukhlis. Code-named CoPlan Black Crescent, it would successfully recruit two double agents to help authorities piece together the links between the MILF, the Abu Sayyaf, and al-Qaeda.[46] Mukhlis would finally be arrested in a CIA sting operation on May 25, 2003.[47]

Abu Sayyaf has proved itself to be more than a mere shakedown operation, though it is that. One of Mukhlis's bombings was carried off with help from an Abu Sayyaf member, who offered to help pay for it by extorting money from restaurants, hotels, even the city mayor.[48] The MILF has been involved in on-again, off-again peace negotiations with the Philippine government and it continues to deny it has any institutional links with al-Qaeda. "There are speculations that there might be some members of the MILF who might have established links," said Eid Kabalu, MILF spokesman. "And that is why we call on the military, the government to again specify, pinpoint this group so that we can conduct a separate or joint investigation."[49] There is overwhelming evidence that the links go to its top leadership, but the government does not want to admit its truth.

When I began doing investigative reports on these links soon after 9/11, CNN ran dozens of exclusive reports. I was stunned at the response. The MILF had so interlinked its cause with the marginalization of Muslims in Mindanao that during a seminar in Manila, I was accused of being anti-Muslim. Several people asked why I was against the peace process. It showed me how successful the MILF's strategy had been in the Philippines. The only hope for a lasting peace in the southern Philippines is to demand explanations from the MILF and determine whether it continues to support radical Islamic groups like al-Qaeda.

Soon after, I began receiving text messages on my cellular phone. First they were routed through common friends—other Filipino journalists who had good relations with the MILF. One text said, "Please tell our good friend Maria Ressa that she is being used by the military." I sent back a message saying the information did not come from the Philippine military but from its regional neighbors. Then the messages began coming directly—veiled threats that made our network take extra security.

For more than a year after she took office, President Gloria Macapagal-Arroyo reversed the all-out war position of her predecessor, Joseph Estrada, that shut down Camp Abubakar and stopped the growth of the MILF. In conversations with former cabinet members under Estrada, I was told the decision to attack was largely influenced by President Estrada's acknowledgment that foreigners were using MILF camps. The fall of his government in 2001 changed that policy. When President Arroyo stepped in, she emphasized national reconciliation and offered peace, even though the MILF used the cease-fire—as it had in the past—as a chance to rebuild its forces. Intelligence reports document the buildup.

At one point, MILF cadres were being trained in twenty-seven camps in Mindanao. "The MILF intensifies conduct of trainings in all MILF camps to upgrade the military capabilities of its fighters"[50] summarizes one report available to President Arroyo.

One document says MILF rebels were going back to camps that had been temporarily overrun by Philippine soldiers and setting up bases again. "The MILF is obviously taking advantage of the existing ceasefire agreement by intensifying recruitment, training, logistical build-up and fortification of positions."[51]

Another document reports on the arrival of foreign trainers in MILF camps and actually lists fourteen names: five from Indonesia, two from Afghanistan, two from Egypt, and one each from Libya, Qatar, Sudan, Saudi Arabia, and Turkey.[52]

Another documents how Jemaah Islamiyah moved its headquarters to Indonesia after the fall of Camp Abubakar in 2000 and how it has switched positions with the MILF. Now it is the MILF that has been given its own barracks and training facilities within the JI camp in Indonesia. It also chronicles how the MILF supplies arms to Jemaah Islamiyah and receives weapons shipments through Indonesia.[53] That relationship would again change after Indonesia began its own crackdown.

Yet another intelligence document shows how the MILF joined an umbrella organization formed by Abu Bakar Ba'asyir, the Rabitatul Mujahideen (RM). Philippine authorities initially thought this was Jemaah Islamiyah's fighting arm. Later, they realized this was Ba'asyir's and Hambali's attempt to bring together Southeast Asian and South Asian extremist groups.[54]

From these intelligence reports, it is very clear Jemaah Islamiyah and al-Qaeda have a solid presence in the Philippines. Yet the government, in its peace talks, continues to offer autonomy to the MILF in its stronghold.

In a surprising turnaround on February 11, 2003, the Philippine military attacked the MILF. For days the military had been bringing in troops and equipment. Members of the Army's Sixth Infantry Division backed by reinforcements—a total of five army and marine battalions—surrounded the MILF's Buliok complex in Liguasan Marsh near Pikit, North Cotabato, the hometown of MILF chief Hashim Salamat. It was a difficult area, but the military knew where the camps were located because of aerial and surveillance photographs taken the previous November. The agent who authorized the aerial run had now been asked to work with military forces. It was clear the MILF had been there a while and, it seemed, were consolidating their forces.

Within a few hours, the military would say more than one hundred rebels were killed—a claim the MILF dismissed as propaganda. But in another sign of the government's disjointed efforts, even as military commanders told their troops to attack, government officials in Manila approved the final draft of a comprehensive peace agreement with the MILF. That afternoon, President Arroyo ordered the military to stop the attacks and return to barracks.

Less than twenty-four hours later, President Arroyo released a short statement reversing her decision: "As of 2:00 P.M. today, I have ordered the armed forces of the Philippines to capture and occupy the Buliok complex fronting the Liguasan Marsh in central Mindanao. The Buliok complex has been identified as the base of operations and refuge area of the notorious Pentagon kidnapping gang and other heavily-armed criminal groups in Mindanao. This campaign which I have ordered is not directed against the Moro Islamic Liberation Front. However, our troops will defend themselves against any force blocking their mission to eliminate criminal gangs in Mindanao. My government is committed to achieving a peace settlement with the MILF. I emphasize, however, that my government is duty-bound to uphold the rule of law and to neutralize all armed criminal elements in Mindanao, wherever they may be."

It was a clear sign of the government's confusion. No word of al-Qaeda. No direct hit on the MILF. The alleged target, the Pentagon gang, had been placed on the U.S. list of terrorist organizations last year, but it was not the real target. By the end of the week, Philippine troops would take over the compound, and the country's highest-ranking general would finally admit they were after the MILF: "What precipitated this action is the massing up of MILF forces in the area," Armed Forces Chief of Staff Dionisio Santiago said from Malacañang Palace. A day earlier, his forces had captured the home of MILF chief Hashim Salamat. Soldiers recovered boxes of documents, including manuals on assassination, ambush, and bombing techniques. Pictures of children holding rifles, and others depicting intensive training, were also found. "It means they're training terrorists," said Major General Generoso Senga, commander of the Sixth Infantry Division. "They're even training child combatants." Officers said they would go through the material looking for links with bin Laden's network.

MILF spokesman Eid Kabalu denied military accusations and said the documents were "planted" by military officials to justify the assault and the violation of a standing cease-fire agreement. No matter the claims and counterclaims, a series of attacks and counterattacks began that pitched Mindanao again into all-out war.

By the end of the month, hundreds would be killed and more than 50,000 residents forced to flee their homes. At one point, the entire island of Mindanao lost power after MILF rebels allegedly blew up at least five power transmission towers that supplied electricity. The military also blamed the MILF for a series of massacres in several villages, claims the MILF denied. By February 27, Armed Forces Chief of Staff Dionisio Santiago said he wanted the MILF declared terrorists: "Economic sabotage, ambushes, name it, they have done it. I think what they're doing and with their refusal to sit down at the negotiation table, it's high time they are out in the category of terrorists."

Yet, in late July, both sides declared a cease-fire and President

Arroyo said she was confident a peace deal with the MILF could be signed by the end of the year. On August 5, 2003, the MILF announced the death of its founder and chairman, Hashim Salamat, who died from a heart attack on July 13. The MILF kept his death a secret until it determined who would succeed him, naming Al Haj Murad, the MILF military chief, Salamat's successor. A civil engineer by training, he is viewed as more moderate than Salamat.

As of this writing, both sides are again attempting to enforce a cease-fire and begin formal peace talks in Malaysia. Several factors have complicated the process. On July 27, 2003, Arroyo faced a mutiny within her military. About three hundred junior officers took over the prime commercial complex in the capital's financial district and held their country hostage for nearly twenty-four hours. Although the siege ended quickly, the mutineers hurled grave accusations against Arroyo's government and the military establishment, charging senior officers of selling arms to the MILF and the government of setting off explosions as an excuse for military aid from the United States. Now investigations are under way, both on the charges and on the identities of the civilian coconspirators of the mutineers—all of these factors, analysts say, leaving this nation vulnerable in the war on terror.

CHAPTER 8

SINGAPORE: AL-QAEDA'S PLAN A

"This is the place where U.S. military personnels [*sic*] will be dropped off from a bus, and they will walk towards the MRT station. And this is one of the regular buses that carry the military personnels from Sembawang [where the Americans live] to Yishun MRT station [the subway]."[1] The voice in the surveillance video explained it as clearly and simply as possible. "Those personnels after they alighted from the bus, they will move towards the MRT station—as you can see from the far left—the people walking towards the MRT station—they will walk the same way as other people. Now being zoomed in is a bicycle bay where the train commuters parked their bicycles in the morning before they board the train, and they will pick it up later in the evening after work." The camera switches to another angle of the same bicycle bay. The narrator talks about a plan to place a bomb in a box strapped to a bicycle and leave it to explode at this strategic stand between the bus stop and the subway station. "This is the bicycle bay as viewed from the footpath that leads towards the MRT station. You will notice that some of the boxes are placed on the motorcycles—these are the same type of boxes that we intend to use." The tape then shows other scenes of the same spot, pointing out an alternative area to park the bicycle, at another point showing drainage holes that "might be useful" to hide explosives.

The tape had been edited from five tapes of raw footage in order to present a Singapore bombing plan to al-Qaeda for approval. The edited master was first given to Faiz bin Abu Bakar Bafana. A former Singaporean, Faiz was a trusted deputy of Hambali. Under Hambali's instructions, Faiz brought the videotape to Afghanistan in 1999 and showed it to Mohammed Atef, al-Qaeda's former military chief, then the third high-est-ranking official. Atef greenlighted the project, telling Faiz to go ahead and buy the explosives and short-list the men needed for the attack.

At first glance, it might seem surprising that al-Qaeda has flourished in Singapore. The tiny city-state is only 18 percent Muslim, and, on paper, it would seem to offer every reason in the world for its Muslims to be modern and law-abiding. Yet Singapore has been so fully infiltrated by al-Qaeda that it was the target of a bomb scheme even bigger than the Bali blasts. The (fairly simple) Bali bombing was a second choice, acti-vated when plans for an extraordinary group of explosions in Singapore were abandoned in their late stages.

Al-Qaeda's appeal to Muslims of all educational and economic backgrounds has consistently been underestimated, even in the wake of 9/11 and even by its smartest opponents. The story of Singapore is a sobering reminder of the depth and strength of al-Qaeda's appeal.

Some people, perhaps many, have chosen the path of al-Qaeda over Singapore's apparent utopian success. Singapore had no homeless; in fact, nearly 90 percent of its three million people lived in govern-ment-subsidized housing. Until recently, everyone who wanted to work had a job. There were more jobs than applicants, and migrant workers from neighboring countries had been imported to fill the gaps. All its citizens are given a stake in the nation through the Central Provident Fund set up by the government—a compulsory savings scheme that gives Singapore the highest savings rate in the world. Add to that the government-subsidized health and education systems that are the best in the region. Corruption has been virtually stamped out of the govern-ment bureaucracy: foreign expatriates and diplomats actually rate cor-ruption in Singapore to be lower than in their own Western countries.[2] The crime rate is so low that when a friend of mine dropped his wallet on the street, a Singaporean picked it up and returned it to him within a day. Even Lee Kuan Yew, the long-time leader who served as first prime minister from Singapore's independence from Malaysia in 1965 until stepping down in 1990, has a hard time believing his success. "In 1965, we were a fairly dilapidated town, not quite recovered from the ravages of war but just beginning to rebuild. At that time, our main preoccupation was how to make a living because the entrepôt trade which had survived and given us a living for one hundred–plus years was going to be replaced by all our neighbors' trading direct. So I had no great visions of transformation. First job was to get investments, get jobs, and we had to get the manufacturing sector started because we needed jobs, and manufacturing created jobs," he says.[3] "After a while, we stumbled on something that was much more effective. I spent two months of the October term—November, December—in Harvard in 1968. I was taking a sabbatical and our EDB, our Economic Development Board, had already been established there in New York, so they got me to meet businessmen. I also spoke to the Economic Club of New York and so on. Then I met them and talked to them. Then I discovered that they were looking for a safe place where they could manufacture their electronics and then bring them back to America. At that time, there was a Cultural Revolution in China. Hong Kong was in turmoil so we became a desirable location, and because the first few succeeded so well—within months, they were up and running and exporting—so we got more and more investments. By 1973, five years from 1968, we had solved our unemployment problem."

I first met Lee Kuan Yew in the late 1980s during one of his trips to the Philippines. Singapore's success had turned Lee into the spokesman for Asian values, which set off a global debate that pitted Western values focused on individual human rights against "the Asian way"—the good of the collective whole. He had boiled his nation's success down to a few simple ideas: a respect for elders and the law, hard work, and the recognition that the needs of society must transcend the individual's. "A Confucianist view of order between subject and ruler—this helps in the rapid transformation of society . . . in other words, you fit yourself into society—the exact opposite of the American rights of the individual," said Lee.

My crew and I left ourselves plenty of time to set up; I had been warned he was a perfectionist. Yet we waited for nearly two hours as an aide came in periodically to inspect our setup. Each time he asked us to turn on the TV lights and checked the thermostat in the room. Finally, after the fourth or fifth time, I asked him if there was anything wrong. He told me, "No, nothing. Don't worry. It should hit 18 degrees soon." Then he explained it to me: Lee Kuan Yew did not want to do a television interview under hot lights until the air-conditioner cooled the room down to his preferred temperature: 18 degrees Celsius (65 degrees Fahrenheit). You could look at this as the absurd height of a controlling personality—or see it as a man who knows exactly what he wants and aims to get it.

That is the kind of attention to detail that created Singapore, and it's apparent when you land at the airport. Singapore's Changi Airport has been voted the most efficient and best-liked airport in the world because it offers just about anything any traveler could desire: shops, massage, live entertainment, Internet access. Going from the plane, through the gate, and through Customs normally takes less than ten minutes. By the time you get to baggage claim, your bags are waiting. Even on a busy day, you will spend no more than five minutes waiting before an attendant opens a taxi door for you. The drive from the airport is an easy ride: traffic is closely regulated. The trees, plants, and flowers may catch your attention; Singapore has more than 3,000 species of palms. Nicknamed the Garden City, Singapore is a carefully planned and landscaped garden. The Ministry of Environment imports about 80 percent of its trees and shrubs. The plants in the center of the highway from the airport are potted. In the early years, fearing an invasion from former civil war opponent Malaysia, the government had wanted to be able to remove these plants in order to turn the highway into a huge airplane runway to evacuate its citizens.

Singapore is serious about taking care of its people, and that leaves it wide open to criticism—the same way the nerd in high school is the butt of jokes because he works so hard. There's the overused joke about the "fine city"—because of all the penalties against spitting, jaywalking, littering. There is even a fine against chewing gum, which at one point was declared illegal: authorities had discovered the subways were slowing down because of the gum stuck between the doors. That kind of academic attention to detail and the study of human behavior is the foundation of much of Singapore's laws and policies. This is a place where politicians don't like to be called politicians because of the stigma of self-interest and demagoguery; here, politicians actually try to focus on public service. They're kept honest in part by an intricate web of social and political links but also because Lee Kuan Yew has been ever watching.

This clockwork island of towering skyscrapers has one of the highest population densities in the world, with over 4,200 people per square kilometer in the mid-1990s. Without careful planning, people and buildings might have turned the city into a concrete jungle. As it is, about 61 percent of the population live on just 17 percent of the land area, a land reclamation program that helps maintain an ecological balance. Singapore is one of only two cities in the world to have a genuine tropical rain forest about a forty-five-minute drive from the city center.[4] Its parks have ecotourism preserves that contain more plant species than the whole of North America.

The man whose vision powered this island state knew when to work hard—and unlike other strongman rulers of Asia, like the Philippines' Ferdinand Marcos or Indonesia's Suharto, he knew when to step down. In 1990, while Singapore's economy was booming, Lee turned power over to Singapore's new prime minister, businessman Goh Chok Tong. A new post was created for Lee: senior minister. "I was in charge of a very young country. I had been in power since its independence, and the risk of succession going wrong and bringing the country down was very real. So I made a cautious choice to preserve what we had achieved: to step down whilst I was still active and can do something to help the new prime minister switch seats with me and gradually take control of a machine that was very tailored to my requirements. So he gradually changed and tailored it to make it less personalized to me, and I think it's not been a bad move. This way was better," Lee told me.[5] He was understated in his reasons, but avoiding the corruption of power is a key accomplishment. Lee has a sterling reputation as an incorruptible visionary.

Born September 16, 1921, Lee Kuan Yew is uncompromising in his goals. Although his ancestors were Hakka Chinese, his parents were Straits-born Peranakans, which comes from the Bahasa word *anak*, or offspring, and means "born here." Peranakans were thought to combine the best of Chinese and Malay cultures. At home, Lee grew up speaking English, Malay, and Cantonese. Later, he would teach himself Japanese, Mandarin, and Hokkien. His fluency with languages often gave him added credibility when trying to convince political constituents of potentially unpopular views and policies. Never afraid to buck conventional wisdom, he wanted "to be correct, not politically correct."[6]

Lee is a product of his nation's colonial past and its history, and his personal experiences shaped the Singapore he created. His education was primarily English: first at Singapore's Raffles College, where he studied English along with mathematics and economics. Despite his outstanding academic credentials and awards, he was subject to discipline like everyone else. When he was late for school, he was caned—hit on the buttocks with a rattan stick. He has since written, "I have never understood why Western educationists are so much against corporal punishment. It did my fellow students and me no harm." During World War II, under the brutal Japanese occupation, he worked for a Japanese government propaganda department. In his memoirs, he marveled at the low crime rate despite the fact that everyone was always hungry. The Japanese were so brutal and the punishments so harsh that people refrained from committing any crime, even at the worst of times. "As a result, I have never believed those who advocate a soft approach to crime and punishment, claiming that punishment does not reduce crime." The penal system of Singapore assigns the death penalty for the possession and sale of drugs. On board the plane before you land, the attendant draws your attention to the fact that Singapore has harsh penalties for drugs; just to make sure visitors know, it's written in red on the immigration arrival card.

After the war, Lee went on to Cambridge in England, where he earned a double first in law (top grades in midterms and finals, a distinction achieved by only about 5 percent of Cambridge's students). It was a time to watch, learn, and assess. "I saw the British govern themselves, and I knew that they had a very sophisticated system, very tolerant society, but their interests were Britain and how the colonies could help Britain be better off. So during those critical years, we met amongst ourselves, Singapore and Malaysian students studying there and decided that we should really come back, form a group, grow into a party and struggle and fight for power," said Lee.[7] While in school between 1946 and 1950, he used the Anglicized name Harry Lee, which he dropped when he returned to Singapore. He married the only person he knew who did better than him academically, Kwa Geok Choo, who also received first-class honors in Cambridge, and he set up a law partnership with her. He soon became involved in local politics and resigned as a partner in the firm when he became prime minister in 1959.

A shrewd political operator, Lee Kuan Yew became known for his traits of honesty, efficiency, firmness, and intolerance. Singapore's government became so entwined with Lee's personality that opposition to him was often portrayed as being against the good of the Singaporean collective whole. In 1973, Lee articulated a vision for himself and for what would soon be his nation of overachievers: "The greatest satisfaction in life comes from achievement. To achieve is to be happy. Singaporeans must be imbued with this spirit. We must never get into the vicious cycle of expecting more and more for less and less. . . . Solid satisfaction grows out of achievement. . . . It generates inner or spiritual strength, a strength which grows out of an inner discipline."[8]

Given the utopian success he and Singapore have achieved since then, why would there be any motivation for terrorism? Singaporean officials have tried hard to address this question, and they have tried harder than most others to combat the threat. Yet they have only disrupted, not eliminated, it—and therein lies an important lesson about the seduction of Islamism.

Not everyone agrees that the search for excellence translates to spiritual meaning. In fact, one of the criticisms leveled at Singapore is that the emphasis on economic development has created a nation lacking in creativity and spirituality. The government's response under Prime Minister Goh Chok Tong has been to focus on building creativity through arts and culture. Yet Singapore's imams went in a different direction. "When we asked our Muslims, 'Why have you become so strict in your religious practices?' they answered, 'Because we are better educated and so understand better what must be observed,' " said Lee Kuan Yew, uncomprehendingly.[9]

Al-Qaeda's recruits in Singapore are not downtrodden or marginalized; they were looking for spiritual renewal. "They want to fill a spiritual void. They want to learn about the religion, and therefore, they went to these teachers in search of the truth—or true Islam," said Wong Kan Seng, Singapore's minister of home affairs, in charge of homeland security.[10] "That's why they were taught these concepts, but they were not stupid people. We had two teams of psychologists who looked at [our] detainees, and we found out that two of them have superior intelligence. Majority of them have above average intelligence, and they were educated, English educated. They have jobs. They have homes. Some of them even have diplomas from the Polytechnics"— Singapore's top schools—"so they are not down and out. They are not poor. They are not the ones who need to depend on a handout in order to sustain themselves, and they have families."

Singapore faced the problem of terrorism head-on: it was the first country in Southeast Asia to admit openly to an al-Qaeda presence. It has been the only nation in the world to be completely transparent about its terrorism investigations, releasing pictures and biographies of everyone arrested under its Internal Security Act. "They were ordinary Singaporeans," said deputy prime minister and defense minister Tony Tan.[11] "They are all of them gainfully employed. There were no obvious resentments. They were all doing well, and yet they were prepared to be engaged in this plot—if necessary—to give up their lives, and when we asked them what inspired them, the fact was that they felt they had to be part of this great cause in order to fight against American interests, and if in the course of the fight, Singaporeans were killed, well, that's the course of events. I think that the inspiration behind such groups is very deep, is something which we'll have to get to the bottom of." A soft-spoken, gentle, and thoughtful man with an infectious laugh, it is clear that MIT-educated Tony Tan has analyzed his country's terrorism problem within a larger context. He knows the war on terror is not the United States against al-Qaeda or the West versus the Muslim world. It is a conflict *within* the Muslim world. "There is definitely a clash between elements in Islam itself—between on the one hand, the radical, extremist, fundamentalist groups who see that the present world is wrong . . . [and] modernist Islam, which sees that Islam's future is not to shun the present world but to be integrated with the present world: to master knowledge, science, technology in order to compete on equal terms with the West."

Tan is not the only official to seek understanding. Home Minister Wong Kan Seng argues that "this issue of terrorism is one that is the most serious one as far as security threats are concerned, and it can also undermine our social cohesion. If we do not tell the people what this is all about, how it develops, and what we are going to do about it, and what we need the people to do about it together, then how can we expect them to know what to do?" Yet even here, al-Qaeda has infiltrated and nearly wreaked havoc.

The Singapore arm of Jemaah Islamiyah reports to the Malaysian leadership group. In the 1990s, there were two main recruiters: Abu Jibril and Mukhlas, both Indonesians in exile in Malaysia. They had no trouble recruiting Singaporeans or infiltrating Malaysians across the border. The voice on the surveillance tape of potential American targets at the beginning of this chapter is that of Mukhlas's brother-in-law, forty-year-old engineer Hashim bin Abbas.

Consider the case of Singaporean Ibrahim Maidin, a good example of how a local can transform into a deadly cosmopolitan. Abu Jibril recruited Maidin and sent him to Afghanistan in 1993 for military training, along with seven other Singaporeans. When they returned, Maidin began to spread Jemaah Islamiyah's radical ideology through religious classes and study groups he put together. Often he would invite guest preachers like Abu Jibril, Hambali, and Abu Bakar Ba'asyir. All but one of thirteen JI members detained in Singapore's first wave of arrests said they had been recruited while attending Maidin's religious classes. What was flabbergasting to Singaporeans was that the thirteen pictures plastered below the newspaper headlines after the arrest weren't outwardly fanatic faces; they were ordinary Singaporeans.

When Maidin was arrested in December 2001, the fifty-one-year-old managed an eleven-unit luxury condominium. Many could guess at his religious commitment because of how he dressed: he often wore a long white Arab-style robe and cap. He cropped his hair short, wore thick wire-frame glasses that tilted slightly to the right, and had a long, flowing, graying beard. "I remember telling Ibrahim right after September 11, 'You better shave off your beard or you'll be mistaken for one of Osama's men!' " one tenant said. "He just laughed." [12] Another tenant described him as "mild-mannered and hard-working." Other tenants said he kept religious texts in his desk, although he did not often talk to them about his beliefs. "Once he was in his office, he rarely came out unless one of us asked him to," said a tenant who had lived in the condominium since before Maidin began working there fifteen years ago. "Maybe he was preoccupied with all this plotting!"

Sometimes when tenants needed work done in their apartments, Maidin would send one of his friends to help—men they later recognized as part of the terrorist group whose photographs were published in the national paper. "Ibrahim would bring them to my flat to fix this or that," the wife of a doctor said. "They certainly didn't look evil."

Maidin and his group were accused of several ambitious bombing plots against Western embassies, American naval vessels, American companies, and a shuttle bus carrying American troops. The thirteen Singaporeans arrested that December had no previous criminal records. They were not particularly pious; they were not members of any mosque in Singapore. They were educated in national schools in Singapore. Yet they espoused a radical strain of Islam that focused on an anti-American agenda. Singapore's deputy prime minister, Tony Tan, was the first official I interviewed in Southeast Asia to peg it to the ideology of al-Qaeda. "One of the major dangers which has arisen is the fact that al-Qaeda has been able to co-opt all these regional elements and movements and given them focus and organization," he said. "Mr. Osama Bin Laden has global objectives, but within that he has been able to accommodate all of these disparate movements and be able to link it with his overall objective. So it's, in a way, a franchising of international terrorism."[13]

Tenants remember Maidin taking a long leave in 1993, telling them he was making the Muslim pilgrimage, the hajj, in Mecca. Instead, he went to military training in Afghanistan. The camps are a crucial part of al-Qaeda's success. Recruits are encouraged to attend "just for the experience of jihad," said Home Minister Wong Kan Seng, "to be part of that group." It changes their thinking. It turned Maidin and his seven cohorts into recruiters themselves. "When they came back, they radicalized the other members with the same cause, and they continued to send some of these other members back to Afghanistan to get the same baptism of fire," says Seng. "They feel that they are a small part of a bigger whole, part of this jihadist struggle against America and against the West," says Tan.[14]

After Maidin was arrested, Singapore officials found letters he had written in his hard drive and diskettes: three to Taliban leader Mullah Mohammed Omar and one to Osama bin Laden.[15] It was clear Maidin believed Afghanistan was the prototype of a successful Islamic state. At one point, Maidin proposed Jemaah Islamiyah join the Taliban, which he said was rejected by the *shura*. One letter to Mullah Omar offered a donation of $1,000. The other asked questions that hovered between faith and ideology, in search of simple answers to naive questions. Since taking over Afghanistan, is Mullah Omar "now the Caliph of all Muslim"? "Should Muslims who live in non-Muslim countries migrate to Afghanistan?" If they do, what happens to the mosques they leave behind? "Is it true that the Saudi King/authority is an American ally and co-operates with the non-believers in many matters?"[16]

Feeling part of a Muslim brotherhood and searching for an ideal

Muslim state has given these Singaporean Muslims a revolutionary zeal and helped fill the spiritual void. "They identify themselves with Muslim causes in Palestine, Chechnya, Kosovo, where injustices are done to Muslims. Every day, their TVs show an all-powerful Israeli army battering the Palestinians," said Lee Kuan Yew. "I'm not saying that if you solve the Palestinian problem, it'll all go away. Al-Qaeda's strategy is for all Muslims, not just Arabs, to rally to fight for all Muslims wherever they are oppressed. And the great oppressor is America, Israel's backer. This call to jihad resonates." [17]

From JI Singapore's inception in 1991 until 1999, Maidin and his Malaysia-based leaders planted sleeper agents. Those years were for indoctrination, and they were effective. Singapore officials say those they arrested, in both December 2001 and September 2002, were true believers. Part of the reason they confessed their plans is because they were proud of what they were doing. They were fighting for a higher spiritual cause, and that gave them a sense of comfort and superiority.

At the time of the first arrests, the Singapore group had about sixty to eighty members, and it differed from al-Qaeda's official membership in that—like Malaysia—it included women, perhaps a reflection of the more tolerant Islamic culture of Southeast Asia. Like Malaysia, JI Singapore has five functional units: operations, security, missionary work, economy, and communications. Compared to the other branches, Singapore's raised the most funds, and it had the most developed operational cells. By the time the cells were broken up, their plans were ready to be implemented.

Given Singapore's economic success, it isn't surprising that Jemaah Islamiyah's members shouldered a large part of the financial needs of the entire organization. While al-Qaeda gave money to the group for specific operations, it was in general self-sufficient, sometimes contributing to al-Qaeda and the Taliban. Members of the Singapore cell donated 2 percent of their salaries in the early 1990s. That rose to 5 percent by the end of the decade. Others gave a fixed sum monthly. Investigators believe that 25 percent of the money Singapore raised went to the Malaysian JI arm. Later, another 25 percent went to the Indonesian arm. Money would be transferred personally, with a Singapore member handing the whole sum to a Malaysian member, who would then be in charge of personally handing 25 percent to the Indonesian Jemaah Islamiyah. The remaining 50 percent of the money

Singapore collected was used for its expenses: sending its members to
Afghanistan and the Philippines for training, purchasing equipment like
walkie-talkies and binoculars, and addressing members' needs.

In the early 1990s, all JI members were encouraged to go to Afghanistan through a relatively complicated route. Since Malaysia was the center of operations, all Singaporeans (and Filipinos) would transit through
Kuala Lumpur and travel with high-level Malaysian JI leaders. Covert
arrangements for their entry to Afghanistan via Pakistan were made by
Hambali. A letter written by Hashim bin Abbas (the voice on the surveillance videotape) shows the fake documents that Jemaah Islamiyah
provided. The letter was written to the "mantiqi" or district chief, whom
Singaporean investigators believe to be Hambali, recommending four
members for training. It identified one man named Nasir as ready for *isti-
mata*—to be a suicide bomber. "Nasir is a bachelor who is good at practical rather than theory . . . we do not have members who are trained
commandos here. However, he needs to write to his mother from a dis-
tant country so that she would not look for him." Hashim bin Abbas also
asked that the recruits be provided with falsified letters of acceptance by
religious schools in Pakistan to serve as a cover story for the recruits'
families and employers to account for the three to six months they were
gone. They also needed them to apply for exit permits from Singapore's
Ministry of Defense. The last document each would need was a letter
from Hambali to their contact in Karachi, who would then bring them
to the training camps in Afghanistan.

By the time the Singapore cells were discovered, JI members had
been sent for training not only to the al-Qaeda training camps in
Afghanistan but to Malaysia, the Philippines, and Indonesia. Beginning
in 1990, Jemaah Islamiyah established small training camps in
Malaysia. By 1995, training camps in Gunung Pulai and Kulai in
Malaysia began to approximate the courses they could get in Afghanistan, including guerrilla warfare, infiltration, and ambush. In 2000, it
added urban warfare to the courses in Malaysia. The much larger new
training operation was in the Philippines at Camp Abubakar.

To the discomfort of its neighbors, Singapore has been the only
nation to state publicly the locations of training camps in the region—
information that investigators gleaned from hundreds of hours of interrogation of captured JI members. Singapore was the first to connect the
dots between what were previously considered home-grown, domestic

conflicts and the broader international movement that has hijacked their nation's Muslim militants. Singapore said that the ideology espoused by al-Qaeda is more dangerous than communism, warning its neighbors that a collective response was necessary to deal with this threat. "Al-Qaeda and similar Muslim terrorists share a deeply-felt sense of Islamic brotherhood that transcends ethnicity and national boundaries," said Lee Kuan Yew in the first speech by any public official to link the devastation in Ambon to al-Qaeda.[18] Unfortunately, Indonesia continued to deny the link between Jemaah Islamiyah and al-Qaeda.

There were multiple terrorist plots hatched in Singapore, ranging from single strikes at Americans there to grandiose schemes to trigger outright cross-border warfare. Singapore's operatives were divided into seven operational cells, known as *fiahs*, each with its own terrorist plots. All of them ultimately were controlled by Hambali. The oldest cell, *fiah ayub*, began surveying potential targets as early as 1997 under the leadership of thirty-nine-year-old printer Mohammed Khalim bin Jaffar. A skinny man with a moustache and a grunge goatee, his short hair emphasizes the largeness of his ears. He first attended Maidin's classes in 1989 or 1990, as well as lectures by visiting preachers Abu Jibril and Hambali, who gave religious talks in the homes of other JI members. It was Khalim who came up with the first plan to target Americans in Singapore by striking the subway station. Living in Singapore's Yishun area, he was familiar with the shuttle bus service used by American servicemen and their families to go from the Sembawang area to the Yishun subway station. With the help of forty-year-old service engineer Hashim bin Abbas, Khalim recorded some of the surveillance videotapes of the target that would be edited into the proposal tape. In 1999, Hashim's brother-in-law Mukhlas told *fiah ayub* members to proceed with their plans against Americans. Khalim drew maps of the MRT station while Hashim took more surveillance videos. During some of these sessions, Hashim took his children with him to help mask his purpose. Those scenes with his family were edited out of the final composite tape.

Later in 1999, after al-Qaeda's Mohammed Atef had seen the tape and greenlighted the project, Khalim made a presentation to al-Qaeda leaders, including Atef. He was sent to Afghanistan by Hambali on a JI training mission from September 1999 to April 2000. He talked to al-Qaeda about his plan, at one point drawing two maps and sketching the station. He dictated details about Singapore to one of Osama bin Laden's aides, who wrote them down in Arabic.

It is unclear exactly why the plan wasn't carried out right away. One plotter would later tell Singaporean investigators he thought members of *fiah ayub* found it too difficult to get the 2 tons of explosives they needed. But that plot did provide a concrete link between Jemaah Islamiyah and al-Qaeda to investigators. After the United States attacked Afghanistan and bombed the home of Mohammed Atef, U.S. troops found the videotape as well as the notes Khalim had sketched in the rubble. Singaporean officials would later match the videotape found in Afghanistan and given to them by U.S. investigators to the original tape found in Khalim's Singapore apartment.

Many other links to al-Qaeda and Afghanistan have since been found. Shortly after the September 11 attacks and the U.S.-led campaign in Afghanistan, Ibrahim Maidin distributed a survey to several JI Singapore members. He wanted to gauge their level of commitment to the cause of their Muslim brothers in Afghanistan. On half a sheet of paper, there was space at the top to write their names. The text began: "I understand my responsibilities and capabilities, and I am prepared for . . . ," followed by nine acts of increasing levels of faith and commitment: offer supplications for the Taliban and the mujahideen; missionary work; contribute ideas to help the Taliban; contribute funds to the Taliban; donate new Singapore shares (stocks the government gives its citizens); conduct sabotage outside Singapore against U.S. interests; support any activity against U.S. interests; conduct sabotage inside Singapore against U.S. interests; and finally, volunteer to be a suicide bomber against U.S. interests. Suicide bombings are rare in Southeast Asia, but in a sign of times to come, three members from one cell surveyed, including Khalim Jaffar and Hashim bin Abbas, checked this highest level of commitment.

While Khalim was making his surveillance tapes, his cell had also been enlisted by Hambali and the Malaysian leadership to focus on Singaporean targets, to foment war between Malaysia and Singapore. The plan was to attack key Singaporean installations, like the Ministry of Defense or the water pipelines, which bring water from Malaysia to the city-state, and make the attacks appear to be acts of war by the Malaysian government. Hambali's plot showed an intimate understanding of the history and the people of both nations: he wanted to revive the ethnic strife that caused race riots in the 1960s and fuel the conflict between "Chinese Singapore" and "Malay–Muslim Malaysia" in the hopes of triggering a jihad in Malaysia against Singapore. Hambali wanted to create the chaos of Ambon: if Singapore thought it had been attacked, it might attack Malaysia, triggering a war. Jemaah Islamiyah could then take advantage of the instability to overthrow the governments of both countries and establish an Islamic state. "It's the same doctrine the communists had," said Lee Kuan Yew. "In a chaotic situation, the organized minority will take over. So their objective is, it doesn't matter what it is, just cause strife within the country, strife between races and countries. In the chaos and the confusion that result, they will thrive and win power." [19]

Fiah ayub members pretended to be joggers while they took photographs of water pipelines at the Bukit Timah Nature Reserve. Others followed a Ministry of Defense official to his home to see if they could plant a bomb in the trunk of his car, which would detonate inside the compound of the Ministry of Defense. Others cased Changi Airport.

In 1999, Ibrahim Maidin became Jemaah Islamiyah Singapore's spiritual leader, handing daily operations to Mas Selamat Kastari. Kastari's plot against Changi Airport shows how domestic and international goals can be intertwined. According to Singapore intelligence officials, Kastari was planning to hijack a plane from Aeroflot, the Russian airline, and crash it into the tower at Changi Airport. Using a Russian airliner would show his organization's support for the Muslims of Chechnya. [20] Kastari would evade Singaporean authorities and move freely in Indonesia for months before finally being arrested in February 2003.

Fiah ayub had other plans against the United States. When Khalim was arrested, authorities found a list of two hundred U.S. companies among his papers. Three companies were highlighted. Officials later realized their officers all held high positions in the American Club in Singapore. Khalim had discussed plans to kidnap or assassinate them.

Another plot involved a marine attack using a small boat against U.S. naval vessels traveling along Sembawang on the northeast side of Singapore. Among Khalim's belongings, investigators found a topographical map with detailed markings showing targets and operational planning. Like the USS *Cole* attack in Yemen, the markings on the map identified a strategic "kill" zone where the channel was narrowest and the target ship would have no room to avoid colliding with a suicide mission. It planned on taking advantage of natural geography to hide the attack boat from radar and visual detection until the last minute.

The plots of *fiah ayub* were never carried out, apparently because the JI Singapore members couldn't implement them alone. They needed help from al-Qaeda, which directed their energies to a far more ambitious and spectacular plot instead.

When Hambali wanted help for his plots in Southeast Asia, he approached Khalid Shaikh Mohammed (KSM). Even as KSM was adding the final touches to his 9/11 plot, he was already thinking ahead. He sent two al-Qaeda operatives to Singapore to activate sleeper cells there, explosives expert Fathur Roman al-Ghozi, and an Arab codenamed "Sammy." Al-Ghozi by this point was highly experienced, thanks to the Christmas bombings in Indonesia and the Manila bombings that followed. The plan was to rig seven truck bombs with 3 tons of ammonium nitrate for a massive set of simultaneous bombings. Members of *fiah musa*, a second JI cell in Singapore, would do the surveillance of potential targets, set up the logistics of the attack, and then when all was prepared, they would leave the country while al-Qaeda suicide bombers arrived to implement the attack. One of the suicide bombers, Ahmed Sahagi, was already in Southeast Asia. The plan called for all seven of them to arrive in Singapore just one day before the actual attack. This is a familiar modus operandi of al-Qaeda attacks: locals do the setup work and experienced al-Qaeda operatives implement it.

For targets, "Sammy" suggested the U.S. and Israeli embassies as well as the U.S. naval base. The Singaporeans were asked for other suggestions. They volunteered the Australian and British High Commissions because they were close to the U.S. embassy as well as commercial buildings used by American companies.

When al-Ghozi arrived, he was introduced as "Mike the bombmaker." The Singaporeans didn't know whether he was Filipino or Indonesian. All they knew was that he was an explosives expert. Together, they worked out an elaborate system of code: none of the cell members were using their real names, and they devised substitute nouns for sensitive words, like *market* for Malaysia, *soup* for Singapore, *terminal* for Indonesia, *hotel* for the Philippines, and *book* for passport, and when talking about their targets, the Americans, they used *white meat.*[21]

The cell, acting as guides for their al-Qaeda agents, cased their potential targets and did video surveillance. "Sammy" held the camera for a shaky videotaping of the U.S. embassy and the British and Australian High Commissions. The two men also surveyed the Israeli embassy, the American Club, the AIA Tower, the Citibank building at 1 Raffles Link, and the Republic Plaza, which held the office of the Bank of America. They transferred the videotapes to a VCD, a video compact disk, which authorities later found. Its title was "Visiting Singapore Sightseeing."

Al-Ghozi estimated the group would need 21 tons of explosives to carry out the attacks. He knew that the Malaysian cell had already purchased 4 tons of ammonium nitrate through the company of JI member Yazid Sufaat, so he told the Singaporean members they would need to find 17 tons of ammonium nitrate. The man he specifically asked to find the explosives was twenty-nine-year-old Mohamed Ellias. Of Indian descent, the hefty-looking Ellias is good looking, with curly, shoulder-length black hair, and big black eyes that look like they would be more comfortable in a bar than in a mosque. Al-Ghozi gave Ellias money for his purchases: a total of $5,500 in two installments. Al-Ghozi also asked Ellias and his other cell members to reactivate an earlier plot against U.S. naval ships docking in Singapore. He asked them to survey the naval bases used by the U.S. military and to find a warehouse where the bombs could be created. Meanwhile, al-Ghozi returned to the Philippines to continue to look for explosives on his own for this and other plots.

Ellias found a friend who knew the dispatch clerk of a company that imported chemicals like ammonium nitrate into Singapore. He contacted the dispatch clerk, who talked to his manager. The manager asked Ellias to see him personally to place the order. All seemed on schedule, until officers of the ISD suddenly swooped in and arrested him.

The authorities were very, very lucky. The attacks could easily have been carried off and the amount of explosives that the plotters were in the midst of assembling would have made the Bali bombing look like child's play. The authorities succeeded because of gossip, luck, and a lot of hard work. It seemed that one of the JI members had bragged to friends, and that was all they needed. Shortly after the September 11 attacks, the ISD got a tip from a Singaporean resident who said that one of his friends claimed to know Osama bin Laden. Mohammad Aslam bin Yar Ali Khan, known as Aslam, a Singaporean of Pakistani descent, also said he fought against the Soviets in Afghanistan. The ISD put Aslam, a member of *fiah ayub*, under surveillance. Although he left the country suddenly on October 4, 2001, on a flight for Pakistan, the ISD continued surveillance of his friends. Among them was *fiah musa's* Ellias, one of Aslam's closest friends. So when Ellias and his fellow cell members met with al-Ghozi and his companion, it was under the surveillance of the ISD. The ISD also watched discreetly while the terror cell cased its potential targets.

Meantime, Aslam had gone on to Afghanistan from Pakistan and fought with al-Qaeda against the United States and the Northern Alliance. Sometime at the end of November, he was captured. When his captors searched him, they found a small notebook with names and numbers scrawled inside, including that of Hambali. That led U.S. investigators to Malaysia.[22]

On December 3, 2001, a newspaper published the first report about Aslam's capture. Afraid his co-conspirators would flee or go underground, the ISD stepped up its operations, which began five days later on December 8. The first wave of arrests began the next day: six people were detained, their houses and offices searched. There were more arrests on December 15, 16, and 17; finally, a total of twenty-three people were brought in on Christmas Eve. Of that first group, the ISD would find thirteen members of Jemaah Islamiyah, who were jailed for two years. Two others were released but not allowed to leave the country—they were fundraisers and supporters of the MILF. The rest were set free.

As Singapore was doing the police work leading to the second wave of arrests in September 2002, officials were debating an overall approach to the terrorist threat within its borders. One of the main conclusions is that Singapore can't solve this problem alone: it must have the help of its neighbors, many of them in various stages of denial. That denial is blasted by Lee Kuan Yew: "The first thing is to recognize that this is our problem, not an American problem. If you think they are only after the Americans, you're wrong. For Jemaah Islamiyah leaders like Ba'asyir and Hambali, they want to seize power here, in Indonesia, and if possible, the rest of Southeast Asia. We know from their Internet exchanges that there are 100 radical groups in Indonesia with a total of several thousand members. Even if you catch all the Bali bombers, that's only one cell—one of many cells."[23]

Singapore knows that its arrests could trigger religious and ethnic rivalries, jealousies and paranoia. "Extremism comes at the expense of inter-racial and inter-religious interaction. It excludes rather than includes," said Prime Minister Goh Chok Tong to Parliament.[24] "It results in the withdrawal of the practitioner into his own communal cocoon, and in a rejection of others who do not share his beliefs. When that happens, the other communities will not only keep their distance, but will also press for greater space of their own. This can break up our social cohesion."

On January 28, 2002, Goh called a meeting of religious and community leaders, asking them to cut across religious and racial divides and lay the foundation for an ongoing dialogue that would prevent paranoia between groups. At Kallang Theater, he asked his people not to discriminate or blame the Malay-Muslim community. He began by telling a story: "A Chinese senior civil servant told me that his mother, in her late sixties, called him immediately after news of the arrests broke out. She had discussed the issue with her friend, who proclaimed that henceforth, she would not get into the same lift with a Malay! Such a reaction is irrational, and of course, wrong. But it is not totally unexpected." He insisted that the government would not allow its Malay constituents to become "scapegoats." "For example, some Chinese companies may shun employing Malay-Muslims henceforth. This would be terribly wrong. It would only aggravate the matter and divide our society." At the same time, Prime Minister Goh asked the Malay-Muslims not to become overly sensitive because the government would institute measures that would target their community: the fact is, the police would be searching for Muslims. He told leaders of the complaint of a Malay friend who said that police at a roadblock were stopping only the cars of Malays. "The Malay friend felt that the police were now targeting Malays because of heightened suspicion of the community following the JI arrests. I told [him] that there was probably a logical, operational reason for this. The police were probably looking for a Malay suspect. As such, there was no reason for them to stop Chinese and Indian motorists. I gave him an example of the police looking for a stolen Honda car. They would not stop the Mercedes, BMWs, Suzukis or cars of other make," Goh told his audience. He then empowered the community leaders he was speaking to: "I do not want to alarm you, but it is prudent for us to work on the assumption that a bomb may go off somewhere in Singapore, someday . . . but if community leaders know one another well, and we have already developed confidence, friendship and trust among the different races and religions, then we will be able to move in together and contain the emotional ground reaction immediately."

In January 2003, the Ministry of Home Affairs published a comprehensive White Paper on Jemaah Islamiyah's activities and the government's response. That paper was distributed not only to Parliament and government leaders but also to the general public. The irony is what the government is asking from its people—to be "critical, evaluative and rational," in effect, to be Singaporean—is exactly the reasons many of the detained members of Jemaah Islamiyah listened to preachers like Abu Jibril, Hambali, and Ibrahim Maidin. They told independent teams of psychologists "they found it too stressful to be critical, evaluative and rational."[25] What they wanted, said psychologists who examined them, is a "no-fuss" path to heaven. Enlightenment values generate their own antithesis. It is almost impossible for rational observers to accept that fact. "They were weak," said Wong Kan Seng. "They have weak minds to be easily persuadable and convinced that this is the way to go." When authorities created psychological portraits of the imprisoned terrorists, two characteristics topped the list: high compliance and low assertiveness. Ironically, these are very much a part of the "Asian way."

The terrorists, in fact, mix Enlightenment values with their opposite—reason together with revelation. Al-Qaeda and Jemaah Islamiyah are learning organizations. "They adapt. They change," said Tony Tan, "and therefore, our security agencies will also have to change their strategy, build up better coordination. . . . They will attack when they think that they will be successful. It's an ongoing effort, and you have to keep at it all the time."

Fathur Roman al-Ghozi was arrested in Manila on January 15, 2002, as he was preparing to leave for Thailand. Based on his information, authorities recovered 1.2 tons of explosives that were slated for Singapore. He was sentenced to seventeen years in prison. On July 15, 2003, he and two Abu Sayyaf members in a high-security prison essentially walked out of jail with the help of Abu Ali, al-Ghozi's explosives supplier, who had been allowed to work as a janitor in the detention facility. President Arroyo said, "I acknowledge the serious problem of corruption in the police organization and I am making no excuses for it."[26]

CHAPTER 9

BALI: AL-QAEDA'S
PLAN B

On October 12, 2002, al-Qaeda pulled off its second-worst attack after
9/11, at the Sari Club in Bali, Indonesia, killing more than two hundred
people. Ironically, it was a Plan B for the terrorists, who had been forced
to abandon bigger plans for multiple bombings in Singapore. The full
story of the Bali bombing has never been told. Thanks to a lengthy confession by one of its early planners, an al-Qaeda operative codenamed
"Sammy"—until now, kept secret by authorities—a remarkable window
has opened not simply into the Bali plot, but much deeper—into the
entire training, organization, and planning of al-Qaeda both before and
after 9/11.

Mohammed Mansour Jabarah, a young Canadian of Iraqi descent, is a
reed-thin, tall boy with a moustache who moved to Canada from Kuwait
on August 16, 1994, but continued to maintain an Iraqi passport. At the
time he was twelve years old, with three brothers: the eldest, fifteen-year-
old Abdullah, thirteen-year-old Abdul Rahman, and the youngest, Yussef.
Mohammed would not be the only brother to join al-Qaeda; Abdul Rahman, just a year older, would actually go to the training camps in
Afghanistan first—less than a month before Mohammed did, in July
2000. (Eventually Abdul Rahman would hit the radar screen of law
enforcement agencies around the world, implicated in the Saudi Arabia
bombings of Western housing compounds in Riyadh on May 12, 2003.)[1]
Although the two middle brothers would turn to al-Qaeda, eldest

brother Abdullah would not. He is considered the black sheep of the family, corrupted by Western values. When a student at university, Abdullah did not get the chance to say good-bye to his brothers when they left for Afghanistan, because he was ostracized for choosing to live with his girlfriend. Today, he freely admits that he likes his alcohol and is surrounded by many women. Rakish and relaxed, he and his friends often smoke pot in the garage of his family home in Canada.

"They made their choices," said Abdullah Jabarah, "I made mine."[2] He ended up with the women, "and they got to pray at the mosque." He said maybe they couldn't adjust to Canada, although "you'd think I would be the one with the hard time adjusting being the oldest. I was fifteen." Now because it's widely known that his two brothers are international terrorists, he is thinking of changing his family name. "They didn't think about me and the impact it would have on me and my parents," he said, refusing to speak specifically about each brother except that "between Abdul Rahman and Mohammed, Mohammed is a crazy bastard. Fucking mad."[3]

It is through Mohammed Jabarah that we get the clearest sense of how al-Qaeda's University of Terror works—partly because he is young. He has an impressionable mind and a great memory, and he is cooperating with authorities. Through him, you see—much like in large university campuses—how classmates meet each other, how they identify faces by whom they hang out with and what class they graduated with, how getting their first assignments is much like getting a first job, and how the alumni network remains ready to be activated for future attacks. To his interrogators at the Federal Bureau of Immigration and the Canadian Security Intelligence Service, he provided one of the most comprehensive portraits of al-Qaeda's manipulative recruitment process, training, and deployment.

Reading Mohammed's files, I get a glimmer of understanding of al-Qaeda's appeal and how it works on young minds, reminding me of my college years at Princeton. For someone who grew up by the boardwalk in Seaside Heights, New Jersey, I spent high school blissfully unaware of many things, including what JAP meant. Middle class and Asian, I thought—a shortened version of Japanese, maybe? Then I went to Princeton and learned about a world I could never have conceptualized—where everyone knows JAP means "Jewish American princess." Princeton introduced me to a whole new socioeconomic hierarchy that

didn't exist for the people I grew up with off Exit 88 of the Garden
State Parkway.

Princeton changed and molded me. It taught me an entire worldview: ideals, methods of analysis, frames of references, modes of attacking and solving problems. Socially, I saw the difference in the way
people dressed, the way they walked, the way they spoke. It changed
the way I dressed, the way I walked, the way I spoke. Going there
opened my eyes, empowered me, made me realize one person working
with like-minded individuals can change the world. Princeton made me
want to change the world.

Above all, there was the Honor Code, which each Princetonian
writes on every single term paper, every single exam: one single sentence that says you have not cheated and promise to turn in anyone
who does—a strict, idealistic way of making university students behave.
Leave the students alone in a room, hand out test papers, and put them
on their honor. It's brilliant in part because it uses peer pressure. Even if
you tried to cheat, can you be sure everyone in the room will cheat
with you by not turning you in? Even worse, are you willing to compromise not just your honor but everyone else's? You're part of a tradition
that dates back hundreds of years, and you can't let the institution,
your friends, and your family down. It's wonderful in its simplicity, and
even during my last exams my senior year, it was always with a feeling
of pride that I wrote that sentence and signed my name: "I pledge on
my honor that I have not violated the principles of the Honor Code."
With me, it left behind the idea that *honor* means something important,
that it is something we all must aspire to—and that not everyone
makes it.

That feeling of exclusivity, of self-discipline, of being part of an
elite who see a vision for a better world, of a tradition for excellence
you must maintain: all that is exactly what al-Qaeda creates in its
global network: from the schools known as *pesantrens* and madrassas,
which begin to train young minds of four or five year olds, to the training camps hidden around the world, to the terrorist cells that carry out
its plots. Certainly, al-Qaeda members want to change the world. Young
Muslim men dream of joining al-Qaeda, of being trained to think and
act like al-Qaeda, of standing up to oppression. Malaysia's prime minister, Mahathir Mohamad, understands the appeal: "The reason why
Osama Bin Laden has been able to recruit people to his movement is

because there is a lot of disillusionment on the part of Muslims because their governments seem to be pussy-footing and not doing anything to defend the Muslims, to stop this oppression of Muslims, the massacre of Muslims, the attack against so many Muslim countries."[4]

Al-Qaeda has been compared to a corporation that franchises terrorism, but it operates at a far deeper level than that by molding young minds at extremely formative stages and providing an ideological cause that includes something Princeton never demanded from its students: self-sacrifice for a greater cause and a guaranteed place in heaven. Instead of an Honor Code, al-Qaeda demanded the *ba'yat*—the oath of loyalty.

It gives scholarships for students who can't afford to attend, and it creates fellowships and grants for other like-minded groups that have special projects they need help with. "Any group who has the ability and the people will send a representative to Afghanistan to meet Osama Bin Laden and pitch a plan for Osama Bin Laden to support," describes an FBI document.[5] In the process, it co-opts those groups into its global agenda—like the Jemaah Islamiyah cell that pulled off the Bali bombing.

Mohammed Mansour Jabarah's recruitment began during his high school summers, in the Middle East. After the family moved to Canada in 1994, both brothers returned to Kuwait during their summer vacations. While there, Mohammed often visited his Islamic teacher, Sulaiman Abu Ghaith, a plump, full-bearded man with a white turban who later, after the September 11 attacks, became al-Qaeda's spokesman, saying things like, "The Americans must know that the storm of Airplanes will not stop, God willing, and there are thousands of young people who are as keen about death as Americans are about life."[6] Back in the mid-1990s, he was doing his part to find young recruits, paying more attention to the Jabarah brothers as they grew older, in particular, fanning young Mohammed's anger by showing him training videos from what he called "the jihad in Bosnia" and videotaped speeches of Abdullah Azzam, Osama bin Laden's mentor.[7] In 1999, Mohammed fastened on the violence in Chechnya, surfing websites and poring over videotapes of the fighting there, most propaganda tapes created by al-Qaeda and given to him by Abu Ghaith. When he returned to

Canada after that summer, age sixteen, Mohammed raised money from friends and neighbors on at least three occasions and transferred more than $3,500 to Abu Ghaith.

The next summer in July 2000, Mohammed's brother Abdul Rahman left for Afghanistan. About a month later, Mohammed met Abu Ghaith in Kuwait, who then paid the younger Jabarah's fare to Karachi, Pakistan. Using a series of guides, Mohammed went from Karachi to Peshawar and then on to a five-hour hike through the mountains to wind up at the town of Torkham, on the border between Pakistan and Afghanistan. There the two brothers met and waited about a week. Since the camp wasn't ready yet, they joined a group of eighteen men at the Sheik Shaheed Abu Yahya training camp, about 30 kilometers (18.6 miles) north of Kabul, Afghanistan. This was *Tahziri*, meaning the "beginning" or the "preparation"—the first course for every Muslim student who wants to go on a jihad. Weapons training included handling antitank and antiaircraft weapons like the Sam-7 and stinger missiles. The brothers were taught how to set explosives and use grenades and mines. The course had a bonus: a two-week program on topography and navigation.

The days were long and grueling. Trainees woke up before sunrise to pray, followed by two hours of physical training: one hour of jogging and an hour of calisthenics. After that, they showered and had breakfast. Then they were divided into training groups for classroom work, which lasted about an hour, before a ten-minute break. They came back to class for another hour, after which they could take a forty-five-minute nap. They woke up for noon prayers, followed by an hour's lecture on the Koran. Then it was time for lunch, after which each group did its assigned chores for the maintenance of the camp until afternoon prayers. The rest of the afternoon was spent on "practical military training"—weapons training, live fire exercises, and explosives training. After dinner came a lecture on the virtues of jihad and its finer points, which lasted until around 8:00 to 8:30 P.M., the time for evening prayers. Only after that could they rest, but even sleep was interrupted by shifts on guard duty for the camp. It was and is a rigorous schedule that instills discipline and the ideology of radical Islam in an environment of brotherly camaraderie. The course lasts for sixty continuous days, during which students are given an entire philosophy of living life and are challenged mentally, spiritually, and physically.

After trainees finished the introductory course, at least in 2000 and

2001, they were given a choice: volunteer and fight with the Taliban against the Northern Alliance, go through more training, or return home. The American students arrested in Lackawanna, New York, for example, had decided to go back home. The Jabarah brothers chose to get more training, open to only the "top-rated candidates on the Basic course" in urban guerrilla warfare.[8] Lasting two and a half months, the course teaches students how to organize cells and gives them advanced weapons training and physical combat techniques, as well as honing their analysis of the risks involved in attacking a building. When Mohammed and Abdul Rahman finished this course, they decided it was time to try out their newly acquired skills by fighting with the Taliban.

Mohammed spent two weeks at the front before returning to Kabul for a course on the Koran, but in early 2001, he was diagnosed with hepatitis by al-Qaeda's second in command, Dr. Ayman al-Zawahiri, and was bedridden for about a month. That January, his brother left Afghanistan to see their parents in Canada and then attend the hajj in Saudi Arabia. He returned to Canada in the spring of 2001.

By that time, Mohammed was taking another advanced course with about forty men—the guerrilla mountain warfare course, lasting another two and a half months. Recruits were taught theories of guerrilla warfare, ambush, and communications skills. The training took place at the Al-Farouq training camp, about 75 kilometers from Kandahar. Mohammed noticed several "white guys"—Westerners—taking his course: two blond Australians about twenty-five and thirty years old, a black twenty-year-old Brit named Abbas, a thirty-year-old Jamaican named Khalid, and a black Frenchman. These recruits, like the Jabarah brothers, were becoming increasingly valuable to al-Qaeda because they defied the expectations and profiles of international law enforcement agencies.

After he finished this course, Mohammed returned to Kandahar and stayed at a guesthouse next to the Arabic Islamic Institute. His brother Abdul Rahman returned to Afghanistan, staying with Mohammed briefly at the guest house. Around the end of June 2001, Abu Ghaith came to visit Mohammed and "popped the question": Did he want to become a member of al-Qaeda? Abu Ghaith told him "this decision could only be made by him but that it might be a good idea to join."[9] It was much like becoming a "made man" in the mafia. Only the best recruits were invited.

At that point, Mohammed had already met twice with Osama bin Laden. (He would meet him two more times.) It had taken some doing. The first meeting Mohammed arranged through personal connections, finagling to get close to bin Laden's secretary, a Yemeni named Bashir. Most of their conversation that first time centered on developments in Kuwait. The second meeting happened just a short while before Abu Ghaith recommended Mohammed join al-Qaeda. At the end of Mohammed's mountain warfare course, Abu Ghaith and Osama bin Laden came to the camp "to congratulate the course graduates."[10] Abu Ghaith asked the graduates to support Osama bin Laden, who then gave a graduation speech and attempted to rally new recruits by telling them "hits" would be coming soon against the United States, " 'hits' severe enough to make the United States forget about Vietnam."[11] It was just two months before 9/11. Mohammed, who had originally wanted to get training so he could fight the jihad in Chechnya or in the Middle East, began to rethink his plans. When he heard bin Laden speak that June, he was tempted to join al-Qaeda and focus on a broader set of enemies.

It was a momentous decision, and Mohammed did not make it quickly. In July, Abu Ghaith visited him in the guest house in Kandahar and talked further about it. In mid-July, Mohammed took an additional one-week advanced course for snipers at the al-Qaeda camp at the Kandahar airport. Jabarah excelled at the course, placing first at the competition held at its conclusion. After that, Osama bin Laden invited Mohammed and the other trainees to his house in Kandahar. In their third meeting, Mohammed watched as bin Laden showed videotapes from the Arabic network Al-Jazeera, which conducted a poll that showed Osama bin Laden was more popular than the United States. Bin Laden looked proud while he was screening the tape.[12]

By that point, both Abu Ghaith and Mohammed had been selected to take part in an elite course for potential bodyguards for bin Laden. The fact they were asked to attend the course is considered a great honor among the Muslim fighters in the camps. The course teaches precision shooting with limited ammunition and tests and hones the student's reaction times. Both men took the course, but neither got the job. Mohammed was offered a spot as a trainer at the Al-Farouq camp, but he turned it down because "he wanted to fight, not train."[13]

Not everyone who attended al-Qaeda's camps became a member.

The camps were part of a weeding-out process, and only the best of the best were invited to join. Mohammed estimated al-Qaeda had about 3,000 to 4,000 members, of whom perhaps 300 to 400 were leaders, each handling up to six cell members. As a student, Mohammed spent much time reading books about his passion (jihad and al-Qaeda), asking questions, identifying who did what and who was calling the shots, what happened when—trying to piece together the history of the organization. He devoured its folklore, the gossip about the men, and their dealings and sometimes double-dealings around the camps.

Al-Qaeda was constantly vigilant and paranoid about double agents and had a continuous screening process. During the time Mohammed was there, several people were being interrogated on suspicions they were spies: an Omani, an Afghan, three Kurds, and a Jordanian. After one particularly grueling interrogation session, the Jordanian committed suicide. It is little wonder that intelligence agencies have struggled to infiltrate bin Laden's organization.

Al-Qaeda's Afghan camp was a perfect jihad university, complete with student dorms, a guest house, a media house to get information out, and its training camps. Mohammed met several second-generation al-Qaeda members: Asad, one of the sons of blind Egyptian sheikh Omar Abdul Rahman, and three of Osama bin Laden's sons, including Saad, rumored to be in training to follow in his father's footsteps. Saad took the mountain warfare training course with Mohammed, who asked the younger bin Laden many questions about common acquaintances. Through Saad, Mohammed learned a man he met at a Libyan guest house in Kabul was Anas al-Liby, who was teaching courses on "surveillance, interception and internal security."[14] A member of al-Qaeda from the days it was based in Sudan, he had one other special task. Because he was tall and bore a resemblance to bin Laden, Saad told Mohammed that Anas al-Liby was sometimes used as a decoy when bin Laden was traveling.

At the Islamic Institute in Kandahar, Mohammed ran twice into a wild-haired man he was told was a member of al-Qaeda. Known as Abd al-Jabbar, he was good friends with a black al-Qaeda member Mohammed knew as Sawari.[15] Much later, Mohammed would find out Abd al-Jabbar was actually Richard Reid, the shoe bomber who tried to ignite explosives while on a transatlantic flight, and that his friend Sawari was none other than Zacarias Moussaoui, linked to the JI cell in

Southeast Asia, now on trial in the United States for September 11–related charges.

Mohammed also met four of the September 11 hijackers in a guest house in Kandahar around March 2001. What impressed him most was that one of the men, Ahmed al-Haznawi, "was very devout and could recite the entire Koran from memory."[16] Al-Haznawi would hijack Flight 93, the plane that crash-landed in Pennsylvania. Mohammed said he was later told by an al-Qaeda member who trained with the hijackers that the plane was headed for the White House. (One of the 9/11 planners, Ramzi bin al-Shibh, however, told authorities it was headed for Capitol Hill.)

Another hijacker was Abdulaziz Alomari, who would be on the plane that crashed into the North Tower of the World Trade Center; the others were Khalid al-Midhar and Salem al-Hazmi, who would be on Flight 77 when it crashed into the Pentagon. Al-Haznawi and Alomari gave motivational speeches in Kandahar, while al-Hazmi often rode a motorcycle around town. In a sign of how al-Qaeda maintains security, Mohammed knew these men under their aliases and didn't find out their real names until after he saw their pictures on the news.

Mohammed learned more details about the planning for 9/11 from an al-Qaeda operative named Ahmed Sahagi, a twenty-five-year-old Saudi national and former bodyguard of Osama bin Laden, later assigned to work with Mohammed. Sahagi told Mohammed he attended an "operational training course" with about twenty to thirty people, a group trained for two years to carry out the September 11 attacks. Ahmed said no one knew exactly what they were training for, only that it was an operation in the United States and that the training included hand-to-hand combat. To show how small and interconnected al-Qaeda's operations were, one of their two trainers, Egyptian Hamza Zubair, taught Mohammed his mountain warfare course.[17]

Two of the hijackers as well as Moussaoui subsequently stayed in an apartment in Malaysia owned by Hambali's deputy, Yazid Sufaat. The key link of the Southeast Asian JI cell to the September 11 hijackers was Mohammed's agent-handler, Khalid Shaikh Mohammed, KSM.

Mohammed pieced together much of the history and interpersonal connections of the men who ran al-Qaeda. For example, Mohammed asked about Ramzi Yousef and found out from one of al-Qaeda's top leaders that KSM was "very close to Ramzi Yousef and a person named Azmurai" who was described by KSM as "extremely tough and brave."[18]

Osama Azmurai—spelled by Philippine authorities as "Osmurai" in intelligence documents—was the pseudonym used by Afghan Wali Khan Amin Shah, one of the operatives from the al-Qaeda cell busted in Manila in 1995. Mohammed said KSM told him that "Yousef and Azmarai were good with explosives, and they were both arrested by the US." KSM admitted he "was in Asia with Yousef and Azmarai during a plot to bomb airliners."[19]

Yousef left another legacy: Mohammed told his interrogators that students at the Darunta camp in Afghanistan were taught how to deal with explosives, poisons, and electronics, including how to use a Casio watch as a timer for a bomb—the technique created and perfected by Ramzi Yousef to avoid airport security, which he used effectively on a Philippine Airlines plane in 1994. Years after he was arrested and imprisoned, Yousef's terrorist tricks were still being taught in al-Qaeda's university of terror.

Mohammed knew KSM's brother, Zahid Sheikh Mohammed, who worked with Islamic charities in Peshawar. Mohammed also said he often saw KSM and Abdul Rasul Sayyaf together and that they were good friends. Again, Abdul Rasul Sayyaf was another link between the dozens of JI leaders in Southeast Asia, including Abu Sayyaf founder Abdurajak Janjalani and most of the JI leaders from Indonesia, who were trained in Afghanistan under Sayyaf's tutelage and patronage.[20] Although Sayyaf has never been labeled a member of al-Qaeda, these personal links are clear. In fact, two days before the 9/11 attacks, it was his connections as a part of the Northern Alliance that assisted two Arabs pretending to be journalists to cut through the security of Northern Alliance leader Ahmed Shah Massoud and successfully assassinate the sole moderate leader who had long fought the Taliban and al-Qaeda. Sayyaf is still dogged by suspicions he helped assassinate Massoud, with the support of al-Qaeda and the Taliban,[21] a charge Sayyaf has consistently denied.

These were the events that interested Mohammed, and he asked questions of nearly everyone he came into contact with—like one of his first trainers, Abu Omar, who was in Sudan with Osama bin Laden, and helped explain al-Qaeda's early years. After the Soviet occupation ended, bin Laden returned to Saudi Arabia, where he continued to try to refine the global connections they had formed. When Iraq invaded Kuwait and Saudi Arabia needed help, bin Laden offered the support of his "Afghan Arabs." Yet instead of relying on Muslims, the Saudis turned to the Americans. After the Gulf War, bin Laden was furious at the continued presence of American troops. He asked Muslim scholars to issue a fatwah, but they were afraid, and he felt marginalized. Eventually, he left Saudi Arabia and settled in the Sudan. That was when Mohammed believed bin Laden started actively targeting America and crafting his plan for a global jihad. Bin Laden began urging Muslims not just to concentrate on their own domestic problems with individual governments, stating, "Like an octopus with many arms, hitting the arms is not productive. The only effective way to kill the octopus is to attack its head"— which bin Laden identified as the United States.[22]

Mohammed heard talk about early operations and the lessons they taught: like al-Qaeda's failed assassination plots against U.S. president Bill Clinton, Philippine president Fidel Ramos, Egyptian president Hosni Mubarak—all of which helped create a special course on assassination techniques taught to advanced members. Another operation that was dissected in front of Mohammed was the 1998 bombings of the U.S. embassies in Kenya and Tanzania. Mohammed had met an al-Qaeda member named Osama al Kini in one of the guest houses in Kandahar. Later, he was told al Kini had taught the truck driver in the Nairobi bombing, a Saudi named Azzam, how to drive. Abdullah Azzam drove the truck in the actual operation, but something went wrong because there were supposed to be two "martyrs." Later, bin Laden himself would tell Mohammed in a one-on-one meeting that the other bomber was supposed to be Mohammed Rashed al-'Owhali, who was also riding in the truck. "He was supposed to fight with a guard and open the gate and have Azzam drive into the compound," bin Laden said. Al-'Owhali forgot his pistol inside the truck, and when he realized the bomb was going to explode away from its target, he ran. Later, Mohammed said he heard the "guy who did not die was arrested by the U.S."[23] as, in fact, happened on August 12, 1998.[24]

Mohammed learned al-Qaeda was run by a "Shura Council"—a leadership council that has been replicated by al-Qaeda–linked groups like Jemaah Islamiyah. While Mohammed was in the training camps, al-Qaeda's Shura Council was made up of Osama bin Laden; his deputy, the Egyptian Dr. Ayman al-Zawahiri; Saif al-Adel, in charge of the security committee; Mohammed Atef, head of the military committee; Abu Mohammed al-Masri; Sheikh Sayid and Abu Hafs al-Mauritania, both in charge of religious teaching; and KSM, who ran the Media House. After the death of Atef, KSM would become the head of the military committee.

There were internal problems, as there are in all organizations. Mohammed learned about rivalry within al-Qaeda. "The Egyptians were the ones who started al-Qaeda with Osama bin Laden, and Osama bin Laden was extremely loyal to them. . . . Many were jealous of the Egyptians' important and expanding role in al-Qaeda," Mohammed told the FBI.[25] He told stories of bin Laden's loyalty: how in 1998 when bin Laden heard criticism against his military chief, Atef (a.k.a. Abu Hafs), he called operatives together and began speaking about the Prophet Mohammed, explaining that the only person who stayed with the Prophet during the most challenging times was Abu Bakr. Bin Laden then went on to compare Abu Hafs to Abu Bakr. "Abu Hafs [Atef] knew of Jihad," said bin Laden, "before most of you were even born." Atef began to cry, Mohammed said. Then bin Laden told his fighters he no longer wanted to hear "negative talk about Abu Hafs." Abu Hafs was an Egyptian military commander.

Mohammed learned that after 9/11, the camp where he took the guerrilla mountain warfare course was completely destroyed, but he was also told that al-Qaeda had evacuated all its people by the time the U.S. air strikes began less than a month after 9/11. Mohammed told his interrogators that al-Qaeda had planned to reorganize after the airstrikes in Afghanistan. "The plan was for al-Qaeda people to stay in Afghanistan," Mohammed said, "go to Tajikistan, Iran or Pakistan to regroup, or to return to their home countries and wait for a call."[26]

Mohammed's own terrorism work and the roots of the Bali plot began shortly after he finished his last course—about the time al-Qaeda was putting together the last touches of 9/11. In July 2001, Mohammed asked for a private meeting with bin Laden.

"I want to join al-Qaeda," Mohammed told bin Laden.[27]

"Well. What courses did you take, and how did you do in them?" bin Laden asked. Mohammed reviewed his record, noting that he ranked first in competitions like the one for his sniper course. "You've done well," said bin Laden. "It's an impressive record."

"But I bring more advantages for al-Qaeda," Mohammed said. "I speak excellent English, and I have a clean Canadian passport. I can travel anywhere, and merge into Western cities better than others who work for you."

"But are you ready to fight the enemies of Allah wherever they are? Are you ready to strike fear into the heart of infidels? Can you declare war on Americans and Jews everywhere?"

"Yes."

"Are you ready to swear a *bay'at* to me?"

"Yes," he told bin Laden.

Immediately, he swore the oath.

As they finished, bin Laden said, "By God's will, the coming hits will change all the borders, and all the borders will be redrawn."

Then he told Mohammed to go meet with "Mohammed the Pakistani" for instructions and money for an operation. Mohammed had graduated and was being sent to none other than KSM.

In the first week of August 2001, Mohammed traveled to Karachi, Pakistan, to meet his agent-handler. Mohammed checked into the Embassy Hotel and called KSM, who came to the hotel and picked him up. They drove to KSM's Karachi apartment. KSM had been expecting him and immediately asked about his English-speaking skills. When they got to the apartment, there was another al-Qaeda agent already there, introduced to him as Ahmed.

Ahmed seemed to be about twenty-five or twenty-six years old. He carried a Saudi passport and spoke with a Saudi accent. Ahmed said he was married and had three children, and his family was with him in Afghanistan. From the way he behaved, Mohammed deduced that Ahmed grew up in wealthy surroundings. A veteran al-Qaeda member, Ahmed Sahagi would become Mohammed's partner, but at that point, no explanation was given for his presence. The two men lived with KSM in his Karachi apartment for three weeks. During that time, KSM taught them "how to travel on trains and buses, how to book travel tickets, and how to conform to local customs when traveling."[28]

"When you first travel to a city, on the immigration form—the arrival documents, list a five-star hotel. When you get there, spend only one night at this hotel, then switch to a cheaper one," KSM told them. "You can use a telephone book to find your second hotel, and you should walk outside, and call from a public telephone to make your reservations. Also, when you leave that five-star hotel, make sure you don't take a taxi so there is no record of your trip."

"In fact," KSM added, "use mass transit—buses and trains—particularly when crossing borders. Security is not as vigilant as in airports. But you should never take taxis from your hotel because what we've found is that taxi drivers are often working for intelligence services. Avoid areas like mosques and Islamic centers—the places authorities would be watching looking for people like us. We must break the stereotypes they have.

"When you get to your next hotel, get a tourist guide book. It will have information on how to get around, and it will list potential targets. The guide book will have the addresses of the United States and Israeli embassies, which you should note down as target potentials. Take down the addresses of the American and Israeli airlines in that city." They too were potential targets for terrorist attacks.

KSM explained how to contact other cell members: "The safest way possible. Try not to use cell phones. Public phones are safer. Once you're in place, find a business center in a hotel or Internet café. You contact the other members of the group by e-mail and wait for a response. Use the code words for whatever cell you're working with, but after that first contact, arrange to have your meetings in public places, like shopping malls. Be careful to understand and merge with local customs. Look at how others dress, whether they wear a beard or not, and imitate what they are doing. Above all, don't call attention to yourselves."

After about three weeks, within days of 9/11, KSM told Mohammed to get ready to go to Malaysia to meet with local members "who were planning an operation against the U.S. and Israeli Embassies in the Philippines."[29] Mohammed would "be the go-between for the local Southeast Asian operatives and al-Qaeda," and his "job would be to provide money for a suicide operation in the Philippines."[30]

"Work with them," KSM told Mohammed. "If they need anything, especially money, advise me, and I'll make sure you get what they ask for."

Before leaving Pakistan, KSM brought Mohammed to Hambali's apartment in Karachi. It was time for the two to meet. Mohammed had seen Hambali once before at the Islamic Institute in Kandahar, and he also remembered seeing Hambali driving a white Toyota Corolla. He knew Hambali was a senior member of the group operating in Asia. At his apartment, Hambali began giving him more details about the planned operations. He told Mohammed he would meet with three men—Mahmoud, Azzam, and Saad—and he gave him a phone number to call once he arrived in Kuala Lumpur. The three men would turn out to be Hambali's deputy for Mantiqi 1: Faiz bin Abu Bakar Bafana (Mahmoud); Jemaah Islamiyah's finance chief, Zulkifli Marzuki (Azzam); and Indonesian Fathur Roman al-Ghozi (Saad), in charge of the actual bombing operations.

One day after that meeting, KSM told Mohammed to make sure he left Pakistan by Tuesday, September 11. Given the secrecy shrouding much of the al-Qaeda leaders' movements and the repeated messages from bin Laden warning of more attacks, Mohammed deduced that something big would happen on 9/11. KSM and Mohammed bought a ticket on a plane leaving Karachi for Hong Kong and on to Kuala Lumpur, Malaysia, after the layover. KSM told Mohammed someone else would join him in Kuala Lumpur and that more details would be e-mailed to him after his arrival. The e-mail address used by Mohammed and KSM was silver_crack2002@yahoo.com using the password "hotmail." Both men knew the password so both could access it. Mohammed set up another e-mail account for communication with Hambali: Honda_civic12 @yahoo.com with the password "frfoosh." After these details were worked out, KSM and Mohammed went to a bank in Karachi and withdrew $40,000. He gave Mohammed $10,000 for his expenses.

Mohammed arrived in Hong Kong in time to watch the airplanes crashing into the World Trade Center. He suspected KSM was behind the attacks, and he was right. (KSM, in his apartment in Pakistan, had several video machines set to record the coverage in anticipation of the attacks.) Mohammed was simultaneously elated and daunted, but he went on to his designated meeting point in Malaysia. When he landed at the capital, Mohammed went to a hotel in the Masjid India section of the city, which is where Hambali told him to stay.

When he opened his e-mail at an Internet café, he found a message from KSM telling him his "friend" was already there. Confused, Mohammed sent back a reply asking KSM whom he was referring to, but before he could receive a response, he thought it might be the Ahmed he had just spent three weeks with. Curious, Mohammed checked nearby hotels and found Ahmed Sahagi, now designated a suicide bomber in the operation. Ahmed had just arrived from Pakistan and told Mohammed the

9/11 attacks were carried out by al-Qaeda; indeed, he was with KSM when the attacks actually happened. KSM was at first disappointed, but soon turned happy when the buildings finally "came down."[31]

After a week together, Mohammed called Zulkifli Marzuki and set a time to meet. Zulkifli was about thirty-five years old and owned a home security outfit, where the meeting was held. Mohammed asked about Faiz, who was on a business trip, and al-Ghozi, who "was in the mountains training with the rebels."[32]

"I'm here to help you," Mohammed told Zulkifli. "If you need anything, let me know."

"Thank you. We're glad you're here. We'll meet with Faiz as soon as he returns," said Zulkifli.

After another week, the meeting was set—this time at a McDonald's in Kuala Lumpur.

"I received the $10,000," Faiz said, leaving Mohammed to surmise its source. "How is Mukhtar [KSM] doing?"

KSM had told Mohammed money had already been sent to their local members. It was obvious that Faiz knew KSM personally and the $10,000 must have come from him.

"In order to get this operation going," Faiz continued, "we need to get in touch with Saad [Fathur Roman al-Ghozi] because he is the one who will find the explosives. May Allah protect him." Faiz then told Mohammed and Ahmed to go to the Philippines to meet with al-Ghozi. "I'll ask him to e-mail you after you arrive in Manila."

At the beginning of October 2001, Mohammed and Ahmed traveled to Manila and checked in at the Horizon Hotel. Overlooking Manila Bay, it sits at a key juncture between Manila and the financial capital, Makati. After a few days, Mohammed received an e-mail from al-Ghozi giving a phone number for Mohammed to call. Within two days, al-Ghozi, acting like a tourist, came to the hotel to meet the two al-Qaeda operatives. Mohammed said al-Ghozi spoke fluent Arabic, and he noted al-Ghozi's al-Qaeda training in explosives.

"I have three hundred kilograms of TNT," said al-Ghozi. "I need a little more time and money before I can figure out exactly how much we need. I know I want at least four tons of explosives."

Al-Ghozi took Mohammed and Ahmed to see the potential targets: the U.S. embassy on Roxas Boulevard in Manila and the Israeli embassy in Makati. "We have a problem with the U.S. embassy," al-Ghozi explained. "It's not a good target. It's set back too far from the road so a truck bomb wouldn't be enough. Maybe we could get a plane to crash into the building. In order to make sure we succeed, we would need at least two operations, but even then I'm still not sure it would be successful. Can we go to Malaysia"—the leadership base—"and talk about what this means?"

Ten days later, Mohammed and Ahmed returned to Kuala Lumpur. Separately, al-Ghozi traveled to the Malaysian capital. Again through e-mail, Zulkifli arranged for a meeting between the plotters. They met at McDonald's at the Pertama Complex mall and then drove around in a van. Using a combination of Arabic, English, and Malay, al-Ghozi explained that the Philippine targets "were not good."[33] Faiz suggested an alternative plan, asking Mohammed and al-Ghozi to travel to Singapore "to videotape targets."

Mohammed and al-Ghozi left Kuala Lumpur and made their way to Singapore separately. Ahmed stayed behind. Mohammed boarded a bus two days after the meeting, and when he arrived in front of the Royale Hotel, al-Ghozi met him there with three Singaporean JI cell members using the pseudonyms Simpson, Max, and Alex. The arrival of the al-Qaeda operative the Singaporeans knew as "Sammy" and the Indonesian known as "Mike the bomb-maker" activated Jemaah Islamiyah's sleeper cell in Singapore. Targets were videotaped and, later in Kuala Lumpur, the leaders of the plot chose seven targets: "the American Embassy, the British Embassy, the British Consulate, the Israeli Embassy, The American Club, the Bank of America and the U.S. Naval Ship Yards."[34] Al-Ghozi estimated they would need an additional 17 tons of explosives, costing approximately $160,000. Al-Ghozi returned to Manila to try to find a source for the explosives.

In the meantime, Mohammed returned to Malaysia where, to save money, he and Ahmed rented an apartment in November. Faiz had told him Malaysia "was their economic base"[35] and so should not be considered a target. Then Mohammed called KSM to ask for money, but his home phone was answered by KSM's secretary, who told him KSM had returned to Afghanistan. Mohammed asked for $50,000 for the Singapore operation. After a week, he received an e-mail telling him to call a phone number in Malaysia and tell the person who answered that he "was from the side of Iqbal."[36] The phone number in Malaysia was answered by a man named Yousef, who met with Mohammed at City

One Plaza on November 7, 2001. Yousef came in traditional Afghan tunic and pants, and Mohammed thought he looked Pakistani and was worried because he seemed unconcerned about security. Mohammed said he believed Yousef was al-Qaeda's money man in Malaysia. Yousef said he had received $30,000 for Mohammed. At the mall that day, he gave $10,000 to Mohammed. Two days later, they met again and exchanged another $10,000, followed a couple of days later by another exchange of the final $10,000. Each time, the money was handed to Mohammed in an envelope: $100 bills tied by a rubber band. Mohammed received the money the Jemaah Islamiyah asked for and immediately contacted Zulkifli and handed him the money.

The plan "was to smuggle explosives from the Philippines by ship to Indonesia and then from Indonesia to Singapore for the operation,"[37] but this could take up to a year and a half if they were to do it safely. In short, Plan A, as devised by KSM well in advance of 9/11, at least in general terms, would not have come to pass until roughly spring 2003, if it had stayed on track. But then came Plan B.

Sometime in mid-December, Hambali returned to Kuala Lumpur from Afghanistan with news that Mohammed Atef, al-Qaeda's military chief, had been killed in the U.S. airstrikes. Furthermore, two days before his death, Atef had told Hambali to push the timetable forward for the Asian attacks. If the explosives are in the Philippines, he said, then attack targets there. Hambali told Mohammed to contact al-Ghozi and "cancel the Singapore operation and pick targets in the Philippines."[38]

"If the U.S. and Israeli embassies are not good targets," Hambali said, "then pick better ones, but let's do this in the Philippines."

A week later, Mohammed opened his in box to find an e-mail from Zulkifli titled "problem." Hambali's deputy, Faiz, had been arrested in Singapore while he was visiting his mother. The Singapore plans, already abandoned, would very likely have been compromised anyway. Zulkifli told Mohammed to get out of Malaysia and flee to Bangkok.

The crackdown had begun in Singapore and Malaysia. The word among the operatives in the area was get to Thailand as quickly as possible. Mohammed and Ahmed were among the first to do so. After about two weeks, Mohammed received another e-mail from Zulkifli giving him a phone number to call in Bangkok. When Mohammed called, he found himself speaking with Hambali. When they met at the Chaleena Hotel in Bangkok the next morning, Hambali told Mohammed to leave Southeast Asia "before his picture showed up in the news."[39]

The last time Mohammed saw Hambali was in mid-January 2002, in southern Thailand: "At that time, Hambali discussed carrying out attacks with his group. His plan was to conduct small bombings in bars, cafés or nightclubs frequented by Westerners in Thailand, Malaysia, Singapore, Philippines and Indonesia. Hambali also stated that he had one ton of PETN explosive in Indonesia."[40] It was a switch to so-called soft targets.

Mohammed Jabarah was arrested in March 2002, part of the post-9/11 crackdown. The Bali plot went forward without him.

Thanks to Indonesian police work in the wake of the Bali bombing, the rest of the story can now be told in considerable detail. Before fleeing to Thailand, Hambali had had a meeting with the leaders of Mantiqi 1 in Johor Bahru. Covering Malaysia, Singapore, and southern Thailand, Mantiqi 1 was the most ambitious of Jemaah Islamiyah's cells in terms of terror plots. Jemaah Islamiyah developed plans on its own, and when Hambali felt his team was ready, he asked al-Qaeda for help, as he had done for Jabarah. Four days after the arrest of Faiz, Hambali was furious and told his leaders to go ahead and push forward despite these setbacks. Then he took his key leaders and went to Thailand to work out Plan B.

In February 2002, Hambali gathered Mantiqi 1's top six leaders and pushed the plan forward. Al-Qaeda had already transferred the money, and explosives had been bought. It was a matter of adapting the plan so they could finish the job. At that meeting were Hambali, Mukhlas, Noordin Mohamed Top, Wan Min Wan Mat, Zulkifli Marzuki, and Dr. Azahari Husin. Specific jobs were handed out by Hambali. Noordin Mohamed Top, a teacher at Jemaah Islamiyah's Lukmanul Hakim school since 1998, was told "to plan bombing" logistics. Wan Min Wan Mat, a lecturer at Malaysia's Universiti Teknologi Malaysia (UTM) and Jemaah Islamiyah's treasurer, was named the plot's bagman. Dr. Azahari Husin, another lecturer at UTM and an engineer who studied in Britain, was Jemaah Islamiyah's top bomb expert and is the author of Jemaah Islamiyah's manuals on explosives and building bombs. Azahari was told "to arrange and execute" the explosives for the attack. Mukhlas, who replaced Hambali as the head of Mantiqi 1 in April 2001, was tasked with implementing the actual attack.

Mukhlas was a charter member of Jemaah Islamiyah and a veteran of the original jihad against the Soviets in Afghanistan. He has known Abu Bakar Ba'asyir and Abdullah Sungkar since 1982, when he became a teacher at the Ngruki school in Solo that they founded. "I know the two vanished from the Ngruki boarding school around 1985 when the security forces came to the boarding school," said Mukhlas.[41] In 1986, he left for Malaysia, where he again met up with the two clerics. That was when he said he swore allegiance to Abdullah Sungkar. Later that year, filled with the zeal of jihad, he left for Pakistan. "Jihad is the utmost form of religious service," he later told the Indonesian police. "After I decided to go, I performed the ritual prayer Istikharoh. In that prayer, I dreamt I met with the Prophet—may Allah bless him and give him peace—and he gave me some advice including an encouragement for me to depart because the journey was following the journey of the prophets, so I left at my own expense for Pakistan. And because I was able to speak Arabic I was able to talk with them and had the opportunity to meet with Islamic clerics," he said.

In 1987, he met Osama bin Laden in Joji, Afghanistan. "The Joji territory was under fierce attack by Russian soldiers," said Mukhlas. "The snow was very thick up to two meters. When the mujahideen prepared to hold an attack on Joji, I joined them. The leader of the mujahideen at Joji and also the camp owner was Sheik Osama bin Laden." In that same year, he also met a fellow Indonesian who would later rise up al-Qaeda's ranks: Hambali.

Mukhlas returned from Afghanistan when the war ended in 1989. He went to Malaysia and worked as a laborer and as an Islamic teacher. After about five or six months, he married Faridah bin Abbas, the sister of another JI member from Singapore, Hashim bin Abbas, whose voice would be heard narrating a JI plot on a videotape found in Afghanistan at the end of 2001.

In 1991, at the urging of the JI leaders, Mukhlas founded a JI school. Sungkar told him he should do this because he "had experienced living at the Islamic boarding school Ngruki, and in Malaysia, an Islamic boarding school teaching the Koran and Sunna was badly needed."[42] The land was paid for by Sungkar. The school's maintenance and electricity bills were paid by Wan Min Wan Mat. Ba'asyir, Sungkar, Hambali, and Mukhlas used the school to preach their radical message and recruit their earliest disciples, including Imam Samudra, the Bali blast coordinator, and Mukhlas's younger brothers—Amrozi, who bought the van and explosives for Bali, and Ali Imron, who confessed to helping make and set off the bombs.

The men who carried out the Bali bombings were no novices. This was not the first time they had worked together on a terrorist plot. They had planned and carried out the Christmas bombings in December 2000 in Indonesia and in Ambon—nearly twenty bombs killed at least nineteen people.[43] The same hierarchy, the same team: Hambali calling the shots; Mukhlas below him coordinating financial and logistical requirements; Imam Samudra as the field commander on the ground; Dr. Azahari advising Dulmatin the bomb maker; and Mukhlas's brothers Ali Imron, who built the bombs and triggered them, and Amrozi, who admitted using the same explosives supplier for the church bombings and the Ambon bombs.

Field commander Imam Samudra was the one who got the job done. An Afghan war veteran who had named his son Osama, he was trained as an engineer and computer expert. He developed his radical views by reading books and using the Internet. He became more radical, he admits, than even the Asian Osama bin Laden, Ba'asyir. "Ustad Abu Bakar Ba'asyir leans towards dakwah [missionary work] and the socialization of Islam while I realize that the society's needs go beyond that. Dakwah no longer suffices for the people. They also need a defense," says Samudra.[44] "That is why I call to fellow Muslims through the Internet by summoning them to jihad in Ambon as well as Poso. . . . For those not able, jihad can also be performed through infaq [donations]. The means which I use to call fellow Muslims to jihad is through the chatting channel on the Internet, by sending out URLs for websites I know." (After he was arrested, prosecutors found a great deal of communication with Ba'asyir on his laptop—along with pornographic photographs of Anglo-Saxon women. Samudra insisted those files had been planted. At one point he lived in the Southeast Asian neighborhood known in intelligence communities as "Terror HQ"—Sungai Manggis, Malaysia. There, Samudra lived next door to Hambali, Abu Bakar Ba'asyir, and Abu Jibril. Soon after, he attended the school set up by Mukhlas.

During the Christmas bombings, Samudra reported to Hambali and Mukhlas, and in turn, he managed Hashim bin Abbas, Mukhlas's brother-in-law. In 2001, he would field Malaysian Taufik Abdul Halim, a member of Malaysia's KMM terror group, in several church bombings, until one exploded prematurely, blowing off his leg and leading to his arrest.

Samudra not only used the Internet to coordinate his operatives; he also added an Asian twist: text messaging on cellular phones. According to law enforcement officials in the region, this is one of the hardest forms of communication to trace. Samudra ran various operatives on the ground: Idris was in charge of handling the money that came through Hambali, Wan Min Wan Mat, and Mukhlas and putting it to use in setting up accommodations and logistics; Dulmatin worked with Dr. Azahari above him and Ali Imron below him to make the bombs; Amrozi, Mukhlas's brother, bought the explosives from the same supplier as the Christmas Eve bombings. "I was given the job of finding the chemicals—chlorate, aluminum powder and sulfur—and of buying a car, any type of car but, if possible, try to get a car with Bali number plates," he later explained to police investigators.[45]

Samudra also recruited a separate cell of five young men—the suicide bombers for the plot. It would be the first time Indonesians would volunteer and carry out suicide bombings. "I asked them, 'Brothers, are you or are you not capable of going on a jihad on behalf of Muslims, even if it means a suicide bombing?' I noted that they shouldn't do it if they felt pressured or to be seen as courageous or to be popular or for any other bad reasons. They should do it only for Allah," said Samudra.[46]

Samudra's operatives kept their targets at Kuta Beach in Bali under surveillance for three weeks. On October 9, 2002, just two nights before the bombing, Mukhlas arrived in Bali to take a look at the targets they chose: the Sari Club and Paddy's Bar. The Sari Club is a well-known hangout in Kuta that has earned the ire of many Indonesians. Patronized largely by foreigners, it's known as *bule* land—the land of whites. A well-known pickup place, it often refused entry to single Indonesian women unless they were accompanied by white men. One Western-educated, pretty Indonesian woman complained to me that she and her friends were not allowed inside.

It was a good target, for it had symbolic importance that reverberated through all of Indonesian society. For three straight nights, Imam Samudra and two of his cell members positioned themselves outside, watching and feeding their hatred. "When we got to Jalan Legian," Imam Samudra later said, "we sat in the car in front of the Sari Club. I saw lots of whiteys dancing, and lots of whiteys drinking there. That place—Kuta and especially Paddy's Bar and the Sari Club—was a meeting place for U.S. terrorists and their allies, who the whole world knows to be the monsters." [47]

A white L-300 Mitsubishi van and three chemicals for the explosives were brought to a house on Jalan Pulau Mejangan in Denpasar, Bali, on the morning of October 12, and the cell assembled the bombs. The seats had been taken out of the van, and twelve filing cabinets, full of chemicals—potassium chlorate, sulfur, and aluminum powder—were placed inside. "They put the three ingredients together, and there was a connecting cable and a detonator. Dulmatin knows about that," explains Colonel Zainuri Lubis, a member of the police investigating team. "He is the one who made the detonator, helped by Ali Imron. When everything was ready . . . they loaded [the cabinets] on gradually and then took the car to the scene of the crime." [48]

There was some strain among the Bali bombers, particularly between Ali Imron and Imam Samudra. Ali Imron seemed to have felt marginalized during the planning stages, and during a bizarre press conference after his capture, where he acted more like a talk-show host than a prisoner, Imron portrayed himself as the key link: the man who built the bombs and pulled everything together at the last minute. "The capability of our group as one of the Indonesian nation [sic] should make people proud," Ali Imron told journalists, drawing stunned laughter from his implication that Indonesians should be proud of what his group accomplished. [49] Imron said they used 1.2 tons of black powder connected to a cable detonator with PETN explosives. They also used 94 detonators that each had 3 grams of plastic explosive RDX and a booster that contained TNT. He said the detonators had been brought to Indonesia from the Philippines.

Samudra had chosen two suicide bombers to bring the van to the Sari Club, but at the last minute, the plotters discovered that one, Iqbal (an alias for Arnasan), who was supposed to drive the car, could drive only a short distance in a straight line—he didn't know how to shift gears or turn corners. Samudra ordered a displeased Imron to drive the van to a T-junction close to the targets with Iqbal and the second suicide bomber, Jimi (wearing a vest full of explosives), alongside. At the intersection, Ali Imron got out, and Iqbal drove the remaining short distance. At the Sari Club, Jimi got out of the van and entered the club, while Iqbal stayed in the van. The plotters set up four separate ways of detonating the bomb, providing three different backup systems in case of failure. The first attempt would be by mobile phone; then a direct trigger switch to be pulled by Iqbal, then a timer in case Iqbal was incapacitated, and finally a trigger in one of the filing cabinet drawers set to go off if it was opened.

Ali Imron said that the first method must not have been used because they had forgotten to attach the cell phone. "The remote, the handphone, is still in the pocket of my friend, Idris."

On October 12, 2002, at 9:00 P.M., Ali Imron placed a box-shaped bomb on the sidewalk outside the U.S. consular office in Bali. He then rode a Yamaha motorcycle back to the house to get the van. At 10:00 P.M., Ali Imron drove the van to the T-junction near the Sari Club. At 11:08 P.M., Idris used his cell phone to make a call to trigger an explosion outside the U.S. consular office. By that time, Jimi, with the vestful of explosives, was inside Paddy's bar and detonated his bomb. That smaller explosion was designed to funnel people to the exit, closer to the site of the van's largest and deadliest blast, so fierce it ruptured the internal organs of the people in the area. The fires that followed burned others alive. The roofs of surrounding buildings were made of thatched material, which magnified the explosions, tearing down a whole city block. More than two hundred people died, and hundreds more were injured in a scene of chaos, destruction, and death.

The bombers rejoiced. Some of them went to pray. Like the 9/11 attacks, the result surpassed what they had imagined would happen. "Firstly, I was shocked because the explosion was extremely intense, beyond expectations," said Mukhlas. "I had estimated that only Sari Club and Paddy's would be destroyed. Secondly, I felt grateful because in my opinion, the planned mission and objectives had been achieved because there were many casualties from amongst American allies including Australian citizens. Thirdly, I sought Allah's forgiveness because apparently there were some victims from the Muslim side."[50]

Amrozi, who by that time had returned to his hometown of Tenggulun, but was nonetheless caught by authorities on November 5, 2002, said he believed foreigners threatened the future of Indonesia. "Because the evil plan of the United States, the Jews and their allies is to colonize," he said. "They want to destroy religions. They destroy by creating challenges to religions, that is, dens of vices"—referring to the Sari Club and

Paddy's Bar.[51] Indonesia's moral fabric was collapsing, said Amrozi, because "foreigners have colonized late night television. What would happen to Bali in ten years if I hadn't bombed it?" he asked the court. "For sure, the morals of Indonesians would be severely ruined because most people would not be going to mosques, churches and temples. The Jews, the Americans and their puppets know very well how to destroy the lives of Indonesians. Destroying our morals is very important to them." Another phrase I heard repeatedly from the Bali bombers was that "there was no other choice but violence."

Imam Samudra stayed in Bali for two days after the bombing and revisited the site to survey the destruction. "I felt that I feared only Allah," he said, "and that my efforts, which had been so small, had caused the deaths of so many people. But if those killed were not Muslims but Americans and Christians, then I was grateful." Later, Samudra created his own website, www.istimata.com, to justify the Bali bombings. His words are strong and passionate.

"This site is not intended as a forum for debate," he wrote.[52] "This site has been created so that Muslims understand that—quite apart from whether they agree or not, are opposed or not—there are a handful of Muslims who feel called to revenge the barbarity of the Coalition army of the Cross and its allies (America, England, Australia, Germany, Belgium, Japan, almost all members of NATO, and so on) toward the Islamic State of Afghanistan, which resulted in tens of thousands of casualties in September, 2001.

"It is as if one believer and another have the same body—if one feels the pain, the other also feels it. For all you Christian infidels! If you say that this killing was barbarous and cruel, and happened to 'innocent civilians' from your countries, then you should know that you do crueler things than that. Do you think that 600 thousand babies in Iraq and half a million Afghan children and their mothers are soldiers and sinful people who should have to endure thousands of tons of your bombs?!?!?

"Where are your brains and your consciences?

"The cries of babies and the screams of Muslim women, which are then conveyed by the diplomatic efforts of a handful of Muslims trying to stop your brutality have not been successful, and there is no way they will ever be able to stop your barbarity.

"So here we are, Muslims!!!

"Our hearts have been wounded and are filled with pain at the deaths of our brothers and sisters. We cannot allow unjust and barbarous actions against our Muslim brothers and sisters in any corner of the world.

"We hereby state that we were responsible for the MARTYRS (SUICIDE BOMBING) that took place in Jalan Legian, Kuta, Bali, on the evening of Saturday, October 12, 2002, and in the vicinity of the American embassy in Jalan Hayam Wuruk, Denpasar, Bali, on the same night."

Samudra threatened to continue the attacks unless three conditions are met: first, for coalition forces to leave Afghanistan: "As long as Coalition forces do not leave Afghanistan, there will continue to be casualties from your countries, wherever they may be." Second was the release of all Muslims held as terrorists: "As long as you regard our brothers and sisters as terrorists and torture them in your prisons, especially in Guantanamo Bay, citizens from your countries will receive the same treatment." Finally, he asked all Muslims to stop helping and supporting the "American infidels who spread slander in Muslim circles" and threatened to treat them "the same way we treat your master, America, oppressor and mastermind of world terrorism."

In a separate website about three weeks after the blasts, al-Qaeda claimed credit for Samudra's and his terror network's handiwork, including the Bali blasts, in its list of global attacks against America and its allies. "By attempting to strike a U.S. plane in Saudi Arabia and by bombing a Jewish synagogue in Tunisia, destroying two ships in Yemen, attacking the Fialka base in Kuwait, and bombing nightclubs and whorehouses in Indonesia, Al-Qaeda has shown it has no qualms about attacking inside Arab and Islamic lands," said the statement on the website. "This is provided that the target belongs to the Jewish-Crusader alliance."

Practically speaking, there is no difference between al-Qaeda and Jemaah Islamiyah, as the latter operates as a subsidiary of the former. The Bali bombing was indeed the work of al-Qaeda, which provided funds, training, and some of the personnel to supplement Jemaah Islamiyah's home-grown recruiting. It was on orders from Mohammed Atef, al-Qaeda's number two (while he was still alive), that Jemaah Islamiyah switched from Plan A in Singapore to Plan B in Bali. The ease with which massive explosives were obtained—enough to kill over 200 people—and the relative simplicity of the plan make it a virtual certainty that something like it will happen again.

A M E R I C A N   M I S S T E P S

Decades from now, I am afraid we will look back to March 19, 2003, the day the attacks began on Iraq, and see it as the beginning of the end of the American empire. With little respect for the millions of people around the world who demonstrated against any attack, and for the United Nations, which debated extensively yet fell short of giving an international mandate, the United States and Britain presented intelligence information that they said warranted an attack, and proceeded to overthrow Saddam Hussein. That information would be challenged and denied by U.S. and British officials just a few months later. By attacking Iraq, the United States became both the hero and the villain of the war on terror, its actions making it the most powerful recruitment tool Osama bin Laden could have wished for. Instead of focusing its forces on al-Qaeda, it squandered its strength on an old enemy, giving Muslims around the world more reasons to distrust its motives. The Pew Global Attitudes Project survey, released in June 2003, showed that public support for the war on terror in most Muslim nations had fallen and measured the fall of public support for America in the world's largest Muslim population, Indonesia. In 2000, 75% of Indonesians said they had a favorable opinion of the United States. In 2003, 83% have an unfavorable opinion of America.[1] I grew up under its once benevolent reign. As a child in the Philippines, the only former colony of America, I went to schools founded by Americans, learning to speak English at the same time I was learning the native language, Tagalog. American ideals and values, tempered by Philippine culture, were etched into me, and I grew up wanting to be part of it. America was the dream. Living there was the Holy Grail.

Yet I also feel the tug of nationalism that has become more complex as I have grown older. It's the dilemma of former colonies, an experience repeated in much of Southeast Asia—the chip on the shoulders that is as much an unspoken part of foreign policy in the region as the indelible experiences of childhood each of the leaders has lived through. It is part of the social fabric—something I could see so clearly while I was covering the negotiations for the U.S. bases in the Philippines. The debate didn't center on the economic benefits—what the United States paid to have their bases here. The issue for Filipinos was national sovereignty. Ironically, the only way the former colonized people could gain power and feel like an equal of their former colonizers was by excluding them. The U.S. bases were shut down in 1992.

At the same time, the colonizers of Southeast Asia serve as models: Filipinos study in the United States, as Indonesians migrate to the home of their Dutch colonizers, as Singaporeans and Malaysians mirror their British masters. But just as the colonizers are emulated, they are hated because they often represent the unattainable. Filipinos of my parents' generation grew up thinking Americans knew better: they were wiser, better informed, possessing a broader worldview. That view was challenged by my generation, which began to catalog the betrayals of the former benefactor. Still, no matter what stand you take on nationalism, all agree America is the land of opportunity. As a child, I remember listening to stories about streets paved with gold and wondering what it would be like to walk there.

After 9/11, Southeast Asians felt tremendous sympathy for America. When the United States toppled the Taliban, it was seen as payback for September 11. But when, in Iraq, the United States proved it could—and would—act unilaterally, hatreds shot to the surface. "The U.S. is behaving in a manner which, in fact, is not something that one likes to see, as a friend of America," said former Indonesian presidential spokeswoman Dewi Fortuna Anwar. "Osama bin Laden has dealt such a blow to the United States that in fact now, the United States is turning against some of its own fundamental values, like freedom, democracy and human rights."[2]

It would prove to be a terrific recruiting tool for al-Qaeda. The divide between Americans and the rest of the world, particularly with Muslim nations, has never been greater. At a meeting of 116 heads of state at the summit of the Non-Aligned Movement, one told me, "If we do nothing, the United States will just pick us off one by one."[3] Dewi

Anwar encapsulated the mood: "The fear is if a major power can remove a government at will because it doesn't like it, the implication is that we are going to see similar happenings in the future. Iraq today, who's next? You know, who's the day after? This is very dangerous for international law. If the argument is Saddam Hussein is a dictator, there are many, many dictators. Is the U.S. going to take out all these dictators? When in fact, in the past, the United States has nurtured dictators."[4]

Ironically, as they feared American aggression, these leaders were also growing afraid of their own people. Within the Muslim world, says Malaysia's prime minister, Mahathir Mohamad, it is growing too dangerous to ally openly with the United States, which is increasingly being seen and portrayed as an enemy of Islam. "We may want to remain uninvolved and avoid incurring the displeasure of the powerful countries, but our people are getting restless," said Mahathir in his speech that opened the summit.[5] "They want us to do something. If we don't, then they will, and they will go against us. They will take things into their own hands."

These are the very nations the United States needs to win over—and the very same people bin Laden wants to sway to his radical views. U.S. actions intended to make the world safer are actually pushing moderate Muslims to take a step closer to the radicals. "The existing superpower projects its own moral and cultural values as eternal and ever-lasting truths, and has arrogated to itself the right to remove, through resort to force and violence, what it considers as standing in its way," said Iran's Mohammed Khatami at the summit. "This is the product of fanatic fundamentalism which, sadly enough, happens to command the greatest might in man's history."

The United States in Southeast Asia has always been something of a bull in a china shop, unwittingly causing destruction despite its best intentions. In the 1950s and 1960s, CIA covert actions in the Philippines and Indonesia fueled the distrust of American motives. Given the history, it is little wonder that the people of the region are primed to hate America if given half a chance. When I moved back to the Philippines in 1986 and began reporting, I began to despair about how my American tax dollars were being used to develop and prop up a largely insensitive, therefore ineffective, diplomatic corps. Coming from both worlds, I could sense the divide and see its effects on America's foreign policy in Southeast Asia.

The American diplomats I knew lived expatriate lifestyles in compounds insulated from the reality of life in the Philippines. As a Fulbright scholar, I dealt frequently with the U.S. embassy in Manila in the late 1980s. Of the many officials I met at that time, only two could understand and speak the native language, cutting off access and understanding to a majority of Filipinos. Perhaps because I'm Filipino American, what bothered me more was a condescending attitude that prevailed among embassy officials. Many were midlevel bureaucrats waiting to get to the next pay grade, impressive only for their lack of creativity and curiosity about the countries they lived in. So many embassy officials pontificated about what America stood for rather than trying to understand the nation they were now guests in and looking to find common ground. Often American diplomats came across as arrogant. As I became friends with some of them, I would point this out repeatedly and was often told, "Maria, they just don't understand us. No matter what we do, they hate us because we are strong"—an argument of the haves versus the have-nots. I don't believe that's true, and anyone who believes that shouldn't be representing America. Often Americans are hated because they show a disregard of others' ways of life and a deep-seated disrespect of other cultures.

Over the years, I met many exceptions, and the American ambassadors in Southeast Asia now are among the most sensitive and knowledgeable—Ralph Boyce in Indonesia, Marie Huhtala in Malaysia, Frank Lanvin in Singapore, Francis Ricciardone in the Philippines—but they are the exception rather than the rule. Because there is a lack of true ground reporting, true diplomatic and intelligence work, much is lost in the translation between cultures.

During the cold war, Southeast Asia was a proxy arena. Nations here were used by the Soviet Union and the United States, often to disastrous results—famously, in Vietnam but less famously and equally disastrously in places like East Timor. There is a historical basis for the distrust of America here. Take a look at America's actions in East Timor, a small half-island colonized by Portugal for 350 years. It was annexed as Indonesia's twenty-seventh province in 1975. There is no reason that the United States should have much interest in this little enclave, yet the U.S. played a role in the calamitous annexation and in the bloody transition back to independence in 1999. Less than a month after 9/11, Osama bin Laden would cite East Timor as one justification for his war against America.

According to State Department documents declassified in 2001, Indonesia's invasion of East Timor received the blessings of U.S. president Gerald Ford and Secretary of State Henry Kissinger.[6] Despite repeated public denials by Kissinger that the United States knew anything about Indonesia's plans, a transcript of a 1975 conversation among Suharto, Ford, and Kissinger shows that Suharto received a green light for his military plans.

The U.S. delegation had just come from China after a meeting with Mao Tse-tung and Deng Xiaoping and had stopped in Jakarta before returning to the United States. It was the second meeting between Ford and Suharto in five months, and each was relatively comfortable with the other. Also at the meeting were Kissinger; his Indonesian counterpart, Adam Malik; Indonesia's minister of state Sudharmono, and U.S. ambassador John Newsom. In the midst of a discussion about guerrilla movements in Thailand and Malaysia, Suharto abruptly turned the topic to East Timor.

"I would like to speak to you, Mr. President, about another problem, Timor," said Suharto. "When it looked as if the Portuguese rule would end in Timor, we sought to encourage the Portuguese to an orderly decolonization process. We had agreement with them on such a process and we recognized the authority of Portugal in the carrying out of decolonization and in giving people the right to express their wishes. Indonesia has no territorial ambitions. We are concerned only about the security, tranquility and peace of Asia and the southern hemisphere." Suharto outlined how a Timorese political party, the Fretilin, unilaterally declared independence, contrary to the wishes of four other political parties, which wanted "integration" with Indonesia.

"The four other parties have asked for integration?" asked President Ford.

"Yes," Suharto replied. "It is now important to determine what we can do to establish peace and order for the present and the future in the interest of the security of the area and Indonesia. These are some of the considerations we are now contemplating. We want your understanding if we deem it necessary to take rapid or drastic action."

"We will understand and will not press you on the issue," answered Ford. "We understand the problem you have and the intentions you have."

"You appreciate that the use of U.S.-made arms could create problems," Kissinger told Suharto, showing that he understood American-issued military weapons would be used "illegally."

"We could have technical and legal problems," added Ford. "You are familiar, Mr. President, with the problems we had on Cyprus although this situation is different."

"It depends on how we construe it: whether it is in self-defense or is a foreign operation," said Kissinger. "It is important that whatever you do succeeds quickly."

The next day, Indonesia invaded, triggering nearly a quarter-century of a bloody fight for independence. Tripartite talks continued for more than fifteen years at the United Nations between Portugal and Indonesia. They led nowhere. The breakthrough happened after Suharto's fall. In January 1999, backed by Dewi Anwar and to the surprise of most of his cabinet, the new president, B. J. Habibie, offered East Timor a historic vote, giving its people a choice between autonomy under Indonesia or independence.

However, Habibie's military had no interest in following his policy. By February, the Indonesian military began actively training and arming pro-Indonesian militias, who with the help of Indonesian security forces began a systematic campaign of violence to intimidate East Timor's people into voting to stay with Indonesia. I met many of these militia leaders, like Cancio Lopes de Carvalho and his brother Nemecio, and was continually struck by a self-righteous patriotism that justified their fight. They believed they were the ones who had suffered and were being cheated. East Timorese also had a long memory, and revenge was a prime motivator. "You have to know that what happened in 1999 was just a result or reaction to what happened in 1975. In 1975, many pro-integration were captured, sent to jail and finally were killed without legal process," Nemecio told me. "There were many kidnappings and murders conducted by pro-independence against pro-integration in 1975."[7]

By April 1999, I was at the United Nations reporting on the diplomatic talks to define the terms of that vote. The UN was tasked to administer the vote and was mediating between Indonesia and Portugal. There were no Timorese representatives directly involved. The gap between reality and the world of diplomacy became apparent when the negotiators emerged and announced that Indonesia would be in charge of maintaining security for the vote. They would be helped by a small, unarmed team of civilian policemen. It was like putting the fox in charge of the henhouse.

Violence escalated in the run-up to the vote. A month before, my team and I went from town to town, chronicling the violations, watching as UNAMET, the UN team supervising the vote, tried to hold the process together. While publicly the Indonesian military and police continued denying any involvement with militia violence, what we saw made liars of them. On August 30, 1999, more than 98 percent of East Timor's registered voters went to the polls, and 78.5 percent chose independence. Yet by the time results were announced on September 4, the violence had escalated to the point that residents, diplomats, and journalists had begun fleeing East Timor. The fires began burning in the suburbs of Dili in the early morning of that same day. Shortly after sunrise, pro-independence Timorese fled their villages, fearing a militia and military reprisal.

Even as I was doing live coverage at the announcement of the voting results, my producer was handing me notes: there was an explosion in another part of town, the ports were being closed, and the main gas pipeline was shutting down. The world had backed a high-risk diplomatic experiment, but the losers were the very people they were supposed to be helping—and anyone else who happened to be in East Timor at that time. The militia, aided by the Indonesian security forces, had begun the end game for East Timor, a scorched earth policy that would destroy its cities within ten days, kill more than 1,000 people, and chase more than 250,000 others across the border into Indonesian West Timor.

The immediate problem was that the UN had trusted the word of the Indonesians. So did the militias. "Not only the Indonesian military but also Indonesian diplomats, government officials, politicians, came to us," said former militia leader Nemecio Lopes. "They promised: just continue struggling for integration. We have arranged it with the UN. It is just a formality. You will come out as the winner of this population. So we were fooled and tricked."[8]

Now, Osama bin Laden defined that conflict as the victory of the predominantly Christian East Timorese against Muslim Indonesians. "Let us examine the stand of the West and the United Nations in the developments in Indonesia when they moved to divide the largest country in the Islamic world in terms of population," said bin Laden on November 3, 2001. "This criminal, Kofi Annan, was speaking publicly and putting pressure on the Indonesian government, telling it: you have 24 hours to divide and separate East Timor from Indonesia. Otherwise, we will be forced to send in military forces to separate it by force. The crusader Aus-

tralian forces were on Indonesian shores, and in fact, they landed to separate East Timor, which is part of the Muslim world. Therefore, we should
view events not as separate links, but as links in a long series of conspira-
cies, a war of annihilation in the true sense of the word."

That message would haunt me on Tuesday, August 19, 2003, after a
truck bomb exploded outside the UN headquarters in Baghdad, right
underneath the office of Kofi Annan's representative, Brazilian diplomat Sergio Vieira de Mello, who appeared to be the key target. Authorities are still investigating who carried out the attack. It could be any of
a number of groups—there is no shortage of hatred and distrust of
Americans in Iraq—but only a few have the operational capability and
training to carry out an attack on this scale. And why were the UN and
de Mello targeted, whose presence only offer aid to Iraqis? Before Iraq,
de Mello played a pivotal role in East Timor. As the head of the UN
there, he was responsible for putting East Timor back together as the
world's newest nation. Well-liked, warm, enthusiastic, he was a sensitive
and healing figure who made it a point to be inclusive of all in a deeply
divided society—a diplomat, pragmatist, and a symbol of the UN at its
best. Was his death another example of how bin Laden has united the
conflicts in the Muslim world in his global jihad? Was this part of his
"war of annihilation against America and the West?"

The greater irony is that in 1999, U.S. president Bill Clinton faced a
choice similar to Gerald Ford's in 1975. After the mass evacuation of
East Timor, a small core group of foreigners remained in the UN compound, where pro-independence residents flocked for safety. Thousands
crowded its open courtyard, sleeping wherever they could find space.
There was tremendous international pressure for the world to do something to stop the violence. It was clear it would take too long for the
UN to send its peacekeepers in. Australia had offered to lead the mission, but they wanted help from the United States. Clinton delayed
making that decision.

On September 8, 1999, Admiral Dennis Blair, commander of U.S.
forces in the Pacific, arrived in Jakarta on what was supposed to be a two-
day visit. He stayed less than half a day. He and his aide went to Indonesia
Armed Forces Chief General Wiranto's office. When they arrived, they
found a table set with sixteen teacups for the expected U.S. delegation.
The table went untouched. Instead, Blair asked for a private meeting with
Wiranto, which lasted about forty minutes.[9] "Despite some official state-

ments that things are getting better," Blair told Wiranto, "the situation is
not getting any better on the ground." He then told him the United States
was severing all military ties with Indonesia and that if things continued
the way they were going in East Timor, he could see it "leading to serious
damage for Indonesia's relationship with the world." He said the situation
must improve dramatically, noting that he wasn't asking for words "but
action which could be verified by outside observers."

The next day, President Clinton, on a stopover in Hawaii en route
to the twenty-one-nation summit of the Asia Pacific Economic Cooperation forum in Auckland, New Zealand, finally publicly stated the
Indonesian military's involvement in the violence. "The Indonesian military is aiding and abetting the militia violence," he said. "This is simply
unacceptable." When he arrived in Auckland, the East Timor issue
dominated the sidelines of the meeting. At last, Clinton met with Australia's prime minister, John Howard, to discuss putting together an
international force to step in.[10]

Pentagon officials did not want the U.S. military to be actively
involved, but a compromise was found. On his way back to the United
States, Clinton stopped at Hawaii's Hickam Air Force Base to refuel. At
the "Distinguished Visitors" lounge, Clinton, Blair, and national security
adviser Samuel Berger discussed what the United States was prepared
to do. Blair proposed a plan he knew the Pentagon would support: follow the Australians and provide backup with U.S. intelligence, communications, and logistics personnel.

Back then, even in its inaction, the power of the United States was
apparent. With time being a crucial element, the UN admitted it would
be unable to move quickly. Australia had been prepared to lead the
mission, and yet it took U.S. initiative and involvement for action finally
to be taken, and a multinational effort to bring troops into East Timor
could get underway. Those days came at the cost of wasted lives.

Nearly three years later, it felt liberating to ask Clinton if he regret-
ted coming in so late. "In retrospect," I asked, "do you think you could
have done more to stop the violence?"

"Maybe," he hedged. "When I became convinced that people here
have suffered so much for so long, not just under Indonesia but also
under the colonial system, after I studied the situation and came to
grips with it, it was the only judgment anybody could reach given the
facts of their existence, and so we supported it. But what happens with

a country like the United States, when you're trying to do the right thing, you tend to see every specific problem through the lens of the general concern we had, which was to promote freedom and the rights of minorities without necessarily making a nation everywhere in the world. And sometimes, it makes us slow in the starting gate to stand up against specific abuses so I can't defend everything we did, but I think we've done quite well since 1999."

Clinton was well liked internationally. In fact, Singapore's senior minister, Lee Kuan Yew, said he felt the United States wouldn't have the image problem it has today if someone like Clinton was explaining and rallying support for U.S. policy. It's a perception that had been echoed by other leaders around the world, a direct blow to the style of President Bush.

Clinton's pushes for action in Kosovo and Bosnia were necessary to rally the international community, just as bin Laden's pushes for jihad in Indonesia and Chechnya were necessary to rally extremist Muslims. The irony is that Clinton often had to fight his own government and people to convince them it was in the interests of Americans to take an active role in the world's conflicts—in effect, to act as a global policeman. The greater irony is that Bush's unilateralism is having a negative effect.

"What really changed in our whole perception of this issue was September 11," argues Paul Wolfowitz. Although only the deputy defense secretary, the soft-spoken former political science professor is the ideologue of the Pentagon and wields significant influence on how U.S. forces will be deployed and used in the future. "Before September 11, terrorism was viewed as something ugly, but you lived with it. Saddam Hussein was viewed as something ugly, something that was for the Iraqi people to take care of. After September 11, terrorism looked different. Saddam Hussein, who played with terrorists and had weapons of mass destruction, looked much more threatening to the United States than just to his own people, and so it changed the calculation entirely. I mean, without that perception of threat, I don't believe the President would have considered it something that American lives should be risked for, as terrible as the regime is—I mean, there is no question the regime was a horrible thing."[11]

"The fact that there hasn't been a substantial cache of weapons of mass destruction—is that an embarrassment for the United States?" I asked him, when we spoke in Singapore after the war.

"No," he answered quickly. "Look, this dictator had twelve years to develop innumerable ways to hide his program . . . he was a man with something to hide, and we'll have to find it."

More generally, Wolfowitz had earlier laid out the difficulties of defeating al-Qaeda. "There is a striking resemblance between this organization and a cancer that's metastasized—if that's the right word," Wolfowitz explained. "It's not something where you just cut off the head and the organization withers. It's cells all over the place. Cells with connections to other cells. Terrorist groups with connections to other groups. Many different governments—terrorists supporting governments with help of one kind and disowning them in other ways. This is not a problem that is going to be successfully dealt with by an isolated action in Afghanistan or the successful capturing of a handful of terrorists." Although they may not have announced it publicly, it's obvious the United States has decided how it would deal with gray areas. "We've really got to just change the whole world climate in which terrorism was once accepted as a sort of necessary evil and understand that in the era of weapons of mass destruction that connection is no longer just something we can live with."[12]

In order to do that effectively—to lead the world and win the war on terror—the U.S. government must be perceived to be credible and working for the common good. There was no outcry after an unmanned Predator drone assassinated a group of al-Qaeda, including one American, in Yemen; the evidence seemed clear.[13] (Wolfowitz noted, "One hopes each time to get a success like that.") Iraq, however, was something else entirely.

Soon after multinational troops entered East Timor in 1999, Senator Patrick Leahy (D-VT) introduced an amendment that forbids the resumption of military ties with Indonesia until concrete reforms are undertaken by the Indonesian military, including the prosecution of the soldiers and militia members behind East Timor's destruction. That ban remains in place since, as of this writing, only one high-ranking officer has been convicted and given a light sentence. The debate now is on whether the United States should again begin working with the Indonesian military.

Wolfowitz knows that the Indonesian military "has enormous problems. I would submit those problems have gotten a lot worse over the last ten years, and I'm not sure I'm saying cause and effect, but over the last ten years, we have had a policy of isolating the Indonesian military.

I wouldn't say it's been a stunning success in terms of promoting a better behavior by the military, a more disciplined behavior by the military." It didn't help that in 2002, two American teachers were allegedly killed by Indonesian soldiers in Indonesia's West Papua province. A joint investigation with the FBI has repeatedly run into obstacles.

The American bull in the china shop twists and turns from Washington, ignorant of its true effects. The world's only hope is for American engagement—working with locals, not against them.

It is similar to a reporter's job. After evacuating East Timor in 1999, I knew I had to find a way to get back inside and begin reporting events again. Most of my colleagues and another team from CNN had decided to go to Darwin, Australia, the launching point for the multinational troops. They were going to wait and come in with the troops. There seemed to be little choice because all routes in were closed, including the airport. I decided on a risky move: fly to West Timor and drive into East Timor by land. It was a dangerous ten-hour drive through areas of lawlessness, but it was also a calculated risk. At that point, I thought, the militia would have started evacuating their families. After all, East Timor had already been destroyed: there was no infrastructure, no running water, no electricity, no food. The only authority I could get on my side to lower the risks was the Indonesian military. I had no other choice because they were the only ones active in that territory.

I knew that members of the East Timorese battalions, 744 and 745, had been recalled and were in West Timor. Most of them had deserted, but they still carried their weapons. I also knew these men were probably the ones who actively helped in the destruction of East Timor. Through personal contacts, I found six Timorese soldiers who were part of 744. I trusted them based on the word of their cousin, a man I had grown to know and depend on. These were the men I chose to protect my team. I knew that I could trust them only so far, but I believed the very sight of them would ward off danger. After all, any potential attackers were either their friends or colleagues. I called it a pact with the devil, and it was. (The irony is that by the time we spent nearly a month together, we had become friends. They understood my view better; I understood theirs, although we never did agree.)

I also wanted official recognition from the Indonesian military and some promise they would help. I knew the top-down hierarchy of the army was falling apart and the power now lay with local commanders. I had heard a convoy of military vehicles was driving to East Timor in the morning, and I wanted us to be part of that convoy. When one of my producers tried to set a meeting with the local army commander, I was told to meet his officers at a favorite karaoke bar to discuss the details. That led to one of the most surreal experiences of my career: singing Hall and Oates duets with the local commander, who had quite a nice voice. Five of his men were with him; five of my team members were with me. At one point, when it was my turn to sing, I chose "Desperado."

In the end, we drove alone and made the harrowing ten-hour trip safely. We were the first journalists to enter East Timor since the destruction had begun, reporting at that crucial and dangerous period days before multinational troops landed. Still, we had needed the military, and we had no choice but to engage. The world faces a similar situation for both the security of Indonesia's democracy and the war on terror. Any conflict situation, any areas of lawlessness, of the breakdown of law and order—these are the magnets for al-Qaeda.

The war on terror, says Wolfowitz, is very different from the cold war: "You knew exactly what the Soviet war plan was and exactly what you had to do to meet it, or the threat you face on the Korean peninsula. Those are very fixed. They are calculable. You need a very big force in place to deal with them. The new threats are unpredictable, widely dispersed, and what you may need is a much smaller force much more quickly."

Should the United States be the global policeman? It's a moot argument. America has—de facto—taken that position by virtue of its power. In a perfect world, perhaps that responsibility could fall on the United Nations, but we live in an imperfect reality, and as East Timor has shown, it takes too much time to pull together a multilateral initiative. The United States can set the standard, and it must do so with an even hand.

I believe the United States can rise above self-interest and act according to its lofty ideals. Perhaps I'm naively optimistic in believing that American attention and international focus could help resolve many of the backwater conflicts that have been allowed to fester, like in Chechnya and Kashmir, recruiting grounds for al-Qaeda. But someone must counter al-Qaeda. If that group has reached around the world and convinced its Muslim followers that if one Muslim hurts, they all hurt, then the United States can do the same for the other side. It's a universal hope—and an act of enlightened self-interest.

"BY TONGUE AND TEETH"

There's a well-known law of quantum physics called the Heisenberg Uncertainty Principle, which holds that you cannot find the location of an electron at this precise moment because the very act of trying to locate it pushes it somewhere else.[1] Simply put: "The very act of observation changes that which is being observed."[2] That's exactly what it's like to try to predict al-Qaeda's next moves. Every arrest, every new piece of information that's released into the public domain, even the book you are holding in your hands, changes the way the group operates. The Jemaah Islamiyah operatives in Southeast Asia have been instructed to change all their cell phone numbers and e-mail addresses when someone they are in contact with is captured. The minute one of their ideas is revealed, they react and metamorphose into something else. All we can do is know what they used to think, what their organization was like, what they used to do. We can't predict exactly how they will change as a result of the moves of law enforcement and intelligence agencies around the world. That's why the war on terror is not something that can be won in one or two years; it is the battle of our generation.

However, another principle of physics provides a useful analogy as well. The first law of thermodynamics holds that every action has an equal and *opposite* reaction. In the case of Western foreign policy, it translates to "blowback," a term first coined by the CIA in classified documents obtained by *The New York Times* documenting the U.S. and British covert operations which helped overthrow the government of Mohammed Mossadegh in Iran in 1953.[3] In doing that, America helped set in motion

a chain of events which eventually led to the revival of Islamic fundamentalism around the world. The Shah of Iran came to power and sowed
the seeds for the Islamic revolution led by Ayatollah Khomeini. The fall
of the Shah of Iran (who was backed by the U.S. government) captured
the imaginations of Muslims around the world because it proved that in
the modern world, Muslims can depose a secular, Western-backed government and replace it with an Islamic state. Its reverberations were felt
as far as the moderate Muslim communities in Southeast Asia, where it
reinvigorated fundamentalist and extremist thought.

The reactions, in the world of terrorism and Islamist ideology, are
not always "equal" but they are always "opposite." In Afghanistan in
the mid to late '80s, when Muslims around the world were invoked to
join the first modern jihad against the occupying Soviet forces, the
United States (as is well known) supported the Afghan resistance. It is
still, today, a defensible policy dictated by cold war realities, but the
consequences were not all managed very well. It became the largest
covert action program since Vietnam, funneling more than $3 billion
through Pakistan's intelligence service, ISI, to build up the "Afghan
Arabs"—all fundamentalist and venomously anti-American—that later
grew into an international network of highly disciplined and effective
Islamic militants. Among the key beneficiaries was Abdul Rasul Sayyaf,
who helped train Osama bin Laden and thousands of Southeast Asian
militants, including the founder of the Abu Sayyaf in the Philippines
and some of the Bali and J.W. Marriott Hotel bombers. Yet as soon as
the Soviet Union was defeated, the United States abandoned the
volatile mix it created, and let Pakistan run its own affairs. Pakistan
was unable or unwilling to dismantle it; indeed, the ISI served as a key
node in the growth of militant Islam. Osama bin Laden just had the
imagination to harness what America had abandoned. Through the
years, more than 25,000 Islamic militants streamed through those
Afghan training camps.

It's not just the United States that has had to deal with blowback,
and is now facing the war on terror, in part, because past actions have
strengthened radical Islam. Saudi Arabia, Pakistan, the Middle East, and
much of Southeast Asia also contributed to the rise of radical Islam.

In Southeast Asia it can perhaps be most clearly seen in Indonesia.
Suharto used covert military operations to support militant Islamic
groups when they served his purposes, and then batted them down and

pushed them into the closet when it was no longer politically useful to have them around. When he turned on them, Jemaah Islamiyah's leaders fled Indonesia to set up their base in Malaysia. Similarly, Indonesian officials' manipulation of conflicts in East Timor and Ambon grew out of their control. Both conflicts have been used by al-Qaeda to win and train more recruits. More broadly, the corruption which once powered Indonesia's political system under one-man rule now threatens to engulf the fledgling democracy and is part of the reason radical Islam is gaining converts from its moderate Muslims, many of whom are sick of the injustices they see around them. Part of Osama bin Laden's appeal is his call for justice for marginalized voices who want to see a better world.

Everyone has heard the saying "absolute power corrupts absolutely," but thanks to blowback, there is always some accountability, some payback. An internal U.S. Defense Department report in 1997 noted, "Historical data show a strong correlation between U.S. involvement in international situations and an increase in terrorist attacks against the United States. In addition, the military asymmetry"—referring to America's supreme military might—"that denies nation-states the ability to engage in overt attacks against the United States drives the use of transnational actions (that is, terrorists from one country attacking in another)."[4]

Osama bin Laden says the reason he attacks American civilians is because they fail to stop their leaders from killing Muslims around the world. His twisted logic should be both a wake-up call and a rallying cry for American citizens because it's true. It is a reason why Americans should care and make sure the same standards they demand domestically are also exercised globally. "People don't just tie a bomb to their bodies and explode themselves," said Malaysia's Prime Minister Mahathir. "It's a very unpleasant thing. Or you pilot a plane into a building. It must be some very, very strong thing moving you to do that kind of thing. We have to know why. Why do they become so angry? Is it because they hate Americans? If they hate Americans, why do they hate Americans? We have to find out."

Many Muslim leaders around the world believe that the way the United States has responded in the war on terror has only strengthened Osama bin Laden's appeal. "The way the United States is trying to defend itself is the wrong way," said Dr. Mahathir, who himself is trying to defend his government against Jemaah Islamiyah's plans to topple it.

"It does want to defend itself. It is exposed to danger. It wants to avoid the danger. But by aggravating the situation, by inciting—almost in a negative way—the people who have a tendency of taking the law into their own hands, they are not doing the right thing." Few Southeast Asians complain about the more than three thousand arrests in the war on terror carried out by the United States and its allies. Similarly, the attack of Afghanistan is seen as justified. But the attack on Iraq is seen by many moderate Muslims as a deep setback, only serving to aggravate the anger within the Muslim world.

It is an anger that dates back to colonial times for Muslims, a tale of treachery, betrayal, self-interest, and, of course, power—with the strong dictating to the weak. During World War I, when Sharif Hussein pulled together thirty thousand Arab tribesmen and allied them with the British in exchange for Arab independence, they fought courageously. Yet even while they were fighting, Britain "was already secretly negotiating with France to divide, after the war, the Arab lands whose independence"[5] they had promised. This happened repeatedly—the future of Arab and Muslim nations decided by European and Western countries. The Balfour Declaration in 1920 placed Palestine under British trusteeship. Jewish immigrants began arriving in Palestine, buying more land, soon triggering riots. On November 29, 1947, the UN General Assembly, at the recommendation of Britain, voted to partition Palestine into two states: one Arab, one Jewish. For Muslims, treachery and power robbed the Palestinians of their homeland.

"Until after the Second World War, the Europeans oppressed the Jews who had migrated to their countries. Every year, they carried out pogroms and inquisitions indulging in the massacre of the Jews. The attempt to resolve the Jewish problem reached a peak during World War II when six million Jews were killed," said Malaysia's Dr. Mahathir. "But after the Second World War, the Jews were still in Europe. To force the Jews out of Europe, they seized the territory of the Arab Palestinians to create the state of Israel. Not only were the land, houses, and farms of the Arab Palestinians seized, but the Arabs were chased out of their land, which became Israel."[6] This is a common Muslim view.

Other non-Westerners have tended to agree. "Palestine belongs to the Arabs," said India's Mahatma Gandhi, "in the same sense that England belongs to the English or France to the French. What is going on in Palestine today cannot be justified by any moral code of conduct."

Unfortunately, despite Einsteinian speculation about reversing time, the clock cannot be turned back. Even if peace in the Middle East is achieved tomorrow, Islamic terrorism and extremism will continue, for the genie is out of the bottle.

The war on terror, it must be said, is not going well. In Southeast Asia, terrorists are escaping from prison, and plenty of evidence suggests that some attacks could have been prevented. Prior to the Bali bombing, for example, the Indonesian government, despite the warnings from neighboring countries, Western nations, and its own military intelligence unit, chose to ignore ominous warnings of an impending attack by a network that had already attacked in 2000 because of political self-interest and infighting between its police and military.

The first man arrested and officially linked to Bali was an Indonesian named Amrozi. When his name was announced by the Indonesian police, I searched through the intelligence documents I had accumulated and found a reference to a "Rozi": He attended a meeting led by Abu Bakar Ba'asyir. The document was the interrogation report of an al-Qaeda operative in custody in Singapore, Faiz bin Abu Bakar Bafana.[7] He said Ba'asyir told him and others at the meeting, including "Rozi," to "hatch a plot to assassinate Megawati."

I pointed this out to my intelligence sources in Indonesia, the Philippines, and Singapore. Before the end of the day, several sources came back to me and confirmed, "Yes, Rozi is Amrozi." I had originally been given the Indonesian intelligence document in April 2002—it was clear Indonesia knew Amrozi was part of a terrorist network more than six months before the Bali blasts.

Then an intelligence source told me they were looking for Amrozi's brother, a man named Mukhlas. In that same Indonesian document, I found several references to a Mukhlas, someone who seemed quite high up in the organization. He, according to the document, replaced Hambali as the leader of Mantiqi 1, one of the four JI territories in Southeast Asia.

"Mukhlas would be appointed to replace him since his name had been mentioned in the mass media as a person wanted by the security agencies," the document states.[8] The man who signed those appointment papers was Abu Bakar Ba'asyir.

Finally, this same document mentioned another Indonesian named

Imam Samudra, alias Abdul Aziz, alias Kudama, who acted as an inter-mediary between Mukhlas and Amrozi.

Based on that one document alone—a document I had more than half a year before Bali—and the confirmation of my intelligence sources, I was able to piece together the terrorist network that carried out the Bali attacks before they were even arrested: Amrozi, the foot-soldier, reported to Imam Samudra. Imam Samudra, the field comman-der, reported to Mukhlas, Amrozi's brother, the leader of Mantiqi 1. Mukhlas reported to Hambali, who works with Abu Bakar Ba'asyir.

A few days after CNN aired a report outlining the structure of this cell, the Indonesian police arrested Imam Samudra. Two weeks later, Mukhlas was also arrested.

The Indonesian police knew of the existence of this particular cell as early as April: I was told they believed these men carried out the Christmas church bombings in Indonesia in December 2000. If the men had been arrested, the deaths in Bali might have been prevented.

Today, although more than ninety suspected JI members have been arrested (as of August 2003), most are members of JI's Mantiqi 1, the cell that carried out the Bali bombings on October 12, 2002, and the J.W. Marriott Hotel bombing on August 5, 2003. Mantiqi 3, which cov-ers parts of Indonesia, the MILF camps in the southern Philippines, Malaysia, and Brunei, remains operational, complete with training camps and al-Qaeda operatives. The story of Mantiqi 3 again shows how the internal rift between the Indonesian police and military intelli-gence has only given the terrorists more time to prepare and carry out their plots in peace.

Nearly a year before the Bali blasts, Spain warned Indonesia of the existence of an al-Qaeda cell and a training camp within its borders. In October 2001, Spanish judge Baltasar Garzón announced he would be sending a commission to Indonesia to look for Parlindungan Siregar, an Indonesian national who Garzón claimed was part of al-Qaeda's cell in Spain.[9]

Known as "Parlin," the Indonesian was the right-hand man of Imad Eddin Barakat Yarbas, a Syrian of Spanish nationality who led al-Qaeda's cell in Spain and traveled frequently around the world to recruit Muslims in Europe, Malaysia, Indonesia, and Jordan. His arrest, along with seven other cell members, capped a two-year investigation by a judge best known for leading Spain's crackdown on the Basque separatist group, ETA, and an attempt in 2000 to try Chilean ex-dictator Augusto Pinochet.

In court documents authored by Judge Garzón, Yarbas is linked to the September 11 attacks. In fact, Garzón claimed Yarbas, also known as Abu Dahdah, had prior knowledge of the operation. His Madrid telephone number was found in the address book of Said Bahaji, charged in Germany for helping the 9/11 hijackers. Yarbas has also been linked to Ramzi bin al-Shibh, who admitted planning the attacks with KSM, and head hijacker Mohammed Atta.

In one phone call on August 27, 2001, an al-Qaeda operative identified only as "Shakur" called Yarbas and gave him a coded message. "I have stopped all communications, and I am much calmer psychologically. In class, we have entered into the field of aviation, and we have slit the bird's throat." He asked Yarbas not to mention their conversation to anyone. "My objective is the objective, and I don't want to go into details," he added.[10]

Judge Garzón, in a court order, said this conversation and others refer to the September 11 attacks: "The extreme measures of security and the cryptic nature of the conversations indicate that they refer to the attacks of 9/11/01."[11]

Spain had been tapping the phones of Yarbas since 1995, and it was through another telephone conversation that they first discovered the existence of an al-Qaeda training camp in Indonesia. The call was placed on July 7, 2001 from Indonesia by Parlin, who is the "leader of one of the existing camps in this country [Indonesia] at the service of Osama bin Laden."[12]

Parlin spent the 1990s in Madrid, where he studied aeronautical engineering. Spanish investigators say he was responsible for sending up to three thousand Muslim fighters from Europe to Indonesia for training. Parlin "recruited mujahideens in Spain to be sent to terrorist-military training camps in Afghanistan, Bosnia, and Indonesia."[13]

Yarbas and another al-Qaeda cell member from Spain, Luis Jose Galan Gonzalez, a.k.a. Yusuf Galan, told Judge Garzón they had visited Parlin in Indonesia and given him money, but they denied the existence of training camps.[14] Yet, in his court indictment, Judge Garzón wrote that Luis Gonzalez had been "sent as a mujahideen to Indonesia with the objective of successfully obtaining a military terrorist training course in the month of July 2001."[15]

Spain says it gave the information about the terrorist cell and its training camp to the United States and to Indonesia. "We gave the Indonesian authorities a wealth of details," said the Spanish police. "From the possible location of the terrorist camp to the details of Parlin and the telephone number which he used in his communications with Spain, but they never came back to us."[16] At one point, there were rumors in Jakarta that the United States had given Indonesia satellite photographs of the camp, but publicly, the Indonesian police quickly denied any links to al-Qaeda and continued to do so until shortly after the Bali bombings.

In a clear sign of the split between Indonesia's police and military intelligence, less than three months later, an Indonesian military intelligence report stated the camp existed and that at least one of its instructors is a member of al-Qaeda. "The training camp led by Omar Bandon consisted of eight to ten small villages located side by side on the beach, equipped with light weapons, explosives, and firing range. Participants of the training are not only from local people but also from overseas. The instructor of physical training in the camp is Parlindungan Siregar, a member of al-Qaeda's network in Spain."[17]

While his police counterpart, National Police Chief Da'i Bachtiar, continued to deny any Indonesian links to al-Qaeda, the head of Indonesia's National Intelligence coordinating body, A. M. Hendropriyono, publicly admitted the camp existed—only to be forced to retract his statement a day later. Months later, Hendropriyono admitted military intelligence knew of the camp's existence. "The training camp was not used by Indonesians, but by foreigners. It was by foreigners, for foreigners," he said.[18] Hendropriyono told me that the tip from Spain led Indonesian law enforcement to discover a training camp near Poso, Sulawesi. It was on a beach, set back on a remote island, off traveled routes. By the time officials got there in December 2001, the camp had been abandoned, shut down, they believed, soon after the September 11 attacks.

Intelligence officials in Indonesia and the Philippines say they believe that the Poso camp was set up by Laskar Jundullah, the JI group headed by Indonesian Agus Dwikarna, now in prison in the Philippines. With the help of al-Qaeda operative Omar al-Faruq and, officials believe, Parlindungan Siregar, Dwikarna set up what would become JI's new training camp for the region. Intelligence documents from Southeast Asia show that after the Philippine government attacked the MILF's Camp Abubakar and shut it down in July 2000, Jemaah Islamiyah moved its training camps to Poso. About that time, Poso, long besieged by periodic sectarian conflict, erupted, spreading religious violence from nearby Ambon. Muslim fighters from different groups moved fighters from Ambon to Poso: Laskar Jihad, Laskar Jundullah, which based its force in Poso, and Laskar Mujahideen, fueling conflict between Muslims and Christians.

Indonesian intelligence officials believed the foreigners who trained at the Poso camps actively participated in that war, much like they did in Ambon. In August and October, Indonesian police detained several foreigners traveling in the area. They were released after they showed a letter on behalf of a charity signed by Agus Dwikarna, saying they were there to help rebuild mosques. Much later, that charity would be linked "to Osama bin Laden and al-Qaeda."[19]

Mantiqi 3 has carried out its own attacks, although far smaller and less sophisticated than the Bali bombings. On October 12, 2002, a few hours before the three explosions in Bali, a small explosion hit the Philippine consulate in Manado, Indonesia. One man linked to Mantiqi 3 was arrested soon after. A little less than two months later, on December 5, two simultaneous explosions went off in Makassar, South Sulawesi, the former base of al-Faruq and Agus Dwikarna. One bomb exploded outside a Toyota outlet, the other hit an American icon, McDonald's, killing two people. That restaurant is a few doors down from a Kentucky Fried Chicken, which had been bombed by a similar explosive the year before.

Within days, Indonesia arrested fourteen people, many known members of Laskar Jundullah. During their interrogations, disturbing information was revealed: the presence of up to ten training camps in this part of Indonesia and the fact that many of those arrested had trained in the MILF camps in the Southern Philippines. Several said their weapons were smuggled to Indonesia from the Philippines. South Sulawesi Police Chief Inspector General Firman Gani said he believed the same source supplied the weapons to this group as well as to the Bali cell's Amrozi.[20]

Local police and intelligence officials were cautious about linking the explosions to the JI network, no doubt for political reasons. Statements from the police were infuriatingly ambiguous. "We are not linking the investigation to the Laskar Jundullah. We are only trying to find

the bombers," the local police spokesman, Subagio, told me. "The criminals are the ones we're trying to find." Asked whether the men arrested
admitted to being part of Laskar Jundullah, he said, "We will know
exactly when we find the two we're looking for. They are the key to
everything, Agung and Hisbullah."[21]

Agung Hamid is the commander of Laskar Jundullah and Hisbullah is his deputy. Both men were often seen in the company of
al-Qaeda operative Omar al-Faruq. "They are all friends, and al-Faruq
also lived at Agung's house in 1998," South Sulawesi Intelligence Chief
Achmad Abdi told me.[22]

Even more alarming, at least two of the suspects told investigators
they were planning a new round of bombing attacks for Christmas and
New Year's in 2002. "They have already prepared the bomb container,
the TNT explosive material for the bombs, bomb detonators, and
bombing sketches," said Police Chief Inspector General Firman Gani.[23]

A new order for fifty bomb detonators had been placed through one
of the men who had been arrested. Meantime, ten detonators had already
been assembled into bombs. Two of these bombs were set off in Poso and
two in Makassar. Two others were sent to Manado. The remaining four
were taken by Agung Hamid, who is still on the run.

It seems clear Mantiqi 3 is trying to get its resources together to
mount an attack. In the last two weeks of July 2003, authorities discovered three different caches of explosives on the island of Sulawesi. The
largest on July 26 included eighteen homemade bombs made of ammonium nitrate, the same explosive used in Bali.

In mid-2002, intelligence officials in Southeast Asia told me there were
at least 12 tons of explosives missing in Southeast Asia, feared to be in
the hands of Jemaah Islamiyah and al-Qaeda: 4.6 tons in the Philippines, 4 tons in Malaysia, at least 4 tons in Indonesia. The 4 tons in
Malaysia were recovered in March 2003—the ammonium nitrate originally purchased by Hambali's deputy, Yazid Sufaat. They were buried
near the border of Malaysia and Singapore at the home of a cousin of
Taufik Abdul Halim, one of the first operatives arrested in Indonesia.
The other caches have not been found.

Al-Qaeda operative Omar al-Faruq told his CIA interrogators that
a Saudi sheikh, using a pseudonym allegedly linked to Osama bin

Laden, wired $74,000 to Abu Bakar Ba'asyir to purchase up to four tons of explosives in Indonesia. "It is very likely," Rohan Gunaratna told me, "that a portion of those explosives was used to construct the device and the devices that were detonated in Bali."

Abu Bakar Ba'asyir was put on trial in Indonesia, along with the members of the Bali bombing cell: Amrozi, Imam Samudra, Ali Imron, Idris, and Mukhlas, among the nearly ninety members of Jemaah Islamiyah arrested through August 2003. Indonesia's fledgling court and justice system has done little to engender trust: since the fall of Suharto, the buying and selling of verdicts has become increasingly blatant, easy in a judicial system backed by a legal code rife with contradictions.

Nevertheless, on August 7, 2003, a Balinese court handed a death sentence to Amrozi, the first of the Bali bombers to hear a verdict. He turned around, smiled and gave two thumbs-up. Days earlier, Amrozi told journalists he was prepared to die a martyr's suicide. "Even though I will soon be dead, our mission will be continued by our children and grandchildren," said Amrozi. "It will never stop. There will be a million more like me who will follow. Their name will not be the same as mine, but they will behave the same as me. And the smile, that too, will probably be different from mine."[24]

The verdict in the case of Abu Bakar Ba'asyir is more ambiguous. Soon after Amrozi's verdict, a Jakarta court said it had insufficient evidence to convict Ba'asyir as the head of Jemaah Islamiyah. Instead, Ba'asyir was sentenced—for immigration and treason charges—to four years in prison, far less than the fifteen years demanded by prosecutors or the maximum penalty of life in prison.

Evidence that Jemaah Islamiyah is planning more terrorist operations and remains capable of carrying them out continues to surface. On July 11, 2003, Indonesian authorities announced the arrest of nine more JI members, including two senior members. Four were arrested in the central Java provincial capital of Semarang while five were captured in the capital, Jakarta. In Semarang, those arrests led to the discovery of a JI base camp where police recovered enough explosives to make ten Bali bombs.[25] Among the materials they seized were 900 kilograms of potassium chlorate (the same explosive used by the Bali bombers), 160 kilograms (four boxes) of TNT, 1,200 bomb detonators, 65 high-explosive boosters, 11 shoulder-launched rockets, more than 20,000 rounds of ammunition, M16 rifles, timers, batteries, maps and other documents.

Within days, the Indonesian government warned about the potential for another JI attack on the scale of Bali or larger. Jakarta police
spokesman Colonel Prasetyo[26] said the men "had confessed to investigators that they had sent eight bombs to Jakarta" before their arrest.[27]
Among the documents, they found a list of churches in Jakarta, plans
and maps for shopping malls, and a list of Indonesian legislators. Police
later said they found plans to assassinate four senior officials from President Megawati's political party. "They were planning to launch a string
of bomb attacks on malls and places of worship and to assassinate several noted figures," said Jakarta Police Chief Superintendent General
Makbul Padmanagara.

It's not the first time that authorities found evidence JI members
were actively plotting another attack. One of the men arrested in that
last raid committed suicide while in custody, but police discovered he
lived a block away from the home of President Megawati and had been
planning to set off a bomb on the road used by her convoy. More than a
month earlier when Idris, the man who detonated one of the Bali bombs,
was arrested, police found that instead of hiding in remote areas of
Indonesia, he had been moving in and out of major city centers, meeting
and plotting attacks with other JI members. He had just finished an operation in Medan, Sumatra: his newly reconstituted cell had just robbed a
bank of $20,000, which they planned to use to fund another attack.

Only when it was too late would police realize which attack that
was—discovering that six of the men they arrested, including Idris, had
started working in January on a plot that would be carried out on August
5, 2003. On that day, a suicide bomber recruited by Idris named Asmar
Latin Sani would drive a utility vehicle toward the lobby of the J.W.
Marriott Hotel in Jakarta's central business district. As security guards
approached him, Asmar detonated the bomb, an explosion so fierce it
decapitated his head, authorities say, and hurled it to the fifth floor of the
hotel. The blast shattered all the windows of the two nearby buildings up
to the thirtieth floor, killing 12 people and injuring nearly 150.

Similar to Bali, the authorities were forewarned. Six weeks earlier,
police had intercepted an e-mail from Asmar to a JI operative, according to Gories Mere, the new head of the Indonesian police counterterrorism task force.[28]

"The e-mail interception that mentions he wants 'to marry as soon
as possible.' 'Marry' is a word, a code word of the JI, 'I want to plant a

bomb,' a suicide bomb. He wants to make a suicide bomb," said Gories Mere, talking about Asmar.

It's unclear what was done in those six weeks, but police knew enough to get DNA samples of Asmar's parents and compare it with the DNA samples at the scene to identify him. "We bring it back to compare with the hand found on the crime scene and also with the blood," said Gories, "to compare it if the DNA is identical as Asmar who has sent an e-mail message to other people on another day."

The funding, said police detective Erwin Mappaseng, allegedly came from Hambali, who sent $45,000 to finance attacks in Indonesia against American interests. Police say they believe the bomb, using explosives left over from the Christmas Eve attacks, was built by the same men who built the Bali bombs: Dr. Azahari Husin working with Dulmatin. Both men remain free. Intelligence sources say they believe Hambali's key deputies, including Noordin Mohamed Top (also wanted for Bali) and Zulkarnaen (who heads Jemaah Islamiyah's elite unit) had converged in Jakarta and were planning more attacks.

Indeed, it is an open question whether the arrests have really stopped any terrorist activity. Leaders and operatives have been replaced quickly. Abu Bakar Ba'asyir was replaced by a man named Abu Rusdan. He was arrested on April 23, 2003, at about the same time as the opening of Ba'asyir's trial. As soon as Abu Rusdan was arrested, he was—just as easily—replaced, and now authorities are trying to find that successor. Seventeen other JI members were arrested at about the same time as Abu Rusdan, including Malaysian Nasir bin Abbas, known to Filipinos as Abu Solaiman, the self-confessed head of Mantiqi 3 and the first agent handler of Fathur Roman al-Ghozi.

Bin Abbas told the Indonesian police of a top-level JI meeting in Puncak, Bogor, in Indonesia held on April 7, 2003. He said at least sixteen JI leaders were there for the one-day meeting—including the heads of all four JI Mantiqis.[29]

On Monday, August 11, 2003, at 10:30 P.M., Thai police, working with the CIA, knocked down the door of a one-bedroom apartment in Ayutthaya, Thailand, a mainly Buddhist town about an hour away from Bangkok. Inside, they found the man George Bush described as "one of the world's most lethal terrorists"—Asia's most wanted man, Hambali.

Thailand quickly turned Hambali over to the CIA, which moved him to an unidentified country for interrogation.

Despite his arrest, the threat alert level has never been higher in Southeast Asia. "This region still faces an unprecedented threat," said Rohan Gunaratna. "In terms of attacks, we will not see an appreciable decline because Hambali had groomed and trained many others to succeed him in the event he was captured."[30]

Soon after the Bali bombings, I began finding JI and al-Qaeda links to Thailand and Cambodia. For Thailand, much of what I was putting together seemed circumstantial: in 1994, Ramzi Yousef plotted to bomb the U.S. embassy in Bangkok and when he fled Manila after the al-Qaeda cell was exposed in 1995, he transited through Bangkok en route to Pakistan; in 2002, JI leaders Agus Dwikarna and Fathur Roman al-Ghozi both were departing Manila with tickets for Bangkok. At best, Thailand seemed a favored transit point until I read the interrogation reports of several JI and al-Qaeda operatives, all of whom said that once the crackdown began in Singapore and Malaysia in December 2001, top leaders were told to flee to Thailand. It was in southern Thailand that Hambali called together a meeting that plotted the genesis of the Bali bombings: to "bomb bars, cafes, and nightclubs frequented by Westerners in Thailand, Malaysia, Singapore, the Philippines and Indonesia."

In December 2002, I received a letter from the Thai foreign ministry spokesman, Rathakit Manathat, reacting to several exclusive reports on CNN. "CNN, quoting sources from intelligence agencies, said that there were terrorist operatives in Thailand," Manathat wrote. "But anyone working in intelligence organizations would know that there is interdependency between intelligence agencies, both domestically and internationally, and surely, Thai intelligence agencies would have been furnished with any vital information on terrorists by its counterparts in other countries."

I responded to the letter politely, standing by the credibility of the documents I had gathered and the intelligence agencies I had named, including the FBI. This missive showed me that either the United States did not share that information with Thailand or Thai officials were not keeping its information ministry in the loop—both instances I've seen in neighboring countries. The rest of the letter rebuked me for causing alarm and potentially harming Thailand's tourism industry. Thailand remained in denial for another six months. During that time, Thai prime minister Thaksin Shinawatra repeatedly lashed out at Western governments which had issued travel advisories for Thailand and vehemently denied any links to terrorist groups like Jemaah Islamiyah or al-Qaeda.

On May 16, 2003, based on a tip from Singapore, authorities in Thailand arrested Singaporean Arifin bin Ali, alias John Wong Ah Hung, and three Thais, all allegedly members of Jemaah Islamiyah who had been plotting to bomb an APEC (Asia Pacific Economic Cooperation) summit to be attended by U.S. president George W. Bush later in the year. Finally in June, Thaksin Shinawatra reversed his earlier statements and admitted Jemaah Islamiyah had a cell in his country with ambitious plans.

The three Thais were arrested in southern Thailand on June 10, while Arifin was arrested in Bangkok nearly a month earlier and quickly deported to Singapore. In interrogations with authorities in Singapore, Arifin said he had been hiding in Thailand since January 2002 and that he was "involved with a group of like-minded individuals in planning terrorist attacks against certain targets in Thailand."[31] Singapore and Thai officials said the JI cell was planning to carry out attacks against five foreign embassies in Bangkok as well as on two popular beach resorts in Thailand, Pattaya, and Phuket.

These revelations and arrests followed similar news from Cambodia. On May 27, 2003, Cambodia arrested two Thais and an Egyptian[32] at the Om al-Qura mosque just north of the capital of Phnom Penh on suspicions they were plotting a terrorist operation linked to a June regional security meeting to be attended by U.S. secretary of state Colin Powell. Cambodia's prime minister Hun Sen closed down the Om al-Qura Institute, which is operated by a nongovernmental organization that receives most of its funding from Saudi Arabia. It was headed by Egyptian Esam Mohamid Khidr Ali. Intelligence sources told me they believe Om al-Qura laundered money and funds for al-Qaeda on a massive scale. Nearly five hundred Muslim students were affected when Cambodia closed down the Institute. Teachers and their families from Yemen, Thailand, Sudan, Nigeria, Pakistan, and Egypt were given seventy-two hours to leave the country.

"We have been investigating with the United States since the terrorist attacks in New York," said Hun Sen, in a speech broadcast on national radio. "From the investigation with the United States, we have found out there is a network of terrorists hiding in Cambodia."

Cambodian officials said they had a list of names they were investigating. Indonesian intelligence sources claim some of those named were discovered in a safehouse in Indonesia.

Nations with weak governments, and law enforcement agencies riddled with corruption and inefficiency, are vulnerable to al-Qaeda, which exploits the cracks in their societies. And although one nation can clamp down hard on a cell, if neighboring countries aren't following suit, the operatives simply retreat into that safe haven. Many Southeast Asian nations have made informal arrangements with domestic radical groups. As early as 1994, KSM told his American interrogators "he was . . . impressed with Hambali's connections with the Malaysian government, which allowed him freedom of movement in return for an agreement to concentrate on targets in Indonesia and not to hit targets in Malaysia."[33] Indonesian law enforcement agencies had the same informal arrangements with Indonesian radical groups, including with JI leader Abu Bakar Ba'asyir, even after the 9/11 attacks. A high-ranking Indonesian intelligence official told me, "The idea was always that we left him alone as long as he didn't do anything within our borders." And, of course, even today in the Philippines, MILF fighters maintain camps where JI and al-Qaeda members find sanctuary and receive training.

What is the worst-case scenario? Consider just one. On June 13, 2003, a combined Thai-U.S. sting operation in Bangkok raised fears al-Qaeda could easily get their hands on radioactive material in Southeast Asia to create a dirty bomb, using conventional explosives to disperse radioactive material.

Forty-four-year-old Thai national Narong Penanam is a respected figure in his home village near the Thai-Cambodian border, where he runs a public elementary school. In June 2003, he was arrested in the parking lot of a Bangkok hotel after he tried to sell what he thought was uranium to undercover Thai and U.S. agents for $240,000. American officials said the material seized was cesium-137, a radioactive by-product of nuclear power plants, believed to have come from Russian stockpiles and taken to Thailand via Laos. Initial reports said Narong had as much as 66 pounds, or 30 kilograms, of the radioactive material, enough to contaminate a major city. In fact, he only possessed one gram, just enough to spike a conventional bomb and strew radiation over the blast radius, which could shut down the area for months for expensive decontamination.

Although Narong had no connections to terrorist groups like JI, he was prepared to sell the radioactive material to anyone who would pay his asking price. We know al-Qaeda has dedicated resources to procure and develop chemical, biological, and nuclear weapons. There is no doubt al-Qaeda will buy what men like Narong offer.

So what can be done now? Aside from the military response and the capture of thousands of al-Qaeda operatives globally, I've pinpointed specific weak points throughout the book which must be addressed to win the war on terror.

For the United States, new global realities demand a reassessment of its foreign policy. It must take into account international opinions and moods, particularly from the Arab and Muslim worlds, and give that as much importance as the domestic impetus for determining policy. That's where the work begins, not in public relations. The more the United States is perceived to be dealing with an even hand, the more effective will be its position as the leader of the global war on terror.

In Southeast Asia, counterterrorism units and legislation must be given higher priority and, more important, counterterrorism personnel must be insulated from politics. In Indonesia and the Philippines, the key figures leading intelligence gathering and investigation have all been replaced more than a year into their work, like I Made Pastika, who led the Bali investigations. Largely prompted by jealousy, superiors shunted him to another position; at one point, I was told he couldn't grant an interview to CNN because publicity had become bad for his career. Pastika's reassignment has cut institutional memory and ensured that experience in fighting terror is frittered away. Both Indonesia and the Philippines are preparing for elections in 2004, and politicians, seeing the high-profile attention given to terrorism, have maneuvered to remove effective counterterrorism agents and replace them with personnel loyal to their political objectives. As one Filipino agent told me, "It's become difficult to work. The generals keep wanting their boys to be part of the unit so they replace the men who have done good work."

To varying degrees, politics again is contributing to the level of denial that remains in place in Southeast Asia about the extent and the depth of the terrorism network. In Indonesia, for example, a recent survey conducted by a national magazine showed that only 21 percent of Indonesians believe Jemaah Islamiyah exists. It doesn't help that the Indonesian government and President Megawati herself have never fully set the record straight, largely because of political considerations. The result is a confused, confusing, and defensive national debate that tends to blame the Unites States and defend Islam rather than focusing on the very real problem of terrorism.

On the intelligence front: although it has improved, true intelligence sharing remains an ideal. Proposals have been made to create a regional databank, but this will also likely remain an ideal until Southeast Asian nations, along with the United States, bring down the barriers of distrust separating individual agencies from truly sharing information.

The financial network set in place by Khalifa, bin Laden's brother-in-law in 1998, remains largely intact. It has grown in scope and continues to operate today. Malaysia, where many of these companies operate, remains defensive about the presence of the financial network. Only after the denial is shed can governments begin shutting down these financial conduits.

Finally, there is the propaganda war, the ideological battle the West is losing. In Southeast Asia and South Asia, it begins with the "pipelines of terror"—the Islamic schools, the madrassas and *pesantrens*, which spread the virulent ideology of radical Islam to children. It progresses to schools established by Jemaah Islamiyah, like Abu Bakar Ba'asyir's Pondok Ngruki school, which continues to operate today. These schools inculcate hatred for non-Muslims and breed new recruits for Jemaah Islamiyah and al-Qaeda.

Al-Qaeda's ideology unites disparate Muslim groups, crossing national and ethnic lines. The West has not done enough to fight ideology with ideology. Law enforcement and military action are not enough. If pursued excessively, they are bound to fail. The United States and its Western allies have become their own worst enemies by acting in ways that reinforce and perpetuate the stereotypes propagated by al-Qaeda. There is only one way to win the global war on terrorism—by supporting the moderate Muslims around the world, and by asking for their help. The operative word is "ask"; Americans cannot dictate or demand. Until and unless the West realizes this and begins to act accordingly, al-Qaeda will find supporters for its radical ideology. Yes, law enforcement is crucial, and military maneuvers against al-Qaeda camps must continue. But the linchpin of the war is the Muslim moderates in every Islamic community around the world, who must once again tell the world exactly what Islam truly stands for. They face a difficult task of trying to cage an amorphous enemy that uses their language and traditions to inspire a primal response.

The Al-Qaeda Manual's preamble is blunt: "Islamic governments have never and will never be established through peaceful solutions and cooperative councils. They are established, as they have always been by pen and gun, by word and bullet, by tongue and teeth."[34] It is through both means that the battles are fought and must be won.

ACKNOWLEDGMENTS

This book holds the experiences of nearly seventeen years of work in television in Southeast Asia, most of that reporting for CNN, which has remained committed to the coverage of international news. Although it is, at times, truly exhausting, it has also given me a front-row seat to history and a life I could never have dreamed of. My thanks to Eason Jordan, gave me room to grow; Steve Cassidy, who taught me as much about human nature as he did about the business of news; Parisa Khosravi, who showed me nothing can stand in the way of a determined will; and Ian Macintosh, who combines diplomacy with keen sensitivity.

CNN's investigative team pulled information from all over the world to piece together the picture of al-Qaeda post-9/11. My thanks to our fearless leader, Fuzz Hogan, for going through the manuscript, and to my colleagues Kelli Arena, Susan Candiotti, David Ensor, Phil Hirschkorn, Andrea Koppel, Carol Cratty, and Kevin Bohn, indefatigable in their pursuit of the facts.

Many of the ideas here I discovered while working for CNN's documentary unit under Sid Bedingfield, who commissioned the one-hour documentary *Seeds of Terror.* Producer Ken Shiffman gathered many of these interviews with me. Jennifer Hyde's constructive comments for the documentary and this manuscript were always astute and encouraging, while Kathy Slobogin's rapier pen showed me the punch of good TV writing.

The Row has honed my writing skills and constantly pushed me to do better: Richard Griffiths, Michael Schulder, Henry Schuster, Paul Varian, Ric Ward, Tim Langmaid, and David George.

CNN has also given me the privilege of putting together my own team in Jakarta and Manila, many of whom I have worked with since 1986, and together we have lived through these events. My gratitude to Taffy Santiago, the nail that holds my professional and personal life together, and our collective den mother; to my cameraman, Rene Santiago, whose presence by my side in any war zone automatically makes me feel safer; my producer-editor, Kathy Quiano, my sparring mate. Joining us later and contributing to the book were Atika Shubert, Armand Sol, Judith Torres, Andrew Clark, Boying Palileo, Nuraki Aziz, Rudy Madanir, Jess Liwanag, Ikbal Wahyuddin, Domeng Magora, and Bambang Pardi.

In each country, there were numerous people who gave generously of their time and insights. Thanks go to Philippine president Gloria Macapagal-Arroyo and her staff, Immigration Commissioner Andrea Domingo, Col. Winnie Quidato, Col. Rodolfo "Boogie" Mendoza, Gen. Jaime Caringal, Col. Fritz Galban, former defense secretary Angelo Reyes, former Pakistani prime minister Benazir Bhutto, Singapore's defense minister Tony Tan and his staff, Singapore's minister of home affairs Wong Kan Seng and his spokeswoman, Chew Peck Wan, Malaysia's former prime minister Mahathir Mohamad, Datuk Zakaria Wahab, Malaysian prime minister Abdullah Badawi, Malaysian defense minister Mohammad Najib bin Tun Haji Abdul Razak, former Indonesian president B. J. Habibie, Dewi Fortuna Anwar, A. M. Hendropriyono, Luhut Pandjaitan, Adm. (ret.) Dennis Blair, Adm. T. McCreary, Adm. Thomas Fargo, Capt. John Singley, and U.S. deputy secretary of defense Paul Wolfowitz. There are many more men and women I cannot name—the intelligence agents and analysts who often have to work under difficult circumstances with very little reward. It is their work that forms the bedrock of this book.

So many others have spent countless hours debating with me or helping sort through information: Rohan Gunaratna, who read through my manuscript, Zach Abuza, Seth Mydans, Anastasia Vrachnos, Lynn Felton, Andrew Henstock, Glenda Gloria, Marites Vitug, Sally Neighbour, Anna Hidalgo, Paula Guinto, Anna Rodriguez, Julie Alipala, Will King, Maria Ebrahimji, Carter Clay, Don Greenlees, and Barbara Gonzalez.

My undying gratitude to the best editor any first-time author can have, Bruce Nichols, who took a lengthy manuscript, found a grain of sand and turned it into a pearl, and to Martha Levin and Dominic Anfuso for believing this TV reporter could write. To my agent, Rafe Sagalyn, who took the time to listen to an idea and found a home for it within forty-eight hours, and Charley Hayward, who opened the first door.

In the final stages, thank you to Elisa Rivlin for a painless and thoughtful legal review; to Tricia Wygal for overseeing the copyediting of the book; to Courtney Fischer and Carisa Hays in Free Press publicity; to CNN's Rick Davis, Marianna Spicer-Brooks, and Lee Rivera, who quickly reviewed the manuscript; and to Eslinda Hamzah, who carried pages of proofs from New Delhi to Hong Kong to try to help me make my deadline.

Finally, my gratitude to my family—my parents, Peter and Hermelina, my sisters, Mary Jane, Michelle, Nicole, and my brother, Peter Ames—for always supporting my far-fetched ideas and projects and forgiving my long absences; and to the two people without whom this book would never have been written: Leslie Tucker, who made me believe good friends are better than psychiatrists, and held my hand through every stage of the process, starting with how to get an agent, reading every draft and challenging my ideas; and Jeanette Ifurung, the turtle, who forced me to write when I didn't want to, encouraged me when I was ready to give up, and always, always challenged me to tell a story.

E N D N O T E S

Prelude: Face to Face with Osama bin Laden

1. Author telephone interview with Mark Phillips, June 25, 2003; interview with Rohan Gunaratna, November 2002.
2. Transcript of tape C189#1 from Terror Tapes.
3. Interviews with U.S. officials traveling to the region, October 2001–April 2002.
4. Off-the-record briefings in the Philippines, Indonesia, Malaysia, and Singapore.
5. Author interview with Ajai Sahni, Institute for Conflict Management in New Delhi, India, on October 17, 2002.

Chapter 1: Pictures Don't Lie

1. Classified Philippine intelligence document, "Foreign Nationals Conduct Training at MILF Camps," August 24, 2001.
2. Philippine intelligence document, Person Report—Mohammed Jamal Khalifa, 1995.
3. Classified Philippine intelligence documents, introduction of *The Islamic Fundamentalist/Extremist Movements in the Philippines and Their Links with International Terrorist Organizations*, a PNP-IC Special Investigation Group (SIG) report released December 15, 1994. It was written by Boogie Mendoza but signed and submitted by Rodolfo Garcia as the Director of PNP Intelligence. Contains all statistics and graphs in appendix.
4. Author interview with Pakistan's former prime minister, Benazir Bhutto, New Delhi, India, November 25, 2001.
5. Author interview with Philippine immigration commissioner Andrea Domingo, February 11, 2003.
6. Author interview with Philippine president Gloria Macapagal-Arroyo, Malacañang Palace, Manila, Philippines, February 21, 2002.
7. Author interview with Philippine president Gloria Macapagal-Arroyo, Malacañang Palace, Manila, Philippines, January 11, 2003.
8. Kenneth Timmerman, "Direct Ties of Iraqi Intelligence Agents to Terry Nichols?" *Insight Online*, April 19, 2002.
9. Carlos H. Conde, "Muslim Cleric Confirms Bin Laden Visit to Mindanao," *Philippine Daily Inquirer*, November 13, 2001.

CHAPTER 2: THE BASE

1. Classified Philippine intelligence document, "Police Tactical Interrogation Report of Catherine Subala Brioso alias Cathy/Carol Santiago," January 15, 1995.

2. Ibid.

3. Spelling according to Philippine tactical interrogation report of Brioso. CIA documents of the Norwegian passport put it under the name Grabi Ibrahim Hahsen.

4. CIA documents summarizing the four passports used by Wali Khan Amin Shah and his exit/entry stamps and visas, 1995.

5. Details for the description of their relationship came from Philippine intelligence, "Police Tactical Interrogation Report of Catherine Subala Brioso."

6. Classified Philippine intelligence report, CM Report #01, January 17, 1995.

7. Philippine intelligence reports, February 5–June 10, 1995, detailing activities of Abdul Majid and Salim (Salem) Ali.

8. Classified Philippine intelligence reports, "Chronological Activities of Rose Mosquera," 1995.

9. Classified Philippine intelligence document, CounterIntelligence Group, "BI of Aminda Castanos Custodio," January 1995.

10. Classified Philippine intelligence report, "Additional Report re BI on Aminda Custodio," February 2, 1995. Aminda's mother, Leticia Custodio, told police that Jane Ramos was the girlfriend of Salem Ali and Adam Ali was the boyfriend of her daughter, Aminda.

11. Classified Philippine intelligence report, "After Debriefing Report," January 20, 1995. Information came from police interrogation of Abdul Hakim Murad.

12. Ibid.

13. Classified Philippine intelligence document, "After Debriefing Report," March 9, 1995.

14. Information pieced together from Philippine intelligence documents and an interview with Pakistan's former prime minister Benazir Bhutto, December 15, 2002.

15. Classified Philippine intelligence document, "After Debriefing Report," March 4, 1995.

16. Classified Philippine intelligence document, "Additional Info," January 25, 1995.

17. Classified Philippine intelligence document, "Debriefing Report No. 2," February 13, 1995.

18. Glenda Gloria and Marites Danguilan Vitug, *Under the Crescent Moon: Rebellion in Mindanao* (Manila: Ateneo Center for Social Policy and Public Affairs, 2000), 205.

19. Classified Philippine military intelligence report, 1991.

20. *Kyodo News International*, February 4, 2002.

21. Ibid.
22. Details of the funding and terrorist plots were found in a classified Philippine intelligence document, "Person Report—Mohammed Jamal Khalifa," 1996.
23. Ibid.
24. Jeffrey Tupas, "The Boy Who Wants to Be a Rebel," *Philippine Daily Inquirer*, December 22, 2002.
25. Information from several sources: classified U.S. intelligence document, "Revelations of Khalid Shaikh Mohammed," April 2003; classified Philippine intelligence document, "Interrogation Report of Ashraf Barreto Kunting," undated; and classified Philippine intelligence document, "Interrogation Report of Abdulmukim O. Edris," May 2003. The three al-Qaeda members sent by bin Laden were Yacub al-Bahr, Abu Bakr al-Suhri and Talha al-Madhani. The two al-Qaeda members in Abu Sayyaf camps on Sept 12, 2001 were identified as Faisal al-Domlab a.k.a. Yacub al-Bahr and Fahad M.H. Hawbani a.k.a. Yasser b al-O Taibi/Azzam.
26. Simon Reeve, *The New Jackals: Ramzi Yousef, Osama Bin Laden and the Future of Terrorism* (London: Andre Deutsch, 1999), 75.
27. Classified Philippine intelligence document, "After Debriefing Report," March 4, 1995.
28. Transcripts of Murad's interrogation in Manila, January 7, 1995, p. 1.
29. Ibid.
30. Ibid., p. 3.
31. Interview with former FBI agent, September 29, 2002.
32. U.S. District Court, *Southern District of New York, USA v. Ramzi Ahmed Yousef et al.*, indictment, 1996.
33. Classified U.S. intelligence document, "Revelations of Khalid Shaikh Mohammed," April 2003.
34. Classified Philippine intelligence document, "Revelation of Murad re PAL Bombing," February 20, 1995.
35. Testimony of PAL stewardess Maria de la Cruz in Manila Air bombing trial, May 30, 1996.
36. Classified Philippine intelligence document, "Revelation of Murad re PAL Bombing."
37. Testimony of Yukihiko Usui at the Manila Air bombing trial, June 3, 1996.
38. Classified Philippine intelligence document, "After Debriefing Report," January 20, 1995.
39. Classified Philippine intelligence document, "Debriefing Report on Abdul Hakim Ali Hashim Murad," February 18, 1995.
40. Classified Philippine intelligence document, "After Debriefing Report," March 31, 1995.
41. Ibid.
42. Classified Philippine intelligence document, "After Debriefing Report," March 9, 1995.

43. Classified Philippine intelligence document, "Debriefing Report," January 20, 1995.

44. Author interview with Philippine presidential spokesman Rigoberto Tiglao, September 16, 2001.

45. Classified Philippine intelligence document, "Additional Information Obtained from Murad," February 8, 1995.

46. Laurie Mylroie, *The War Against America: Saddam Hussein and the World Trade Center Attacks* (Washington, D.C.: American Enterprise Institute, 2001), p. 204.

47. Classified Philippine intelligence document, "Debriefing Report," February, 1995.

48. Ibid.

49. Author interview, September 14, 2001.

50. Philippine police classified document, "After Intelligence Operation Report re Neutralization of International Terrorists," February 27, 1995.

51. Ibid.

52. Conversation as relayed by Aida Fariscal to the author on several interviews beginning February 12, 2002, and ending April 28, 2002. Fariscal spoke in Tagalog, the native language of the Philippines. It is a far more flowery and descriptive language than English, and some of the idioms she used have no direct translation to English. In those instances, I used the literal translation.

53. Trial in New York of Bojinka plotters, U.S. District Court, Southern District of N.Y., September 1996.

54. Classified police documents—a file retrieved from Ramzi Yousef's laptop computer entitled "Bojinka."

55. Classified Philippine intelligence document, "Significant Revelations of Murad: Tactical Interrogation Report," February 20, 1995. Grammatical errors as written in report.

56. Stephen Jones, *Others Unknown* (New York: Public Affairs, 1998, 2001). Also telephone interview with author.

57. Author telephone interview with Michael Johnston in April 2002. Johnston is one of the lawyers for the relatives of the victims of the Oklahoma City bombing who filed a case against Iraq in a federal district court in Washington, D.C., in March 2002.

58. Jones, *Others Unknown.* Jones traveled to the Philippines and met with Edwin Angeles before he was released from prison in 1996.

59. Murad's confession became part of an FBI 302 report that was referenced in Timothy McVeigh's March 1997 Petition for Writ of Mandamus, Case No. 97-1109.

60. Account of Ipil raid based on videotapes and news reports as well as Glenda Gloria and Marites Danguilan Vitug, *Under the Crescent Moon: Rebellion in Mindanao.*

61. ABS-CBN television interview, April 1995.

62. Classified Philippine intelligence document, "Tactical Interrogation Report," January 13, 1995.

63. A rendition has the same effect as an extradition, but it is done quietly behind the scenes and officially has no legal backing.

64. Author interview, Manila, Philippines.

65. Author interviews with intelligence officials from Southeast Asia, February–December 2002.

CHAPTER 3: THE ASIAN OSAMA BIN LADEN

1. For more details, see the International Crisis Group briefing paper, "Al-Qaeda in Southeast Asia: The Case of the 'Ngruki Network' in Indonesia," August 8, 2002.

2. Author interview, Jakarta, Indonesia, September 14, 1996.

3. International Crisis Group briefing paper, "Al-Qaeda in Southeast Asia: The Case of the 'Ngruki Network' in Indonesia."

4. Author interview, Jakarta, Indonesia, September 14, 1996.

5. Ibid.

6. Amnesty International, "Indonesia: The Imprisonment of Usroh Activists in Central Java," ASA 21/15/88, October 1988, p. 4.

7. Ibid.

8. Author interview, Jakarta, Indonesia, August 8, 2002.

9. Quotes are taken from a series of lectures given by Abu Bakar Ba'asyir. Variations of these messages appear in nearly all his public appearances.

10. Indictment, Abu Bakar Ba'asyir. Indicted in central Jakarta District Court on April 11, 2003.

11. Author briefing with high-ranking Indonesian intelligence officer, August 2002. He quoted from a letter describing Sungkar's meeting with bin Laden. The letter was intercepted by Indonesian authorities.

12. Author interview, Jakarta, Indonesia, August 8, 2002.

13. Author interview, Singapore, February 20, 2003.

14. Author interview, Jakarta, Indonesia, August 2, 1996.

15. Informal lunch, Jakarta, Indonesia, June 29, 1996.

16. Author interview, Jakarta, Indonesia, June 24, 1996.

17. Author interview, Jakarta, Indonesia, August 27, 1996.

18. Colin Johnson, "Survey of Recent Development," *Bulletin of Indonesian Economic Studies*, vol. 34, No. 2, August 2, 1998, p. 51.

19. Author interview, Jakarta, Indonesia, May 21, 1999.

20. Author interview, Jakarta, Indonesia, September 19, 1998.

21. Press conference quoted in the *Jakarta Post*, May 29, 2002.

22. *Tempo Interaktif,* May 30, 2002.

23. Author interview, Jakarta, Indonesia, October 16, 2002.

24. Author interview, Jakarta, Indonesia, February 15, 2003.

25. Confidential briefing, Indonesian intelligence officer, August 2002.

CHAPTER 4: TERROR HQ

1. Press conference, October 16, 1997.
2. Author interview for *CNN Presents* documentary, February 28, 2003.
3. Author interview, January 28, 2003.
4. Anthony Spaeth, "A Code of Their Own," *Time Asia*, September 2, 2002.
5. CNN, *Inside Asia*, February 9, 2002.
6. Author interview, December 18, 2002.
7. Author briefing, Malaysian intelligence source, February 14, 2003.
8. Zachary Abuza, "Tentacles of Terror: Al-Qaeda's Southeast Asian Network," academic paper, November 21, 2002.
9. Classified Philippine intelligence document, "Faiz Bin Abu Bakar Bafana," March 31, 2002.
10. Singapore white paper on JI, January 7, 2003.
11. Interview with regional intelligence officials and Rohan Gunaratna, author of *Inside Al-Qaeda* (New York: Columbia University Press, 2002).
12. CNN interview.
13. Wong Chun Wai and Lourdes Charles, "Hambali Plotted Terror Campaign," *The Star* (Malaysia), January 1, 2003.
14. Simon Elegant, "Asia's Own Osama," *Time*, April 1, 2002.
15. Author interview, Special Branch source, February 14, 2003.
16. Classified U.S. intelligence document, "Revelations of Khalid Shaikh Mohammed," April 2003.
17. Wong Chun Wai and Lourdes Charles, "Hambali Used RM2 Million Collected from Donations to Fund His Extremist Operations," *The Star* (Malaysia), January 1, 2003.
18. Classified FBI document, March 28, 2003.
19. Ibid.
20. Ibid.
21. Elegant, "Asia's Own Osama."
22. Mark Fineman and Richard C. Paddock, "Indonesia Seen as 'Weakest Link' in Anti-Terror War," *Los Angeles Times*, February 16, 2002.
23. Classified Philippine intelligence document, "Faiz Bin Abu Bakar Bafana," March 31, 2002.
24. Ibid.
25. Author interview, January 28, 2003.
26. Author interview with Singapore's home minister, Wong Kan Seng, January 29, 2003.
27. Classified Philippine intelligence document, "Faiz Bin Abu Bakar Bafana," March 31, 2002.
28. A classified regional intelligence report of Faiz's interrogation reveals Faiz maintained the following companies were linked to Jemaah Islamiyah: Alran Salam Sdn Bhd, owned by JI-front Tadika Luqmanul Habin Syafalec; Mawashi Corporation, a construction firm; Min Hwa, a printing press;

MNZ, an auditing firm; Madina Kebab, a buy-and-sell business of processed meat and supplier of food products to restaurants; Al Amin Sdn Bhd; Syafatex Sdn Bhd, engaged in import and export of textiles.

29. Wong Chun Wai and Lourdes Charles, "Terror Suspect Awarded Pipe Project," *The Star* (Malaysia), January 1, 2003.

30. Classified Philippine intelligence document, "Faiz Bin Abu Bakar Bafana," March 31, 2002.

31. Wong and Lourdes Charles, "Hambali Used RM2 Million Collected from Donations to Fund His Extremist Operations."

32. *United States of America* v. *Zacarias Moussaoui*, appellee brief, U.S. Court of Appeals, Fourth Circuit, No. 03-4162, p. 51. Unsealed May 13, 2003. Full document available at www.findlaw.com and cnn.com.

33. Author interviews with U.S. sources, independently confirmed by Susan Schmidt and Ellen Nakashima, "Moussaoui Said Not to Be Part of 9/11 Plot," *Washington Post*, March 28, 2003.

34. Author interview, Singapore, January 29, 2003.

35. *United States of America* v. *Zacarias Moussaoui*.

36. As part of his defense, Moussaoui, acting as his own lawyer, was allowed to conduct a pretrial deposition via videoconference with one of the men he worked with in Malaysia, another Hambali deputy, Faiz bin Abu Bakar Bafana. The quotes from the appellee brief come from that deposition, which took place in the latter part of 2002.

37. *United States of America* v. *Zacarias Moussaoui*.

CHAPTER 5: BLACK NINJAS AND JIHAD IN AMBON

1. Author interview, Banyuwangi, Indonesia, October 22, 1998.

2. Ibid.

3. Ibid.

4. Ibid.

5. Ibid.

6. "Operasi Ninja, Operasi Intelijen," *Gatra*, October 31, 1998.

7. Author interview, Jakarta, Indonesia, May 14, 1999.

8. World Evangelical Alliance, "Indonesia: Violence Resurges in Ambon Massacre," Religious Liberty Prayer List, May 1, 2002.

9. This color coding of fighting groups, I was beginning to realize, was also cultural. I would see it again in Kalimantan, where brutal beheadings were carried out by the yellows, the Dayaks, against the reds, the Madurese.

10. Human Rights Watch Asia, *Indonesia: The Violence in Ambon* (March 1999).

11. "Laporan Tim Pencari Fakta DPW Partai Keadilan Maluku Tentang Kerusuhan Idul Fitri 1419H Berdarah di Ambon," Chapter III, updated as of February 6, 1999.

12. Author interview, Ambon, Indonesia, February 25, 1999.

13. Author interview, Ambon, Indonesia, February 26, 1999.

14. Author interview, Jakarta, Indonesia, March 5, 1999.

15. *Indonesia: Overcoming Murder and Violence in Maluku*, ICG Asia Report No. 10 (Jakarta/Brussels, December 19, 2000).

16. Rajiv Chandrasekaran, "Indonesian Style Taliban Fights for Islamic Law," *Washington Post*, May 4, 2002.

17. Author off-the-record interviews in Washington, D.C., October 2002.

18. Ahmad Suaedy (ed.) *Premanisme Politik* (Jakarta: Institut Studi Arus Informasi, 2000), p. 59.

19. Untitled Indonesian intelligence documents.

20. Rajiv Chandrasekaran, "Diplomats Worry About Indonesia's Tolerance of Islamic Radicals," *Washington Post*, October 13, 2001.

21. Suaedy, *Premanisme Politik*, 113–115.

22. Untitled Indonesian intelligence documents.

23. *Gatra*, March 25, 2000.

24. Author interview, Washington, D.C., March 21, 2003.

25. *Jakarta Post*, May 9, 2000.

26. *Indonesia: The Search for Peace in Maluku*, ICG Asia Report No. 31 (Jakarta/Brussels, February 8, 2002), p. 7.

27. SiaR News Service, June 27, 2000.

28. Jaffar Umar Thalib, "Declaration of War," broadcast on Radio SPMM, the Voice of the Maluku Muslim Struggle, May 1–3, 2002. Text published by Berdarah on May 8, 2002.

29. Reyko Huang, "In the Spotlight: Laskar Jihad," CDI Terrorism Project, Center for Defense Information, March 8, 2002.

30. International Crisis Group, *Bali Bombing: Rift Emerges Within Jemaah Islamiyah* (Jakarta/Brussels, December 11, 2002), p. 26.

31. Classified Philippine intelligence document, "Rabitatul Mujahidin Terrorist Activities," June 30, 2002.

32. Author interview, Manila, Philippines, July 12, 2002.

33. Classified U.S. intelligence document, "Interrogation of Omar al-Faruq," September 9, 2002.

34. Classified Philippine intelligence document, "Agus Dwikarna," July 2, 2002.

35. Classified regional intelligence document, August 25, 2000.

36. Classified U.S. intelligence document, "Involvement of Agus Dwikarna and Laskar Jundullah with Al-Qa'ida: Organization and Plans of Laskar Jundullah," early March 2002.

37. Classified U.S. intelligence document, September 9, 2002.

38. Classified U.S. intelligence document, September 9, 2002. "Omar Al-Faruq was dispatched by Abu Zubaida and Ibn Shaikh al-Libi to the Philippines in 1995 along with Al Mughira Al Gaza'tri, an Al-Qaeda camp commander."

39. Classified Indonesian intelligence report, "Umar Faruq," June 2002.

40. Classified U.S. intelligence document, September 9, 2002.

41. CNN interview, Jakarta, Indonesia, November 7, 2002.

42. Others who attended the meeting, according to a CIA document, were

Yasin from Malaysia, al-Bukhari from Singapore, and Abdul Azis al Kahar from Sulawesi. Al-Bukhari handed money to Yasin, who was tasked to buy the weapons al-Faruq would need for the assassination attempt. Yasin went to Malaysia and the Philippines to buy the guns, but he later claimed he couldn't get the weapons back into Indonesia. JI operatives say he stole the money.

43. Classified Indonesian intelligence report, June 2002.

44. Dwikarna was the regional head of Al Haramain, which funneled money from al-Qaeda. The reports suggest al-Faruq was a go-between, working closely with Ahmed al-Moudi, the foundation head in Jakarta, as well as the overall leader of the foundation, Saudi national Sheikh Bandar, who visited Indonesia often because he had a wife in Surabaya, Indonesia's second largest city. Al-Faruq admitted Al Haramain is associated with Kompak, Agus Dwikarna's group in Sulawesi. (Information from classified Philippine intelligence report, August 2, 2002.)

45. Classified U.S. intelligence document, September 9, 2002.

46. Interviews with Philippine intelligence officers who questioned Fathur Roman al-Ghozi. By February 2003, al-Ghozi had confessed his role. Additional information came from Faiz bin Abu Bakar Bafana, detained in Singapore, who said Hambali told him he had ordered the attack. Hambali's and KMM's involvement chronicled in these two intelligence reports: classified Philippine intelligence report, "Rabitatul Mujahidin Terrorist Activities," June 30, 2002; and classified Indonesian intelligence report, "Statutory Declaration: Faiz Bin Abu Bakar Bafana," September 4, 2002.

47. Classified Indonesian intelligence report, "Statutory Declaration: Faiz Bin Abu Bakar Bafana," September 4, 2002.

48. Ibid.

49. Classified Philippine intelligence report, "Debriefing on Fathur Roman Al-Ghozi," February 12, 2002.

50. Faiz's brother Fatih Abu Bakar Bafana is a member of Jemaah Islamiyah's Singapore cell and is now in custody in Singapore.

51. International Crisis Group, "Bali Bombing: Rift emerges within Jemaah Islamiyah" (Jakarta/Brussels, December 11, 2002). Among those who attended the final planning meeting were Hambali, Zulkifli, Agus Dwikarna, and JI leader Abu Fatih.

52. Classified Indonesian intelligence report, "Interrogation of the Suspect M. Rozi alias Amrozi alias Chairul Anom," November 26, 2002.

53. Classified Indonesian intelligence report, "Statutory Declaration: Faiz Bin Abu Bakar Bafana," September 4, 2002.

CHAPTER 6: GANGSTERS IN THE PHILIPPINES

1. Gracia Burnham, press statement, Manila, Philippines, June 10, 2002.

2. Gracia Burnham with Dean Merrill, *In the Presence of My Enemies* (Wheaton, Ill.: Tyndale House Publishers, 2003), pp. 265–266.

3. CNN interview, Q&A, May 7, 2003.
4. Classified Philippine intelligence document, "Person Report: Mohammed Jamal Khalifa," 1995.
5. Classified Philippine intelligence document: "Interrogation reports of Edwin Angeles, former Abu Sayyaf founder turned double agent." Undated transcript.
6. Author interviews, Philippine and Pakistani intelligence sources, November 2001–March 2002.
7. Classified Philippine intelligence document: "Interrogation reports of Edwin Angeles, former Abu Sayyaf founder turned double agent." Undated transcript.
8. Rodolfo Mendoza, *Philippine Jihad, Inc.*, September 11, 2002, p. 28.
9. Emily Clark, "In the Spotlight: Abu Sayyaf" (Washington, D.C.: Center for Defense Information, March 5, 2002).
10. Jim Gomez, "Philippine Rebels, Bin Laden Linked," Associated Press, June 20, 2000.
11. Clark, "In the Spotlight," p. 35.
12. Surname withheld for protection. Interview with Cheche Lazaro for the Probe Team, April 2000.
13. Interview with Cheche Lazaro for the Probe Team, April 2000.
14. Confidential Philippine intelligence report, "Biographical Data: Haj Aldam Tilao a.k.a. Abu Ahmad Sabaya."
15. CNN interview, Q&A, May 7, 2003.
16. Interview with Cheche Lazaro for the Probe Team.
17. The last hostage, Filipino diving instructor Rollando Ullah, would not be released until 2003.
18. Author interview, Manila, Philippines, September 10, 2002.
19. Author interview, Zamboanga, Philippines, September 7, 2000.
20. Author interview, Manila, Philippines, September 12, 2000.
21. Author interview, Zamboanga, Philippines, September 7, 2000.
22. Reuters quoting police sources on Jolo.
23. Numerous allegations against President Estrada were made, including by former German hostage Werner Wallert in a CNN interview, Q&A, August 14, 2002.
24. Mendoza, *Philippine Jihad, Inc.*, p. 36.
25. Burnham, *In the Presence of My Enemies.* p. 16.
26. CNN interview, Basilan, Philippines, January 20, 2002.
27. Pekka Mykkanen, "Greed of Philippines Army Elements May Be a Security Hazard for US Troops," *Helsingin Sanomat*, February 3, 2002.
28. Ibid.
29. CNN interview, Q&A, May 7, 2003.
30. Burnham, *In the Presence of My Enemies* p. 199.
31. Ibid.
32. Interview transcript, *Mindanews*, June 8, 2002.

33. Burnham, *In the Presence of My Enemies,* p. 303.
34. Ibid., p. 304.

CHAPTER 7: THE NEW CALIPHATE

1. Interview with Nida'ul Islam, May 1998.
2. Special report, Philippine Intelligence Command: "The Islamic Fundamentalist/Extremist Movements in the Philippines and Their Links with International Terrorist Organizations," December 1994.
3. Rohan Gunaratna, *Inside Al-Qaeda: Global Network of Terror* (New York: Columbia University Press, 2002), p. 175.
4. Al-Jazeera Interview with Osama bin Laden conducted by Jamal Ismail in 1999 in Afghanistan.
5. Special report, Philippine Intelligence Command: "The Islamic Fundamentalist/Extremist Movements in the Philippines and Their Links with International Terrorist Organizations," December 1994.
6. Ibid.
7. Ibid.
8. Rigoberto Tiglao, "Moro Reprise," *Far Eastern Economic Review,* December 26, 1996.
9. "Philippines C: Commissar of the Faith: For MILF Chief, Autonomy Isn't Enough," *Far Eastern Economic Review,* March 28, 1996.
10. Classified Philippine intelligence document, "The Moro Islamic Liberation Front Briefing," 2000.
11. Classified Philippine intelligence document, n.d.
12. Glenda Gloria and Marites Danguilan Vitug, *Under the Crescent Moon: Rebellion in Mindanao* (Manila: Ateneo Center for Social Policy and Public Affairs, 2000), p. 112.
13. Interviews with regional intelligence officials and terrorism expert Rohan Gunaratna between Sept. 2001–Nov. 2002.
14. Classified Philippine intelligence document, "TIR on Pandu Yudhawinata aka Yudha/Abu Muhammad," December 8, 1999.
15. Briefing with Chow Peck Wan, Ministry of Home Affairs, November 15, 2002.
16. Classified Philippine intelligence document, "TIR on Pandu Yudhawinata aka, Yudha/Abu Muhammad," December 8, 1999, p. 9.
17. Ibid., p. 9.
18. Classified Philippine intelligence document, "CoPlan 'Pink Poppy.'"
19. Ibid.
20. Ibid.
21. Author interview, Manila, Philippines, February 10, 2002.
22. Background briefings, Philippine intelligence sources.
23. Ibid.
24. Classified Philippine intelligence document, "Spot Report Re Apprehension of Suspected International Terrorist," December 16, 1999.

25. Classified Philippine intelligence document, "Development Report Re Arrest of Suspected International Terrorist," December 16, 1999.

26. Donald G. McNeil, Jr., "French Hold Suspected Terrorist Tied to Bin Laden," *New York Times,* June 28, 2000.

27. Author interview, Atlanta, Georgia, September 20, 2002.

28. Background briefings with Philippine intelligence sources.

29. Classified U.S. intelligence document, September 2002.

30. Classified Philippine intelligence document, "Summary of Information: Umar Faruq," October 2002.

31. Ibid.

32. Ahmed Ressam, the millennium bomber, in court testimony admitted al-Qaeda was training operatives in the use of cyanide. In raids near Paris in December 2002, French police recovered cyanide from a suspected al-Qaeda safehouse. In February 2002, the antiterrorist police took nine Moroccans into custody. They were allegedly planning to poison the city's water supply with cyanide. Finally, when KSM was captured on March 1, 2003, computer files and diskettes discovered in his possession showed al-Qaeda was capable of manufacturing cyanide.

33. Classified U.S. intelligence document, September 2002.

34. Ibid.

35. Classified Indonesian intelligence document, "Interrogation of Mohammad Nasir bin Abbas," April 18, 2003.

36. Classified Philippine intelligence document, "Debriefing Report: Faiz Bin Abu Bakar Bafana," March 31, 2002.

37. Classified Indonesian intelligence report, "Interrogation of Mohammad Nasir bin Abbas," April 18, 2003.

38. Classified Philippine intelligence document, "Debriefing Report: Fathur Roman Al-Ghozi," March 8, 2002.

39. Classified Philippine intelligence document, "Debriefing Report: Cosain Lapinig Ramos a.k.a. Abu Ali," August 19, 2002.

40. Colonel Rodolfo Mendoza, Philippine intelligence report, "Philippine Jihad, Inc.," September 11, 2002, p. 198.

41. Classified Philippine intelligence document, "Debriefing of Fathur Roman Al-Ghozi," February 12, 2002.

42. Classified Philippine intelligence document, "Debriefing Report: Faiz Bin Abu Bakar Bafana," March 31, 2002.

43. Classified letter dated December 6, 2000 with MILF document and budget attached.

44. Classified Philippine intelligence document, "Debriefing Report: Haji Mukhlis Yunos," May 27, 2003.

45. Background briefing with Philippine intelligence officials, May 2003.

46. Classified Philippine intelligence document, "Al-Qaeda Cell in the Philippines: An Investigation," May 20, 2002.

47. Background briefing with Philippine and U.S. intelligence sources, June 2003.

48. Classified Philippine intelligence document, "Special Report on the General Santos City Bombings," June 10, 2002.
49. CNN interview, Cotabato City, Philippines, March 12, 2002.
50. Classified Philippine intelligence document, "MILF Intensifies Training Activities," June 19, 2001.
51. Classified Philippine intelligence document, "MILF Forces Re-Occupy AFP-Overrun Camps," July 24, 2001.
52. Classified Philippine intelligence document, "Foreign Nationals Conduct Training at MILF Camps," August 24, 2001.
53. Classified Philippine intelligence document, "MILF Arms Stored at Jemaah Islamiyah Camp in Indonesia," April 5, 2002.
54. Classified Philippine intelligence document, "The Southeast Asian Terrorist Network," September 20, 2002.

CHAPTER 8: SINGAPORE

1. Transcript of surveillance videotape provided by Singapore government.
2. Political and Economic Risk Consultancy, adapted from the *Economist*, 1995. With 0 as the rating for no corruption at all, most Western nations were given a rating of 2 for corruption. Singapore was rated 1.
3. Interview with CNN, February 9, 2002.
4. The other city that still has primary rain forest is Rio de Janeiro, Brazil.
5. Author interview, Singapore, July 23, 1999.
6. Lee Kuan Yew, *The Singapore Story* (Singapore: Prentice Hall, 1998), p. 571.
7. Ibid., p. 74.
8. Lee Kuan Yew speech, 1973.
9. Interview with Lee Kuan Yew, *Far Eastern Economic Review*, December 12, 2002.
10. Author interview, January 29, 2003.
11. Author interview, May 31, 2002.
12. *Singapore Straits Times*, January 13, 2002.
13. Author interview, May 31, 2002.
14. Author interview, February 21, 2003.
15. Singapore Ministry of Home Affairs white paper, "The Jemaah Islamiyah Arrests and the Threat of Terrorism," January 7, 2003.
16. Ibid.
17. Interview with Lee, *Far Eastern Economic Review*.
18. Lee Kuan Yew, "The East Asian Strategic Balance After 9/11," speech delivered on May 31, 2002.
19. Interview with Lee, *Far Eastern Economic Review*.
20. Interview with Singapore intelligence sources.
21. Classified FBI document, March 2002.
22. U.S. intelligence official briefing, October 2, 2002.
23. Interview with Lee, *Far Eastern Economic Review*.
24. Speech by Prime Minister Goh Chok Tong during the parliamentary debate on the President's Address, April 5, 2002.

25. Singapore Ministry of Home Affairs white paper, p. 17.
26. Statement from the Presidential Palace, July 17, 2003.

CHAPTER 9: BALI

1. James Hookway, "Authorities Pursue Suspected Ringleader with Two Pass-ports," *Asian Wall Street Journal*, May 15, 2003. Abdul Rahman Mansour Jabarah was killed in a firefight in Saudi Arabia on July 4, 2003. For details see Josh Meyer, "Saudi Police Kill Two Al Qaeda leaders, Two Others in Clash," *Los Angeles Times*, July 4, 2003.
2. Institute for Defense and Strategic Studies, NTU Singapore, interview conducted in Canada, May 28, 2003.
3. Ibid.
4. Author interview, Kuala Lumpur, Malaysia, February 28, 2003.
5. Classified U.S. intelligence document, "Information Derived from Mohammad Mansour Jabarah," FBI, August 6, 2002, p. 30.
6. Taped al-Qaeda message played on Al-Jazeera, October 13, 2001.
7. Classified Canadian intelligence document, "Mohammad Mansour Jabarah," CSIS, p. 2.
8. Ibid., p. 4.
9. Ibid., p. 6.
10. Ibid., p. 5.
11. Ibid., p. 6.
12. Ibid.
13. Ibid., p. 7.
14. Classified U.S. intelligence document, "Information Derived from Moham-mad Mansour Jabarah," FBI, August 6, 2002, p. 22.
15. Ibid., pp. 12, 14, 25.
16. Classified Canadian intelligence document, "Mohammad Mansour Jabarah," CSIS, p. 2.
17. Classified U.S. intelligence document, "Information Derived from Mohammad Mansour Jabarah," FBI, August 6, 2002, p. 7.
18. Ibid., p. 14.
19. Ibid.
20. Interrogation reports of numerous Jemaah Islamiyah members arrested in Indonesia and Malaysia, including the head of Mantiqi 3, Nasir bin Abbas a.k.a. Abu Solaiman.
21. Classified U.S. intelligence documents, "Information Derived from Mohammad Mansour Jabarah," FBI, August 6, 2002, p. 37.
22. Ibid., p. 30.
23. Ibid., p. 22.
24. Criminal complaint against Kenya bombing suspect al-Owhali, United States Information Agency. Available on the web, http://usinfo.state.gov/topical/pol/terror/98090103.htm.
25. Classified U.S. intelligence document, "Information derived from Moham-mad Mansour Jabarah," FBI, August 6, 2002, p. 29.

26. Ibid., p. 31.

27. Conversation recreated from CSIS and FBI documents based on the interrogation of Jabarah.

28. Classified U.S. intelligence document, FBI, August 6, 2002, p. 6.

29. Ibid.

30. Classified CSIS documents, p. 2.

31. Classified U.S. intelligence document, FBI, August 6, 2002, p. 7.

32. Ibid., p. 8.

33. Classified U.S. intelligence document, "Information Derived from Mohammad Mansour Jabarah," FBI, August 21, 2002.

34. Classified CSIS document, p. 4.

35. Classified U.S. intelligence document, FBI, August 6, 2002, p. 9.

36. Ibid., p. 10.

37. Classified CSIS document, p. 4.

38. Classified U.S. intelligence document, FBI, August 6, 2002, p. 10.

39. Ibid., p. 11.

40. Ibid.

41. Indonesian Police interrogation report, "Ali Ghufron alias Mukhlas," December 13, 2002.

42. Ibid.

43. Romesh Ratnesar, "How an Al-Qaeda Bigwig Got Nabbed," *Time*, August 25, 2003.

44. Indonesian Police interrogation report, "Imam Samudra," October 21, 2002.

45. Indonesian Police interrogation report, "Amrozi Bin H. Nurhasyim," November 14, 2002.

46. Indonesian Police interrogation report, "Imam Samudra," November 29, 2002.

47. Indonesian Police interrogation report, "Imam Samudra," December 16, 2002.

48. Interview with Sally Neighbour, ABC Australia for Four Corners, aired June 2003.

49. Ali Imron press conference, February 11, 2003.

50. Indonesian Police interrogation report, "Ali Ghufron alias Mukhlas," December 14, 2002.

51. Amrozi court statements, June 12, 2003.

52. Indonesian Police interrogation report, "Imam Samudra," January 12, 2003.

Chapter 10: American Missteps

1. The Pew Research for the People and the Press, Pew Global Attitudes Project survey at www.people-press.org.

2. Author interview, Jakarta, Indonesia, February 16, 2003.

3. Summit of Non-Aligned Movement in Kuala Lumpur, Malaysia, February 2003.

4. Author interview, Jakarta, Indonesia, August 5, 2002.

5. Opening speech by Malaysian Prime Minister Mahathir Mohamad for the Summit of Non-Aligned Movement, Kuala Lumpur, Malaysia, February 24, 2003.

6. Department of State telegram, December 6, 1975, declassified June 26, 2001. Obtained by the National Security Archive under the Freedom of Information Act, available at www.nsarchive.org.

7. Author interview, Suai, East Timor, May 13, 2002.

8. Ibid.

9. Author interview, U.S. Defense official, September 8, 1999.

10. Don Greenlees and Robert Garran, *Deliverance: The Inside Story of East Timor's Fight for Freedom* (Allen & Unwin: Australia, 2002), p. 256.

11. Author interview, Singapore, May 31, 2003.

12. Author interview, Washington D.C., November 5, 2002.

13. The CIA predator drone strike in Yemen happened in November 2002. My interview with Wolfowitz on November 5 was the first public statement by a U.S. official that admitted responsibility and promised more.

POSTLUDE: "BY TONGUE AND TEETH"

1. The only way to locate an electron is to enclose the system and shoot another electron at the suspected location. You can then measure exactly how much that second electron was deflected and that will show you where your first electron *was* at the time you decided to look for it. We can never know exactly where an electron is at any precise moment. That is the Heisenberg Uncertainty Principle.

2. Quote from a character in the HBO series *Six Feet Under.*

3. Classified CIA documents behind the CIA's operations in Iran in 1953 were leaked to the *The New York Times* and published on the web. A copy can be found on www.nsarchives.com.

4. Chalmers Johnson, *Blowback: The Costs and Consequences of American Empire* (New York: Henry Holt, 2000), p. 9.

5. Queen Noordin, *Leap of Faith: Memoirs of an Unexpected Life* (New York: Miramax Books, 2003), p. 58.

6. Mahathir Mohamad, Opening speech for the 54th UMNO General Assembly, June 19, 2003.

7. Indonesian intelligence document obtained by CNN in April 2002.

8. Ibid.

9. From Spanish Court Order given by Judge Baltasar Garzón to justify detention of eight men believed to be members of al-Qaeda's cell in Spain, November 18, 2001, p. 5.

10. Ibid., p. 17.

11. Ibid., p. 17.

12. Ibid., p. 5.

13. Ibid., p. 5.

14. Kathy Marks and Elizabeth Nash, "Bali Bombing: Spain Claims Its Warn-

ing over Indonesian Terror Cell Went Unheeded," *The Independent*, October 21, 2002.

15. Spanish Court Document, November 18, 2001, p. 15.
16. Marks and Nash, "Bali Bombing."
17. Classified Indonesian intelligence document, "Al-Qaeda Infrastructure in Indonesia," February 2002.
18. Author interview, Jakarta, Indonesia, April 2002.
19. Background briefing with Indonesian intelligence officials, April 2002.
20. "Suspects in Makassar Bombing Rise to 16," *Tempo Interactive*, December 14, 2002.
21. Author interview, Makassar, Indonesia, January 17, 2003.
22. Ibid.
23. "Bombers Planned Christmas Eve Bombing," *Tempo Interactive*, December 14, 2002.
24. Darren Goodsir, "Amrozi Smiles at Death: I Will Be a Martyr," *Sydney Morning Herald*, August 1, 2003.
25. Peter Kammerer, "Escalation of Jemaah Islamiyah's Terror Campaign Forecast," *South China Morning Post*, July 16, 2003.
26. Like most Indonesians, he only has one name.
27. "Indonesian Police Warn Militants Distributed Eight Bombs," Associated Press, July 15, 2003.
28. Radio interview with Australia's ABC Radio AM program, August 7, 2003.
29. Classified Indonesian intelligence document, "Interrogation Report of Mohammed Naser Bin Abbas," April 18, 2003.
30. Author interview, Singapore, August 17, 2003.
31. Singapore's Ministry of Home Affairs Statement, "Arrest of Jemaah Islamiyah Fugitive Arifin bin Ali alias John Wong," June 10, 2003.
32. The two Thai nationals arrested were Hajichiming Abdul Azi, thirty-six years old, and Muhammadyalludin Mading, forty-one years old. The Egyptian was Esam Mohamid Khidr Ali, forty years old.
33. Classified U.S. intelligence document, "Revelations of Khalid Shaikh Mohammed," April 2003.
34. The Al-Qaeda Manual, "The Al-Qaeda Document, vol. 1" (Alexandria, Va.: Tempest Publishing, 2002), p. 8.

INDEX

Abbas, Faridah bin, 183
Abbas, Hashim bin, 155, 183, 184
Abbas, Mohammed Nasir bin, 134–36,
    154, 215–16
Abdi, Achmad, 212
Abu Bakar Bafana, Faiz bin, 77–78,
    102–3, 135–37, 143–44, 178, 207
    arrest of, 181
    Jabarah meeting with, 179, 180
Abu Ghaith, Sulaiman, 167–70
Abu Hafs, *see* Atef, Mohammed
Abu Jibril, 75–77, 155, 162
    recruiting for JI of, 150–51
    in Sungai Manggis, 75, 184
    Thalib rivalry with, 94–95
Abu Rusdan, 215
Abu Sayyaf, 12, 21, 31, 32–33, 40, 97,
    104–24, 138
    al-Qaeda training for, 25–26, 27, 109
    Basilan branch of, 28, 109
    bombings by, 27
    brutality of, 109, 110, 118–20
    children kidnapped by, 110
    civilian support for, 111, 116
    Cruz and, 113–14, 120–21
    demands of, 109–10
    development of, 26
    foreigners targeted by, 108
    greed of, 112–16
    hostages killed by, 118–20
    impact of Janjalani's death on, 109, 113
    Ipil attacks of, 41–43
    Jolo branch of, 109
    kidnappings by, 104–7, 108–21
    media and, 113–15, 120–21
    members of, 26–27
    merge with al-Qaeda rejected by, 134
    military connections of, 107, 111, 120
    Palawan kidnappings of, 116–18

poverty and, 111
    Sipadan hostages of, 112–16
    splintering of, 109
    Urban Guerrilla Squad of, 27
    U.S. actions against, 120–23
    U.S. focus on, 13
    Yousef and, 25–26, 27, 110
Adel, Saif al-, 174
Afghanistan, 2, 19–20, 50, 107
    Asians in jihad in, 12, 21, 126–28
    JI members in, 70, 73, 76, 78
    Soviet Union in, 12, 126, 204
    terrorist training camps in, 9, 12,
        70–71, 77
    U.S. airstrikes in, 175
Agustina, Mira, 100–101
airport security, 25, 28–31, 173, 177
al-Farouq training camp, 169, 170, 175
Al-Fatah mosque, 86–87
Algeria, 132, 133
Al-Haramain Foundation, 96
Ali, Adam, *see* Yousef, Ramzi Ahmed
Al-Jazeera, 170
Al Mukmin school, 48, 50, 51, 57–58,
    75, 102
Alomari, Abdulaziz, 172
Alongan, Yusof, 131, 133
al-Qaeda, 1–2, 4, 61, 167, 171, 212,
    219, 220–21
    anti-American sentiment used by, 4,
        205–6
    assassinations of members of, 200
    in Cambodia, 216
    comparison with mafia of, 169
    conflicts within, 96–97, 175
    early operations of, 174
    e-mail use by, 177, 178–79
    estimated size of, 171
    evacuation of Afghanistan by, 175

243

ABOUT THE AUTHOR

MARIA RESSA, CNN's lead investigative reporter in Asia, has lived in Southeast Asia for more than sixteen years. In 1988, she was named CNN's Manila bureau chief and, in 1995, became CNN's Jakarta bureau chief. In addition, Ressa has traveled extensively and reported from India, Kashmir, China, South Korea, Japan, Australia and the United States. Videotapes of her coverage of terrorism were found in what experts believe to be Osama bin Laden's private videotape collection in Afghanistan.

Ressa graduated from Princeton University. She was awarded a Fulbright Fellowship to the Philippines in 1986, where she attended graduate school at the University of the Philippines. Among the awards she has received are the Asian Television Award in 1999 for Indonesia, the SAIS-Novartis International Journalism Award in 2000 for her work in East Timor, the Ferris Professorship of Journalism in 2001, and the National Headliner Award for Investigative Journalism in 2002.

Printed in the United States
By Bookmasters